The Five Elements

Volume I

The Movement of Life
through
Body, Mind and Spirit

by

Dr. Christa-Maria Herrmann

Second Edition Paperback

Published by
Paul Coughlin Ltd.

The Five Elements, Volume I
*The Movement of Life
through Body, Mind and Spirit*

Copyright © Christa-Maria Herrmann 2000
All Rights Reserved

First Edition Paperback First Published in 1996.

No part of this publication may be reproduced, stored in a retrieval system, or transmitted, in any form, or by any means, electronic, mechanical, photocopying, recording or otherwise, without the express permission of the publisher in writing.

The right of Christa-Maria Herrmann to be identified as the author of this work has been asserted by her in accordance with the Copyright, Design and Patents Act, 1988

Author
Christa-Maria Herrmann.
/www.5element.org.uk/cmherrmann/
Email: cmherrmann@5element.org.uk

Publisher
Second Edition Paperback.
Published in the UK by
Paul Coughlin Ltd. Coventry.
/www.coughlins.com/publishing/
Email: publishing@coughlins.com

Printer
Printed and bound in the UK
by Welton Print Ltd.
Royal Leamington Spa,
Warwickshire.
/www.welton.print.dial.pipex.com/
Email: welton.print@dial.pipex.com

ISBN 0 9537 900 0 2

Other books by the same author:

The Five Elements, Volume II
A Contemplation of Relationships
Paul Coughlin Ltd, Coventry, UK 2000.

Dewdrop in Tomorrow's Ocean;
A Story of Reincarnation and Spiritual Awakening.

The Way of Raku
Patten Press, Penzance, Cornwall, UK 1988.

Case study in Self Awareness,
Monash University, Melbourne, 1978.

Guru and Disciple;
Contemplation of a Sansktit hymn;
SAT Bhavana Trust, Mumbai, 1999.

CONTENTS

Forward 7
Acknowledgement 8
Dedication 9

PART I 11

THE MOVEMENT OF LIFE 11
Prologue 12
CHAPTER ONE 17
The Movement of Life in the Body 17
The Concept of Body-Mind-Soul 24
The Concept of the Auric Body 29
The Concept of the *Nadis* and *Chakras* 34
CHAPTER TWO 43
The Movement of Life in the Meridians 43

PART II 63

THE MOVEMENT OF LIFE AND THE FIVE ELEMENTS 63
CHAPTER THREE 67
Invocation of Earth 67
Character of Earth 70
Associations to the Earth Meridians 74
The Cycle 81
CHAPTER FOUR 103
Invocation of Metal (Air) 103
Character of Metal (Air) 106
Associations to the Metal Meridians 111
The Cycle 115
CHAPTER FIVE 139
Invocation of Water 139
Character of Water 144
Associations to the Water Meridians 147
The Cycle 152
CHAPTER SIX 171
Invocation of Wood (Space/Ether) 171
Character of Wood (Space/Ether) 173
Associations to the Wood meridians 182
The Cycle 185
CHAPTER SEVEN 203
Invocation of Fire 203
Characteristics of Fire 206
Associations to the Fire Meridians 211

    The Cycle 219
    CONCLUSION 232
PART III **235**
  RESTORING THE BALANCE IN THE ELEMENTS 235
    Prologue *236*
  CHAPTER EIGHT 247
    Balancing the Earth Element *247*
  CHAPTER NINE 259
    Balancing the Metal Element *259*
  CHAPTER TEN 271
    Balancing the Water Element *271*
  CHAPTER ELEVEN 283
    Balancing the Wood Element *283*
  CHAPTER TWELVE 295
    Balancing the Fire Element *295*
  POSTSCRIPT 309
    The Movement of Life as Seen by Sages, Saints and Scientists *309*
  NOTES 341
    About The Author *350*

Forward

I am very happy to see that Christa-Maria Herrmann has written this book entitled THE FIVE ELEMENTS which describes the circulation of the five elements; earth, fire, water, wood and air through the body and the environment according to the Chinese medical and Taoist systems. The conception of life and the universe, which she uses in her book relates to Hindu, Buddhist, Christian and Taoist beliefs.

I was personally very interested to see that she has added her own experiences of the five elements as well as making relevant references to views of modern science. This kind of synthesis of Eastern and Western, ancient and modern knowledge and understanding is exactly what is required right now. By following one system, religion or viewpoint we receive only a partial view of any given situation because our views are coloured by cultural and historical factors.

Taking the best of the good news and positive information from all the traditions we can find many new and innovative solutions to our personal, mental and physical health difficulties, as well as finding solutions to the complex social and environmental problems now besetting the global village at the beginning of the third millennium.

Through the balancing of our five inner elements and the healing of the five outer elements we can create inner peace and thus contribute towards the development of world peace. I hope that the readers of this book will use it as a resource on their personal paths to healing and peace.

T.Y.S. Lama Gangchen Rinpoche
Kunpen Lama Gancen
Via Marco Polo 13
20124 Milano
Italy

ACKNOWLEDGEMENT

This book contains work from many great writers and visionary thinkers; it is to these that I owe my greatest debt, whether they be dead or alive. Sincere gratitude for their original creativity fills my heart.

But there are also others that helped, special thanks go to Sonia Moriceau, my Shiatsu teacher, whose guidance was essential to finding the door to understanding my own body, she also sowed the seed for this book and gave valuable advice and criticism. Furthermore I would like to thank the SYDA Foundation, who allowed me to use some of their materials; and the venerable Thich Nhat Hahn who gave personal permission to use his poem "Peace is every step" in it's entirety. Direct quotations are, as is customary, marked with footnotes, thoughts might be "quoted" from memory and in this form, they have become my own.

In order to distinguish some nouns, which have become specialised terms in this context, I take the liberty to use capitalised letters; (example: the Earth; Air Element, Metal Energy; Water-person; Bladder-organ-network). The usual spelling is retained, where the word is used in their common meaning.

Last but not least many thanks to my good friends Belinda and Val whose untiring help and feedback, typing and correcting of the manuscript cannot be praised highly enough.

Furthermore my gratitude extends to Tina and Martin Ramirez, whose enthusiasm for the contents and editorial work carried the book to fruition.

DEDICATION

If only we would understand the songs of the birds, if only we could interpret the pattern of the clouds, if only we could tune into the whispers of stones, we would not need books. But as we don't, we need help to understand life and ourselves. To truly understand we need guidance and grace.

I would like to offer this book, with immense gratitude, at the feet of my Gurus and teachers from whom I receive both, without them I would not be on this path.

In the Bhagawat Purana (ancient Indian scripture) Lord Dattarcya lists 24 Gurus, people, nature, elements - who taught him well; ultimately he exclaims: "Learn above all, from the rhythms of your own body." I like to join him.

I hope that this book can pass some of the guidance I have received on to others. To those who are on the path to understand themselves and those who are lost on the many paths of understanding, it might give assistance and encouragement to follow their own quest and find their own personal understanding. To those who are practitioners in the field of complimentary medicine, it might be of help in observing and interpreting the state of health of their patients, as well as helping to foster their own well-being.

The emphasis here is not to explore any specific concept, neither East nor West, neither Oriental nor allopathic medicine, but to find the common ground in both, to see beyond separating individual concepts to the common source, which bind us together. For to those caught in the trap of arguments and contradictions, of rationalising and analysing, it might help to feel the words of many self-realised men and women and be encouraged by them, to seek such experiences for oneself. For the path and the purpose are the same: just following the path will change our relationship within the ultimate "Play" that is life.

PART I
THE MOVEMENT OF LIFE

PROLOGUE

Chinese sages, Indian saints, European mystics, quantum physicists and modern biologists agree that we are made of the same 'stuff'. Each have, due to their unique experience, tradition and culture different ways of expressing the nature of THAT, yet they agree: all that exists is ultimately made out of the same. In that depths, we are all One. This might sound farfetched, because it seems to belie our everyday experience. We see the objects out there in the world around us and surely they are different from each other; we see the tree, the car, the cat, the other person quite objectively and distinctly as individual shapes.

But what we see, is not what is. We see a table, yet it is wood, or more over cells, or carbon. So far we can follow, but once we reach the atomic or subatomic level most of us are lost. It is said in the Vedas (ancient Indian scriptures) that normally we look at the waves of the sea and we see many waves, each wave has a shape and activity, each one rises and falls. From the point of the wave, that is totally correct, each wave exists and it can say, "Look at me, I am a wave", but the wave overlooks the fact, that is part of the ocean. It could equally say, "Look, I am the ocean". Only in rare moments when the surface is shining like a mirror and all distinctive features are gone, then recognition dawns: yes the source is ocean. What is the difference between the two statements? Isn't the wave ocean, the ocean waves? The difference lies in the perception of self as separate - or as part of a greater whole. The consequences of that self-perception are two totally different views of the universe. Yet with still deeper contemplation one recognises that both wave and ocean consist of one and the same; they are both forms of water.

Our modern scientists have come to similar insights. Einstein recognised some of this when he said: "Life and death flow into one, and there is neither evolution nor destiny, only Being". Einstein saw the ocean, but he did not realise that he was not an onlooker, but part of that ocean, that we are indeed a "unified field" as R. Sheldrake calls it, or a web where "consciousness and matter is married in one intricate order with n-th dimensions", as D. Bohm calls it; or - a subjective participatory universe, as H. Skolimowski calls it (more in the Postscript). Most up to date scientific insight agrees with what sages have "seen" already thousands of years. How come? These "seers" or *rishis* were just as capable as we are of dividing nature up into space, time, matter and energy. That does not need scientists, but they had a different approach; they turned their backs on looking *at* things and decided to observe the inner play of energies. There they found a different reality and declared that their existed a unified field in which all existed *para* (beyond) our normal perception. This fourth dimension, they called *turiya*. "They said that the fourth state can be directly experienced only after the mind has transcended its normal activity, which requires the special technique of meditation"[1]. After stepping into the awareness of this fourth dimension, the sages could utter: Aham Brahmasmi,... I am the universe.

Turning inwards through meditation, and contemplation one finds the entrance to the world of energies behind our everyday perception, a fourth dimension. Different cultures used different names: divine spark, pure consciousness, face of God, the energy state where all is known, and more. Many agree that this is the place of our origin and the space where we are healed.

There is a lovely story to illustrate this. A lady visited a Yogi who lived in a cave in the mountains of the Himalayas. He asked the lady in, served her tea and then talked through the afternoon. When dusk came, the English lady said her "thank you" and told the Yogi how much she had enjoyed his company, how much she had learned. She continued to say; if the Yogi ever came to England, please, would he come to see her, she would be delighted to return his hospitality and would welcome him into her house. So please, would he accept her invitation and visit her in London.

PART I

The Yogi folded his hands, in the greeting *mudra* of respect and said: "I am London".

Very well, but what does this mean for us, for you and me? It means that the thousands of year old split between sacred and profane, has been an illusion, a construction of our minds. It is not an illusion in the sense of a mirage, where nothing is there, - but an illusion where we only see the tip of the ice-berg. Our senses are only able to perceive so much, and then our mind makes us believe: this is all there is! This illusion roots in ignorance! We share existence on many levels, be it physical, mental or in more subtle areas like emotions and subtle energies with planets and our sun, earth and mountains, rivers and seas, animals and plants. Even the air around us and our own bodies share an essence, an original energy that is "beyond the human". The latter is the definition of the Oxford dictionary of "Divinity". In this way we all share the divine, share sacredness.

This awesome realisation led ancient wise people to investigate the nature of this shared ground, and they found <u>five categories</u>, or base energies in which we can observe and experience our universe: fire, earth, water, plant - and animal life that breathes, and the space that contains all these. They contemplated the nature of these FIVE ELEMENTS in great detail. We can follow there investigation. We too are sometimes aware of the awesome power, when we are alone in the forest, watch a sunset, listen to music or experience the earth shaking in an earthquake, we too feel divinity of the universe, but for the rest of the time ...? We conveniently put it away - and focus on what "we can see with our own eyes", because we believe what the body says, what the wave shouts: "Look at me I am a wave", and we constantly work to prove our illusion to ourselves. Why are most of us so scared to admit, that we are the ocean? Why are we so scared to admit the divine in us and all of creation?

If we look towards other cultures we find the awareness of the sacred is kept alive in daily activities. The Balinese family would not dream of starting the day without giving thanks to the divine life-force by offering flowers and food at the entrance of the house. In the Far East people light incense and offer prayers to the ancestors before the day starts, to acknowledge the continuity of the divine through generations. In India no festivity is complete without chanting the divine names of God. In *ashrams* and monasteries around the world, food is offered to the divine, and blessed before each meal. In Christian households children used to be taught to give thanks before meals and to pray at bedtime. In Celtic Cornwall mothers give thanks to the divine, by burying the afterbirth of a baby under special trees, a gesture of spiritual gratitude. Some Australian Aboriginals and the American Indians both have ceremonies where drops of their blood drip onto the earth; a gift of life given back in gratitude to the divine source.

The key though, to understand and honour our shared divinity lies beyond all rituals and traditions, or indeed spiritual practices in an attitude of mind. We have to learn to constantly observe our mind and body to keep our awareness on this truth. We have to ask us, how do we approach things and issues, what tricks is our mind and body playing? In other words, we have to be "mindful". We have to direct our mind, to look deeper, beyond the superficial individual and separate appearances our senses perceive. Once we mindfully observe ourselves, body and mind and our environment, we like the ancient sages will find that we share with all that exists, five types of energies, we call them the FIVE ELEMENTS. They are what we can perceive through our senses, but they also are more than individual forms. Without widened or deepened perception we are stuck in the frame of our individual minds[2], we remain separate.

Because we look at ourselves as separate objects, we also look at God as a kind of separate object; out there, away from us, a threatening, authoritarian force that is pitted against our will. Either a force against which we have to prove our free will, a power to whom we are delivered (*kismet*) or we shrug our shoulders and so divine will becomes the ogre that releases us from responsibilities. God's will has been blamed throughout history in either of these roles, to justify anything from personal illness and misfortune, to killing others, taking territory, and all cruelties imaginable, with no understanding that we simply are to blame ourselves; for we are THAT.

God is not out there, but in here as our life-force, our prana, our 'movement of life'. The only way to get into contact with the divine, is to penetrate our own mind, to go beyond our mind, and find out who we really are. The way to do that is through meditation; meditation is the key to explore our intrinsic nature from the physical to the sacred. From here, we can understand and carry out our responsibilities of healing ourselves and fulfilling our purpose.

Chapter One

The Movement of Life in the Body

At the base of modern western thought, including the understanding of our bodies, was the Cartesian view of the world based on the Newtonian model of reality. Just as the world, the body was looked upon as an intricate mechanism; a type of grand machine that is controlled by the brain and the peripheral nervous system, the ultimate biological computer. Along with this perspective "a dichotomy of mind and body has been imposed on human beings. The body is divided in order to comprehend the phenomena of life such as anatomical structures, cells, tissues etc. Health has come to be viewed in terms of the state of our physical components"[1]. This leads to such absurd concepts as taking eggs from aborted foetuses to implant in infertile women, in disrespect of the emotional implication for the future mother or the child. It is commonly believed that such actions are due to the fact that science has advanced marvellously. That is true. The scientist invents the method of splitting the atom, but it is up to us how to use knowledge. The scientific mind discovers the way of how to implant eggs from aborted foetuses, yet it is our responsibility, our moral and ethical attitude that decides what we do with that knowledge. We are neither slaves to the scientist's discovery nor to his dissecting world-view. Yet our medical profession too often behaves as though science is absolute truth to be obeyed.

The doctor's perspective, in fact, traditional medicine as a whole, has changed very little, despite the change in physical and biological science and or their holistic consequences. By and large physicians still see the body as a machine, as do the majority of people. For what we and physicians have yet fully to understand, is how the insight of science and mysticism can be applied to the body and the field of medicine. Some have made a start. "We are beings in dynamic equilibrium with a universe of energy and light of many different frequencies and forms"[2].

Chapter 1

Sharing the energy with all that exists poses a problem, how do we distinguish between the energy in us - and around us?

The Japanese tradition talks about *Rei-Ki*, "*Rei*" being universal energy, and *Ki* as the personal Life force. Ki generally means "an intangible and all pervasive energy which exists everywhere". *Yet Ki* is also the power that animates life, and it is the force underlying the rhythm of nature, which in the human body is represented by breathing... Although you can get a feeling for what *Ki* is like, *Ki* can never be pinned down. It can be compared to the atmosphere in general, such as the atmosphere of a place, the 'air' about a person and specially ones feeling"[3]. Breathing is the most visible manifestation of the exchange of *Ki* with our environment; it is often used to illustrate all other types of energetic exchange[4].

The Chinese *Chi*, or *Qi*, is an energetic substance that flows from the environment into the body, similar to the Hindu term, *prana*. It is probably the most commonly used term to describe vital Energy, and is compared to rivers and oceans of the Earth, due to which the planets move and the sun shines. "Only because of Chi man lives and breathes. The wise of old charted its way in the body. Its origin was the *Tao*... It has two aspects, a kind of brother-sister team called Yin and Yang"[5]. The difference between the Japanese term and the Chinese one, both frequently used in complementary medicine, is that Chi is more universal, yet includes body energy, whereas Ki is more focused on the body, yet not exclusively body energy.

The Indian tradition thinks of creative life-energy as female and calls her Shakti.

Whichever word we prefer to describe the energy in the body, Shakti, Chi, Ki, Life-force, Movement of Life, they are - in essence, no different from their more universal partner, Shakti, Rei-Ki, Universal Energy etc. 'Both' are one, yet in two forms interdependent and synergetic constantly in movement. For energy to move in the right direction and purposefully, it needs to be intelligent and conscious. Without intelligence matter would be undirected, formless and chaotic. Intelligence makes the difference between the house designed by an architect and a pile of bricks. The body must be credited with an immense fund of "know-how". Every cell is not only programmed by its DNA, but furthermore empowered by knowledge, which R. Sheldrake calls a morphogenetic field. (e.g. the knowledge of rate of dividing in the production of two new cells)[6].

Once the conscious, intelligent life force leaves the body at death, the physical matter is slowly degraded into a disorganised collection of chemicals. The larger life force reabsorbs that matter back into its body of universal energy. This process is no different from a wave that falls back into the ocean, its individual performance spent. In this sense death is just a change of form of energy, energy which is itself immortal; neither born nor unborn, nor yet to be born. Or more scientifically stated: "there is a law of conservation of mass... physical matter is permanent although it may change its form"[7]. Matter becomes energy, energy becomes matter.

Energy has vibrations, different energies can be recognised by different vibrations. "The vibrational mode of a physical body is a reflection of the dominant frequency at which it resonates. Although the energetic levels of a human vary from moment to moment and day to day, each physical body tends to vibrate at a particular frequency. There are many factors, that contribute to the total frequency expression"[8]. The main frequency-band characteristic for a particular body accounts for personal trends, characteristics, dominant tendencies and even personality?

Vibration can be changed, in particular through other vibrations. For this purpose music and chanting have long been, and still are, used in Ayurvedic medicine[9], as are voice workshops in some areas of complimentary medicine. In the Bradford Hall Clinic in England, Dr Guy Manners has, for twenty years, investigated music and found that each organ in our body has an ideal tone combination, signifying health. From that he has built a machine to produce these sounds to be used in clinics all over the world to assist in healing. Sound is also used to enhance altered states of consciousness. A lot of New Age music is aimed at opening *Chakras* (see about *Chakras* in detail later). Drum music, for instance, relates to the base *Chakra* and is said to connect to the earth; rock music increases the energy flow to a fast pace through the second *Chakra*. Consciously applied music could change life dramatically be it in healing or simply in daily life. The work of A. Tomatis needs to be mentioned here, who has studied the human ear over fifty years and treated people successfully with sound, curing deafness and even such complex illness as schizophrenia, paralysis and illiteracy.

Further studies are necessary into the effect on the human-energy- field of such subtle vibrations as solar and stellar energy; by geocosmic frequencies, by intrinsic "disturbances" such as our emotions, nutritional and environmental factors and so on. What energies and vibrations are thrown out by the radio, television, microwave oven etc.? Research has already shown that our newest status gadget, the cellular mobile phone increases the risk of brain-tumours rapidly. What vibrations are given off by violent video tapes, news reports of war or even "simple things" like Concorde's sonic boom? What is their effect on our own vibrations? Really we know very little about our bodies or, in terms of being an energy field!

We all think we do know our own body, but do we? But do we take notice of it? Or do we wait until we find ourselves in situations where life shouts so loudly at us that we have to listen; do we wait until our bodies scream:

"Listen, listen to me! I have manifested a cancerous growth, but you still don't change your lifestyle, you don't listen. What else do you want me to do? Or …"Listen to me, is one heart attack enough, or have I to manifest another before you slow down?" Or,… "Listen to me or do you want me to break your other hip before you change the direction of your life?" Or,…"Listen, listen to me, I am tired, give me some rest before I collapse, or I shall manifest more than just the flu". Or, …

"Listen, listen to me, the way you relate to your mother is wrong. Will I have to stiffen up the left side of your body even more before you notice?"[10]. Or, or, or...

Our bodies are vibrating energies, our bodies have consciousness, our body has intelligence, so science and mystics tell us, when, then, will we listen to it, when will we learn from our own bodies?

In the Bhagavad Gita, Lord Krishna compares the body to a field. He says to Arjuna, This body is called "the field",

> The wise who understand such things
> call the One who knows this
> the knower of the field
> I, the knower of this field
> and every field, hold it that
> you must understand this
> it is true knowledge to know the knower
>
> What is the nature of the field
> who the knower is and its powers
> I will lead you to understand all that.
>
> The Bhagavad Gita 13; 1-3.[11]

Why does Krishna call the body the field? A field is of earth, abundantly creating new life, like the womb of a mother. A field is brought to life by pure water that is essential to nurture and nourish everybody; it is warmed by the Fire of the Sun which is life giving to all. It is rich in minerals and trace elements needed for all grains, flowers, fruits, trees to grow and surrounded by air, which provides prana, for everything to grow animate and inanimate. The field occupies space, its whole inherent purpose is to be space in which things can happen. So the field, like the body is made up of the five primal elements. So far we said, all that exist is made of one all-pervasive, divine and intelligent energy. Now we see that this, whether in a field (environment) or the body is classified into five different categories, aggregates, characteristics, states or **ELEMENTS**.

The Five Elements are the gross manifestation of the ultimate energy. It is said that in ever decreasing subtlety the ONE, most subtle energy became Two (absolute Space and Movement). The movement has *three gunas,* three states of being *(sattvic, rajastic, tamasic)* - stillness, action and inertia; a mixtures of these brings about first the Five Elements; out of these then all of Creation arises. Thus the One became two, and duality appeared, the "Two" became "Five"; the Five are finally of such gross substances that our senses can perceive them. They are the meeting point of the lowest level of the subtle abstract energies on its way to manifestation. In this way they are at the same time the highest level of abstraction for physical manifest form. One could say the FIVE ELEMENTS are the pivotal point between the manifest, visible world and the subtle energetic world. Because of this central position they are a door to either world - to either perception. Observing the physical Five Elements can open understanding to the subtler world, and they are a gate through which the spiritual and subtle energies touch our physical world.

Our body is physical form and as such equipped with five physical organs of perception. The human mind can only register what it perceives through these senses; "energies" have to take form for us to register them; the subtle has to become manifest for us to understand it. So somehow our universe and body has to manifest and eventually to dissolve again through these gates into the One Supreme reality that we all are.

The importance of the Five Elements is thus immeasurable and evident in all cultures and traditions. Contemporary Europe had lost this knowledge amongst other ancient wisdom in the last few hundred years. It was revived a few decades ago with the spread of Chinese and other complementary medicines. It is not without significance, that the Five Elements, which effect all existence came back to us via the knowledge of the body.

Under the mechanistic view our body consciousness was reduced so much that it was almost destroyed. We had lost sight of its role and neglected it. Yet without consciousness the body has no power, no insight, it cannot do anything by itself. Looking back to the analogy of the field, it becomes obvious. With the body, as with the field you can do what you want; you can turn it into an apple orchard, or a flower garden. You can split it into little plots and build a house for people to live in, on it; or you can make it into a cemetery and it will receive the dead. You can also do nothing and let thistles and thorny bushes grow on it. Just as the field the body itself is willing to do our bidding, it serves us. It is ours to do with what we want. We can train to be a boxer, become a potter, a wise man or a fool, a good man or a bad man. We can do with this body what we want - and men have done anything to it from reaching enlightenment to crippling it, selling it and humiliating it.

If this is done to a body, then there must be a doer! Who treats the body like this? To find out you need to understand your body, listen to it, observe it and know it. But who does this listening; who does this knowing? The material body itself is inactive, harmless, neutral, is a process, yet in every cell in all aspects constantly decisions are made. There is constant awareness of what needs to be done. Who knows what needs to be done?

If you see somebody else's beauty and you get jealous, there is no sense in cutting your eyes out, the eyes are not at fault for seeing, they act according to their nature, but our *egos*, our conditioned minds they tell us to be envious, jealous. The mind suffers, therefore we have to purify our minds and get to "Know the Knower" behind the scenes; our true Self, our true nature, then it is a pleasure to be in the body. The body then is free to become the creative instrument, the creative tool of the divine energy. It can fulfil its true nature, its purpose.

There is a story told about a saint who, when his death approached, thanked everybody, bowed to the five elements and his Guru, then with folded hands thanked his body: "My dearest body, with your help and grace I saw God. I thank you. I may have often neglected your needs and frightened you. I have made you suffer but you have always helped me. I am in your debt. You gave me a quick and perceptive mind. Sometimes I unknowingly wronged you, even though, you always helped me, did everything you could for me! Whatever I did, you returned only friendship and support. Without you I could not have followed my spiritual path, would not have realised God". With these words he left his body behind.

> The rich
> will make temples for Shiva
> What shall I
> a poor man do?
> My legs are pillars
> the body the shrine
> the head a cupola of gold.
>
> Listen, O lord of the meeting river,
> things standing still shall fall
> but moving ever shall stay
>
> Ba sa vanna 820[12]

The Concept of Body-Mind-Soul

Now let's have a closer look at the anatomy of the energetic entity we have so far just called "body". The most commonly used description in the West is that of a triadic entity, body-mind-soul. A new branch of medicine, the vibrational medicine, sees this triadic body as "subtle energy fields, condensing and influencing electromagnetic energy fields, which in turn condense into matter i.e. chemicals. Then Chemistry condenses and creates structure, structure has to carry out certain functions, which then reinforce the structures, whose state then gives feedback to the chemistry, which in turn, influences the electromagnetic field; which then reflects on the subtle energy field. Thus the body is soul and soul is body"[13]. This revolutionary sounding statement is saying no more than that the body is in essence not only physical matter (machine), but is of the same nature as subtle and spiritual energy. A thought that leads deeply into philosophy and religion: it supports, the above that we are *a* form of divine, all pervasive self-aware energy. This body of energy has three aggregates of existence, yet all are consciousness. Starting with the highest level, we call it the soul. Soul is consciousness aware of itself. The consciousness of the Soul is what is called in today's literature the SELF or Higher Self (by contrast to the *ego*).

The consciousness of the mind is that part which is the observer, the "knower" (as experienced in meditation), and the consciousness of the body is apparent in its ordered "know how". Let's look closer at the latter two.

Even if one looked very carefully, one "would never see it (the body) the same time twice. Ninety eight percent of the atoms in your body were not there a year ago. The skeleton that seems so solid was not there three months ago. The configuration of the bone cells remains somewhat constant, but atoms of all kinds pass freely back and forth through the cell walls, and by that means you acquire a new skeleton every three months. The skin is new every month. You have a new stomach lining every four days"[14]. So what actually appeared a solid body is more akin to a river. "It is as if you lived in a building whose bricks are systematically taken out and replaced"[15]. Who or what keeps the blueprint, the architect's plans, for the body to look the same today, yesterday and tomorrow? The process seems even more daunting if one visualises that through respiration, digestion, elimination etc. the bricks are constantly changed with stones from the surrounding world (Food, Air, Water, Interactions etc.). Some "intelligence" has to guide this process, so that we do not collapse in a heap of "matter".

As for the mind, we usually associate it with the brain. We are used to think that our brain is the intelligent leader that guides all processes. Brain cells are only one kind of cells with a special task; all cells have an intelligent centre in their nucleus, which reproduces itself and receives and gives messages. Thus it seems that the whole building has consciousness. "Neurophysiologists have long sought the area of the brain that is the centre of free will and decision making. Although they may identify regions of grey matter that participate in the process of executing commands, researchers will look long and hard before they ever discover the real seat of consciousness in the brain. The brain albeit a complex bio-computer, still needs a programmer to instruct the nervous system of how to perform and what acts accomplish what. The conscious entity, which uses this bio-mechanism of the brain and body is the human spirit or soul"[16]. R. Gerber further states, "human beings are more than flesh and blood, proteins, fats and nucleic acids. The body would be a pile of disorderly chemicals were it not for the animating life-force that maintains and organises molecular substances into living, breathing, thinking individuals... It is a unique form of subtle energy that has yet to be fully grasped by scientists"[17]. This guiding, knowing energy is what the biologist Rupert Sheldrake calls the morphogenetic field (becoming into form) and it is embedded in ever larger unified fields or the conscious order as David Bohm calls it.

It seems that mind, body and soul are like parallel universes. Anything that happens in one, leaves tracks in the other, they communicate through neurotransmitters. They are different forms of conscious energy in one unified field.

The implications of this view are enormous, and although not new, little notice has been taken in the Western way of life or general "science". For if one looks at the mind-body-soul not as three entities in relation to each other, but as one unified field, then it implies that we do not have a soul as such, or a divine spark as theories of old suggest, but we *are* divine as a *whole entity*. We are en-souled on all levels of being. If I am such a divine being, then you are such a divine being as well! There is only one thing left:

--See--God--in--Each--Other--

Well, if you and I are divine beings, then what does the word divine mean. We have said earlier, that by definition divine means: beyond human. We are human and we are beyond human. We are human and divine, this latter quality we have not realised. To realise this fully, and not only understand it with our intellect is what the much thought-after goal of "self-realisation" means.

How do I meet, treat the divine being that is you? How do I relate to a divine being, which is alive and ordinary human being? Not a picture of Jesus, not a statue of Shiva, to treat them as divine is relatively easy! But how do I treat <u>you, the divine being</u>? Jesus was man; Christ was God; he was human and divine. He had both natures in himself. But we -? Knowing that you have God-nature too surely there is only one way for me to treat you that is - "with love and respect". Well said, that is easy as long as "you" are abstract, but once I know you?

> Do I treat the rude child with love and respect?
> Do I treat the aggressive neighbour with love and respect?
> Do I treat the dishonest businessman with love and respect?
> Do I treat my domineering mother with love and respect?
> Do I treat my cheating husband with love and respect?
> Do I treat the burglar with love and respect?
> Do I treat the murderer with love and respect?
> I would have to be a saint!

Thich Nath Hahn's poem describes this problem well.

> Call me by my true names.
> Do not say that I'll depart tomorrow
> because even today I still arrive.
> Look deeply: I arrive in every second
> to be a bud on a spring branch,
> to be a tiny bird, with wings still fragile,
> learning to sing in a new nest,
> to be a caterpillar in the heart of a flower,
> to be a jewel hiding itself in stone.

Chapter 1

I still arrive, in order to laugh and cry,
in order to fear and to hope.
The rhythm of my heart is the birth and
death of all that are alive.

I am the mayfly metamorphosing on the surface of the river,
and I am the bird which, when spring comes, arrives in
time to eat the mayfly.

I am the frog swimming happily in the clear pond,
and I am also the grass-snake, who, approaching in silence,
feeds itself on the frog.

I am the child in Uganda, all skin and bones,
my legs as thin as bamboo sticks,
and I am the arms merchant, selling deadly weapons to Uganda.

I am the twelve-year-old girl, refugee on a small boat,
who throws herself into the ocean after being raped by a
sea pirate,
and I am the pirate, my heart not yet capable of seeing
and loving.

I am a member of the politburo, with power in my hands,
and I am the man who has to pay his ' Debt of blood ' to
my people,
dying slowly in a forced labour camp.

My joy is like Spring, so warm it makes flowers bloom in
all walks of life.
My pain is like a river of tears, so full it fills four oceans.

Please call me by my true names,
so I can hear all my cries and laughs at once,
so I can see that my joy and pain are one.
Please call me by my true names,
so I can wake up,
and so the door of my heart can be left open,
the door of compassion[18].

The Concept of the Auric Body

Let us now look at another much used "anatomy" of the body. An easy way to understand the principle is to look at a flame of a candle. From the obvious view it is a source of energy, warmth and light. Looking closer we see a centre and a blue flame, around that are many different layers of less intense heat and light, or "ever subtler" layers of energy.

"The human energy field is the manifestation of universal energy that is ultimately involved with human life. It can be described as a luminous body that surrounds and interpenetrates the physical body, emits its own characteristic radiation and is usually called the 'Aura'. Based on their observations, researchers have created theoretical models that divide the aura into several layers. These layers are sometimes called Bodies, and they interpenetrate and surround each other in successive layers. Each succeeding body is composed of finer substances and higher 'vibrations' than the body that it surrounds and interpenetrates"[19]. The layers are defined by locations, colour, brightness, form, density, fluidity and function and are grouped into different systems. Here is not the place to go into detail, suffice to say most people describe four to seven layers, even up to twelve. To give you a taste, just dim the light in your room, and put your outstretched fingers in front of a white wall, soft focus your eyes, and most likely you can see some kind of luminous outside rim of your hand. If there is a "New Age" or "Health Fair" near you, you could probably get an auric photo of yourself. It displays the electromagnetic fields around you.

From the scientific point of view the layers are not just "beautiful visual expressions". Each "layer can be considered to be of a higher vibration, occupying the same space as the levels of vibration below it... thus we have seen seven bodies, all occupying the same space at the same time, each one extending out beyond the last". This refutes the common impression that the aura is like rings around the body; there are no such separate rings, but seven fields of energy, of different sizes, vibrating at different rates, and - as we will see - interacting; in this way they form a complex, unified field. The first four of these "individual" yet "connected" fields are the etheric body, the emotional, the mental and the astral. East and West are in agreement on these. The latter three, however, are not so universally mentioned: the etheric template, celestial and ketheric or casual body. The last two layers being of spiritual nature of such high frequency that Barbara Brennan wrote: "When we bring our consciousness to the seventh level of the aura, we know that we are one with the Creator"[21].

The etheric body is supposed to be of a state between energy and matter, "like a sparkling web of light beams"[20]. The second is associated with feelings, and the vibrations they have in all their many states; a fluid body that changes as our emotion changes.

The mental body is of fine substances "associated with thought and other mental processes".

The astral body further out from the others is obviously dealing more with the environment, and the vibrations that effect us. It is influenced by other organisms and objects, thus feeding the environment to our mental body, influencing those vibrations that by the thought process in turn have an effect on our feeling body. This in turn is manifest in our physical body.

Both, this and the mind-body-soul approach describe energy fields, of increasing vibrations feeding each other, interconnected to the one above and below. If we consist of fields of high and low frequency energy in constant flux, then there are, perhaps people who have more or less of the low frequency areas than average. An unusually high amount of lower frequencies could possibly account for illness or behavioural problems. There must be, by inference, also people who have higher frequency vibrations. These might be specially gifted people.

Furthermore if some people have higher frequencies than others, could there not be people with altogether higher frequencies? People who have "purified" their lower energy fields and raised their energies to such extraordinary level that they do not have the same lower energy bodies, but are pure spiritual energy? Then they would have no body! That could explain the trans-cultural phenomena of angels and celestial beings. One step below that would be people who have a body - just, but are on all other levels of such high frequency that they are almost pure energy, pure consciousness? In old times the wise recognised these beings as living Gods.

People that are in such an exalted state have existed in all regions. We call them Saints and "they incarnate for the ordinary human being that 'other-ness' which brings wholesome meaning to life. Our age and society is characterised by the eclipse of the sacred." Mankind seems no longer to produce them, perhaps because the dominant ideals and aspirations today are expressions of the baser values of consumerism and individuality. We have, by and large, lost the knowledge to recognise these people, haven't we? But in the East, especially in India and in strong Catholic countries, we still find them. "Saints are like us, and yet qualitatively different from us. They are totally human, yet believed to be focal points of spiritual force fields, in the sense that they literally alter the quality of the energy that surrounds them"[22].

Meditating on that different energy frequency within, the Kashmir Shaivist's saint Lalleshvari said, while gazing up at the glaciers crowning the mountains of Kashmir "Water freezes into ice and ice -grazed by the suns rays- melts into water. Just so, all pervading consciousness congeals into the ephemeral material universe. But when matter is grazed by the compassionate glance of God, it releases itself once more into all pervasive being"[23].

We influence each other's pulsation, or frequency rates. "The pulsation rates in one person's field induces a change in the pulsation rates of an other's field. It works just as tuning forks do"[24]. Really this is something that happens all the time, unnoticed, in families. When a person is ill in the family, let's say a child, the mother usually spends a lot of time supporting and looking after the child; by this the healthy, higher frequencies of the mother transfer and influence the child's lower ones. All people in the family, in a normal give and take situation, pass on such health-giving frequencies. This accounts for people, usually, getting better more quickly at home than in a sterile hospital atmosphere. The whole of the healing arts including spiritual healing, laying on of hands, *Rei-Ki* etc., is related to transference of energy, a lifting from the lower frequencies to the higher ones.

If the energy frequencies are vastly different, like in that of a "divine" person (one with very high, pure frequencies, as introduced earlier), the energy field of any person in their presence will be drastically affected; and their frequencies raised. This is why people in all times have travelled far to sit in the energy field of their Guru. In Tibetan Buddhism, Kashmir Shaivism, general Hinduism, Advaita Vedanta, Siddha Yoga or even Zen Buddhism, such Masters, such Siddhas, "perfected Beings", or to use the more familiar Indian word, such Gurus, are and have always been recognised. Their deliberate influence on our energy fields is called *shaktipat* (the giving of *shakti*, life-energy). It makes me wonder whether originally baptism was carried by the same understanding?

Sometimes, when this increased energy frequency runs through a person, it releases energy blocks on all levels in the receiver and will then have to be dealt with. The receiver may contact old traumas and the physical, structural or emotional release might follow, which can be painful and disturbing. The Indians call these happenings *kriyas*. In my experience, they can range from bouts of tears to the changing positions of bones and/or spasmic release of energy. But they are always relatively short lived and can be helped by such medicine as arnica or 'rescue remedy'. They stop as soon as the higher frequencies have adjusted or cleared out the lower frequencies.

Let us return to the view of a body as many different vibrating energy fields, commonly called auric bodies. As with the previous approach, this has far reaching consequences for medicine as well as our daily life. One would have to question, whether the mere removal by operation of an organ would deal with its disfunctioning energy field. For example, a cancerous growth might be removed, but that would not alter the energy pattern. An operation, let's say a removal of a gallbladder, would not effectively change the pattern that caused the manifestation. Is it still there in another level; until changed! Unless the energy-level is adjusted, the cause is still there ready to manifest new problems of some kind linked to the field of influence of the gallbladder? The organ, the manifestation of the lowest frequency has been removed, but not the cause. Healing is only effective if dealt with on all levels. A change is needed in the life organism in total, on all, even the subtlest, energy levels. The effect of this could include changes in the personality, lifestyle, or even consciousness.

How far does our energy field extend? Imagine a room full of people, not just occupying say: two by two by six foot, but instead needing a space of six by six by nine foot? We would need bigger rooms? Think about the question of when do you make contact? When do you start to interfere in somebody else's space? In what way would our architecture or transport system have to change? Visualise the above personal space via crowded skyscraper living such as in Hong Kong or New York; imagine an underground railway at rush hour! Does the problem of mass-hysteria have its roots here? What about the hooliganism in football crowds, or simply a full classroom situation and how about inner-city crime. Ortega y Gasset's theory of mass-hysteria suddenly makes more sense.

And how about our intimate relationships, where does our space start in the matrimonial bed, where does intimacy start, where invasion? How about people, who are forever tired, are they spending endless energy, constantly converting theirs or other people's low frequencies into higher ones? Are they working hard although doing "nothing" just because they are surrounded by people with the "wrong" frequencies? Instead of taking pills, people who feel unwell, tired and without energy ought to look at their way of living, maybe even the place they are living and the earth's vibrations in that place. How much our everyday life needs to change if we take notice of these concepts is anybody's guess. It is relevant here in so far, as it shows how far removed we are from respecting people as divine beings. Beings with a personal energy field, which is constantly changing and working at converting lower energy frequencies to higher frequencies.

The latter in fact might be the purpose of our human existence as we reach out to return back to the light we came from. This process is called doing *Sadhana*, spiritual practices, which Allama Prabhu describes something like this:

> I have made a garden out of my body
> my mind is the spade
> With it I dug up the illusions, like weeds
> I broke the clods of worldliness.
> I raked the earth and sowed the seeds of the spirit
> My well is a thousand-fold lotus
> My waterwheel, my breath,
> My subtle nadi is used to channel water
> To prevent the five oxes of the senses
> from trampling my crops
> I have set up a fence
> all around of patience and poise.
> Behold, O Lord of Caves![25]
> Day and Night I have watched
> To protect my tender seedlings.[26]

The Concept of the *Nadis* and *Chakras*

Let us now look at an eastern system of 'anatomy' of the body; a system by which energy from the universal aspect of the divine, is thought to be absorbed by *chakras* into the human energy field.

The Oriental system of *chakras* (Sanskrit for wheels) is not separable from the system of *nadis*, specific subtle energy channels that transport the energy to the cellular structure of the physical body. "This energy is in turn translated into hormonal physiological and ultimately cellular changes throughout the body"[27]. There seem to be at least seven major *chakras*, but may be as many as three hundred and sixty. Each one is associated with a nerve plexus and a major endocrine gland and a psychic perceptual function. Both *nadis* and *chakras* could be described as "specialised step-down transformers (that) translate the effect of etheric, astral and higher vibrational inputs into biological manifestations via our unique endocrine system"[28]. This statement shows that the anatomy of the auric body and *chakras/nadis* are not to be separated. The *chakras* and the *nadis* could be understood as connecting doors to the auric bodies representing an extensive network of fluid like energies "which parallel the bodily nerves in their abundance. In the Eastern Yoga literature, the *nadis* are symbolic of the fine roots of the lotus, which distribute the life-force and energy of each *chakra* into the physical body. Various sources have described up to seventy two thousand *nadis* or etheric channels of energy in the subtle anatomy of human beings. These unique channels effect the nature and quality of nerve transmission within the extensive network of the brain, spinal cord and peripheral nerves. Dis-functioning at the level of the *chakras* and *nadis* can, therefore, be associated with pathological changes in the nervous system. In addition the hormonal link up between the *chakras* and endocrine glands suggests even further complexities of how a subtle energetic systems imbalance can create abnormal changes in the cells of the entire body"[29].

There are three main *nadis: ida, pingala and sushumna*. They are incomparably subtle hollow tubes that criss-cross each other in the centre of the spine, like the caduceus symbol of medicine confined in the spinal column. The *chakras* themselves are seen as absorbing and transforming energies from the environment (much like the astral body of the auric system); each *chakra* being associated with a different frequency. Energy of high frequencies enter in the crown *chakra* and are transformed down through the others to wherever it is needed, in addition each *chakra* also can metabolise energy horizontally.

Here we have to realise a common misconception, we often think of facts as static, provable, having one definite description. So people get disoriented when "facts" do not fit into the expected box. The varying number of *chakras*, as well as their varying functions, are no exceptions. The *chakras* are seen as living aspects of an organism. Depending on the frequency the *chakra* metabolises specific elemental energy and is attached to that element. In the Buddhist system they are especially changeable. What aspect one looks at depends entirely on the "inner scientist" and his own observation in the laboratory of meditation. In this way the element attached to the *chakra* can vary, according to his intention. The Buddhist system is more concerned with the dynamic flow. "The transformation of the current of cosmic or nature energies into spiritual potentialities; these *chakra* are the points in which psychic forces and bodily functions merge into each other; they are focal points in which cosmic and psychic energies crystallise into bodily qualities, and in which bodily qualities are dissolved or transmuted again into psychic forces"[30]. The natural elements and their qualities are more detached from their natural prototypes, and thus the same centre does not "necessarily always represent the same element or property. The symbolism of the elements moves on many planes; nature, abstract concepts, sense perception, and equally on emotional, psychic, intuitional and spiritual planes. They are like things in a state of flux"[31]. This will account for discrepancies in the following over-view.

A Westerner might see this with doubtful eyes, yet it can be appreciated for what it is, namely a dynamic principle, a living organism whose movements are not predictable, not bound by limiting laws. By comparison Ayurvedic medicine, puts relatively more emphasis on these centres as junction boxes for the respective *nadis*, metabolising energy in connection with

The Movement of Life in the Body

the elements of nature[32]. This gives the *chakras* a so-called more objective content in the form of permanently attached Elements, seed-syllables (sound) etc.

Here is a short summary (frequencies are measured in THZ=1 multiplied by 10 to the power of 12 Hertz)[33].

Muladhara, the base *chakra* is associated with a frequency of 460 THz; is associated with the colour red and the element of earth. It's associated with the adrenals, the sacro-coccygeal plexus, the spinal column and kidneys. It's associated with raw physical energy, the will to live and new learning skills - but also with the colour yellow, a square or a cube and with the meditation symbol of the Buddha Amoghasiddi who stands for the 'all-accomplishing', karma-freeing wisdom and the seed-syllable 'AH'. In the Tibetan system this and the next *chakra* have been combined under the name *Sang-Na*, it is seen as a four-petalled Lotus with the syllable 'Lam', the vehicle of an elephant and the Wind (energy current that is associated with the Ratna family of Supreme Healer Ratnasambava)[34].

Svadhisthana, the second *chakra* is associated with the frequency of 500 THz; the colour orange, the element of water, the gonads, the reproductive system, the sacral plexus or hypogastrian plexus. It is associated with the quality of love, giving and receiving pleasure, sexual energy and also with the whole negative side of the system of nutrition (separation, assimilation, rejection, elimination). It is also associated with the shape of a crescent, the colour white, the seed syllable 'Vam' and deepening meditation.

Manipura, the third *chakra* is associated with the frequency of 520 THz; the colour yellow, the element fire. It is associated with the pancreas, stomach, liver, gallbladder, nervous system, epigastrian plexus and the solar plexus. It is associated with spiritual wisdom, consciousness of universality of life and healing. It is associated with purification of the digestive fire and also the shape of a triangle, the colour red, the seed syllable 'Tram' or 'Ram' and the wisdom of equanimity, - as

Chapter 1

well as the wind, energy current of the Karma family of the Supreme Healer Amoghasiddhi.

The Navel Centre is also associated with the element of water, in the sense of transformation and "assimilation of subconscious material"[35] - and as such with a white disc, symbolising mirror-like wisdom. The Naval *chakra* is also associated with the Meditation and healing Buddha Ratnasambava, that symbolises generosity and giving spiritually and materially .

Anahata, the fourth *chakra*, is associated with the frequency of 570 THz; the colour green, the element air, the thymus, the heart plexus, the vagus nerve, circulatory system. It is associated with love to human beings and openness to life, hearing of divine sounds (*nada*), with the residence of the individual souls (in Hindi - *jivatma*). It is associated as well with the shape of a hexagram, the colour grey-blue, the seed-syllable 'Yam', the deer (symbol of speed/air) and the supreme Healer Akshobya and the *dharmadatu* wisdom; the wind (energy current), white in colour with a seed-syllable 'Hum', and the symbol of ultimate integration.

Vishuddha, the fifth *chakra* is associated with the frequency of 630 THz; the colour blue, the element is ether, space (or wood). It is associated with the thyroid, bronchial and vocal apparatus, lungs, alimentary canal, cervical ganglia and the medulla. It is associated with the senses and sense of self within society, talking and assimilating - but also with the symbolic shape of a semi-circular bow, the colour white, the syllable 'Ham', also the shape of a circle. It is associated with the Buddha Amitabha, the embodiment of discriminating wisdom of inner vision; and his seed-syllable 'Hri'; the energy current or wind has the colour red and is associated with the Pema family of the Supreme Healer Amitabha.

Ajna, the sixth *chakra* is associated with the frequency 710 THz; indigo blue, "the element is the spirit" and it is associated with the pituitary gland, lower brain, left eye, ears, nose, sympathetic nervous system, hypothalamus, ability to carry out ideas, capacity to visualise and understand mental concepts, mind and cognitive and visionary facilities, - although separately mentioned, mostly the *Ajna* is linked in Tibetan scriptures with the crown chakra. The seed-syllables are 'Ham' and 'Ksam' (or So-ham); but the main syllable is that of a short, or half 'A'.

Sahasra, the seventh *chakra*, is associated with the frequency of 430 - 750 THz; the colour white and the "element of light", the pineal gland, the upper brain, right eye, cerebral cortex, and the cerebral spinal nerve system, the integration of personality. It is associated with spiritual aspects of mankind, the house of God, unconditional joy, the soul's place to become one with God. Together with the 6th *chakra,* it is associated "with 'the blue flaming drop', the *bindu*, the symbol of the element 'space' or 'ether'. Its Lord is Vairochana, who embodies the 'wisdom of the Universal Law', and who is embraced by the 'Mother of Heavenly Space'. His seed-syllable is 'Ohm' " [36].

The current or wind is associated with the colour blue, and the Sangy Buddha family of the Supreme Healer Vairochana. The symbol is the thousand petalled Lotus, sometimes linked directly with the Serpent power of Kundalini; leaving the other six centres behind[37].

> A shining of light
> each wheel a fountain
> Water drawn up through its centre
> pouring itself into the vessel
> splashing, gurgling, overflowing
> into the next, only to rise
> up, out of the Absolute
> pouring energy into the being
> flowing, overpowering, energising
> onto the next
> for our gathering
> eternally giving
> from Self, to Supreme Self.

Chapter 1

Kundalini Energy, the potentiality through which the wise reach highest spiritual power, lies dormant in the *muladhara*, at the base of the spine. It can be awoken, and when freed, ascends in the *sushummna*, the central channel, in the spinal nerve column, and pierces and cleans it as well as each *chakra* in turn, up to the *sahasra*. All beings are potentially capable of waking this source of spiritual energy and when it happens, there is a notable transformation in the consciousness of ourselves. The symbol for this strong symbol is found in most cultures, from the Hopi Indians in North America to the Kung people of the Kalahari Desert in Africa. We find it in carvings of spirals and snakes on Celtic stones in Ireland and Scandinavia, and as the snake symbol of Egypt and the serpent deities of the Aztecs and Australian Aboriginals.

The function of *Kundalini* energy, as well as the *chakras*, is to convert energy into us-able higher frequencies for us, and this changes our awareness of the immediate surroundings and body-awareness.

Let's turn to some specific examples. It is customary to embrace people when causally meeting a person. Ask yourself: "Do I really want to take this person's energy into my heart *chakra*, or am I doing it out of politeness, or even displaying false love and affection?" Are you true to yourself and respectful of others?

Do you feel tired and lifeless? Could it be that your base *chakra* is not metabolising energy properly? If you have lower backache, say, in the sacrum, could it be that the sacral chakra is not working effectively and reflecting problems in the reproductive organs? Is it hard to meet your child's need for love because your heart *chakra* is closed? How can you open a *chakra*? How can you encourage a *chakra* to metabolise more energy? What restricts its work? Listen to your body, what experience is blocking it, or even dislodging the *chakra*?

A new way of thinking about health and illness and everyday life is required. Aryuvedic medicine and Tibetan medicine have used the *chakras* and *chakra* balancing for thousands of years[38]. Imagine someone has thyroid problems, the thyroid itself can be taken out, and that is just what conventional medicine might do. But the thyroid is linked to the fifth *chakra* and the fifth auric field. Therefore it is associated with the bronchial and vocal apparatus; but on a psychological level (the emotional auric body) it is connected to the sense of self or self-worth in society; a place of security in society, a sense of belonging.

It is also related to the will. So the person might well ask him/herself, 'am I willing to surrender to the powers of the universe or do I expect them to harm me? Is my fifth chakra closed , because I expect "never to be able to do or be what I want?"'.

Now let's compare this to the mind-body-soul approach. There the neck is seen as a bridge between the mind (head) and the body. Thoughts and ideas get expressed or repressed here. Here we swallow more than food. We take in. We also express feelings, or if unable to we have to swallow them. If we are not allowed to choose the place and task in society, our job, profession or even friends that we want, then we have to swallow our interest, creativity, anger and frustration. Such swallowing back or "blocking" can amass energy and lead to hyperactivity in that area, e.g. ulcers, coughing; even goitre. Now removing the thyroid does not help the person to assimilate and express what they feel, what they want or what to do in society or in life. They still imagine the universe wills them ill. Nothing has changed, the *chakra* is still closed, the fifth level of metabolising energy is still not working, so where does the problem go now? Does it manifest itself in another illness in that same region, e.g. the ears, mouth, teeth?

Instead of having the thyroid removed and/or spend the rest of their lives swallowing pills; it could be suggested that the person addresses the real problem. Consider a change of job, or addressing their mistrust in the universe or take charge of their lives rather that feeling victimised by life itself, or perhaps just seek an outlet for pent-up emotions.

This short example is not intended to be a case study, nor is it in any way complete it is merely demonstration how the three concepts of anatomies of the body as a unified field of energy can work together.

Chapter Two

The Movement of Life in the Meridians

I suggest:

Lie on the floor flat on your back. Allow your attention to come gently to your feet. Tell yourself to let go of any tension in your feet; then take your awareness to your ankles and consciously let go of any tightness you feel there. Take your mind to your calves; be aware of any tension there and let it go. Let your awareness move to your Knees and thighs and let go of any tension you become aware of. Allow your attention to focus on your buttocks and let go of any tension there; then travel up your spine vertebra by vertebra and relax any tension you feel by consciously letting go. Now imagine gentle hands sweeping any tension out of the muscles along your spine, - relax your back. Let go of any tension in your shoulders; let go!

Then put your awareness in your arms and hands and let go of tension there. Focus your awareness on the front of your body, become aware of the rising and falling of your belly, and let go of any tension in this area. Just watch with your mind's eye the rise and fall of your belly; all tension of the organs in the abdominal area flows out on the out breath; let it go. Then draw your awareness to your chest and just observe its rise and fall; all tension is released in that rise and fall. Now let your awareness go to your throat and jaw and feel the tension, let it go. Then feel the cheekbones, the ears, feel the cartilage, feel the skull, let it go. Allow the attention to go to the nose, feel the breath, in and out, easy, no tension. Focus your mind on your eyes, the sockets; let the eyes relax as if sinking back into black velvet; let go of your mind. Stroke your forehead and your skull with unseen hands; relax the tension in your head; let it go!

You are completely relaxed, yet fully aware of your body. Just sink into that awareness. Then let go of even that[1]. When I lay there in the stillness of my body I became aware of a flowing sensation in me, a floating, and then a feeling as though honey or molten gold flows through me. First I become aware of it along the spine and then in the sacrum, a warm flowing, glowing feeling. Then the inside of my arms seem to have light streaming through them! The back of my legs start to "sparkle". The back of my head feels like a "Spaghetti Junction", then suddenly there is physical activity there, even though I lie perfectly still. The "Spaghetti Junction" seems to smooth out, stretching as though someone said "Ah-h-h-h" and something flows over the crown of my head. It is as though an unknown universe moves inside me, it flows, streams, glides! While in that total relaxed state of awareness, I witness the energy working in my body, it is flowing, like water, in a sort of line from the back of my legs to the crown of my head. What is it that I witnessed?

Ancient sages felt and saw this energy and they recognised disturbances in this flow and ways to redress these imbalances. 5000 years ago in India the Science of life, Ayur-veda was developed and needles used along these lines to balance the energy flow. This is mentioned in the Vedas. From earliest times the Buddhist University (Takshshila) too taught such techniques. Although the knowledge went into the background in its country of origin, through travelling monks it flourished in China.

Consequently the Chinese have for thousands of years recognised, studied and used these energy flows and have developed a whole system of such "rivers of energy".

Chi, the divine energy, flows through twelve such channels and they called them 'meridians'. There are different approaches to these meridians. Some, like the traditional acupuncture system, envisage them as absorbing energy "into the human body via portals of energy on the skin". Others see them as being more flexible, and loosely processing energy along these specific lines, and pay less importance to the individual points. All focus though on the end points. Try to remember the picture of the man by Michelangelo, with his hands raised straight over the head. Now imagine a group of (lines) meridians enter at the fingertips, journeying through the body and gathering the heavenly energy of *Yang*. Other such lines start at the toes journeying upwards, gathering the energy of the earth, the *Yin* energy.

S. Masunaga, in this century, focused on the energy- flow, proposing that the energy can be contacted anywhere along the line. Others treated the meridians as fixed body parts especially scientists such as the Russian Iyzak Bentov and Dr. Valerie Hunt. They have measured the epidermis on points along the meridians and found that these have unique properties, their electrical resistance is lower than that of the surrounding skin by a factor of ten to one. They also found that the electrical quality is influenced by different states of consciousness such as waking , sleeping and meditation or a state of "dis-ease".

Kim Bong Han suggested that the meridians have an actual tubular structure that can be measured. Dr. Hiroshi Motoyama has not only measured the electrical characteristics of various meridians but has, with a device called AMI (Machine diagnosed imbalances) taken some sort of photos akin to the Kirlian photography. Electrography or Kirlian photography is a technique whereby living objects in the presence of high frequency, high voltage low current electrical fields are photographed. Semyon Kirlian pioneered this technique at about the same time as H.S. Burr measured electric fields around living objects at Yale University in 1940. Today it is common at any 'health fair' that you can have your hands, feet or aura photographed in this way[2].

The danger of these "fixed" approaches lies in compartmentalisation, thus completely missing the point of the wise of old who saw that the energy does not only flow in these rivers, but is flowing in different levels (bodies) or energy fields constantly interacting in nth-dimensions. The above work led to extensive use of "meridian photography" especially in Japan, where it is reputed to be used for selection of employees as it reveal potential weakness and thus future state of health or rather illness. Such futuristic and ethically horrific approach has a strange by-product. They help convince people, especially in the traditional medical world, that we are indeed beings of intelligent energy, and that meridians are part of our "physical anatomy". In fact, "the meridian system is the key interfacing system between the etheric and the physical"[3], and that "energy flows through the body in exquisitely organised patterns, or channels called meridians"[4].

W. Ohashi and S. Masunaga have re-directed the understanding of the meridian system away from such calcifying studies that approach the meridians as though they were a new body part. Ohashi and Masunaga revived the original concepts where meridians are embedded in an understanding of the body as something in constant flux in itself, as well as with nature. The movement in side the body corresponds with nature according to the five Elements. This idea is found in the Japanese as well as in the Chinese tradition; yet the roots of this approach go back to the spiritual traditions of India[5] where the *rishis* saw the world as belonging to five realms, that of the Earth (e.g. Artharva Veda XII, I), the Fire (e.g. Rig Veda 1, 36), Air-breath (Artharva Veda XI), Water, the King of the Cosmos (Artharva Veda IV, 16 ff), and Faith, that which kindles the fire, that through which comes light (Rig Veda X 1, 51 ff).

As we have mentioned previously, the elements represent the characters of different energy fields. By and large, the theory of the meridians cannot, without altering or even negating its uses, be separated from the context of the elements. To talk of the elements, which imprint the meridians with their character, is one way of grasping the concept of transforming energy from the outside into useful frequencies for us. Meridians are energy of higher frequencies than what we normally term physical and visible. Yet the vibration of meridians is so close to the surface that they can be felt, or rather their effect can be felt as "full or empty", as there or lacking; as tense and repellent, as slack and needy, contracted or flowing, cold or warm, or as the Japanese call it, *kyo* or *jitsu*.

What is this touch that can perceive such subtlety? Touch really is "the brain reaching out into the world using specialised nerve cells to register certain information"[6]. All the five senses are tools of the brain. "The world we see, taste, smell (and touch) is such an interpretation by our brain of various energy fields". When bar magnets come together with their north poles facing each other, the magnetic field pushes them apart. If these were thinking magnets they would "feel" something solid between themselves and recoil. To the observing eye – there is nothing there, yet to the "observer" inside the magnet, the subjective one, it is tangible and exists without a doubt.

What we feel and experience is always subjective to our brain, only, we are told by others, it is not. Let's assume we could take that filter of conditioning out. With pure awareness we would feel energy without any interpretation of quality or characteristics. Now this is exactly what trained healers should do, they clear their personal attachment and focus with intention thus the pure power of their consciousness contacts energy. Shiatsu is a healing praxis, which combines both touch and intention, in order to help the natural flow of energies through the meridians. "As do healers of Aryuvedic medicine, Taoist healers, American Indian medicine men/women, Hunza healers or healers of the Christian Essener tradition. It is important to understand that such forms of healing through touch and intention are based on the belief that the tissue, which composes our physical form, is fed not only by oxygen, glucose and chemical nutrients, (which of course are themselves forms of energy) but also by higher vibrational energies"[7].

How can the intention of the healer be enough to "feel" and energies the body?

It is because intention, like "thought itself" is pure energy. Just take a minute to think about the consequences of such a statement. Thoughts are energy! Thoughts can pass through other fields of energy, and like other energy they can turn to matter. My thoughts influence then and perhaps create what is around me. If I had the ability to concentrate the thought energy enough, I could manifest objects. Is that not what seems so unbelievable to us, when holy men of the East reputedly manifest objects (sweets, ashes) seemingly out of the air; in our time of Satya Sai Baba or Nityananda are examples[8].

If thought is energy, that can become manifest through focus, then the thought "I hate you" has the same effect as saying it. Another example: think "Peace" and there will be peace. A colossal statement, yet, it makes us aware how much we need to be aware and conscious if the energy field theory is right.

We said earlier, that cells have intrinsic intelligence; we can now add that thought can become intelligent manifestation in cells, and meridians move intelligent energy. Energy follows a triadic rhythm of rest (ground, stillness or balance), of motion (action, creation) and destruction (dissolution). The same rhythm is followed by the meridians; they can be in balance, in motion or activity, or in dissolution, emptying themselves. In constant interaction with their surroundings, they too follow this triadic rhythm as we touch they change.

Think of a pebble that has just been thrown into the water and making ripples, a second stone is thrown in making ripples; one field of energy patterns interferes with the other. We throw in a third, a fourth etc. All the rings interfere with each other. Nothing in the universe is without such interference, or "participation". This means that the triadic rhythm of the meridian will constantly be interfered with, changed, thrown off course, blocked by another rhythm. This is the nature of being alive! Being alive is - constant change.

When the interference is prolonged and follows repeatedly the same pattern, it would become a reason for severe disturbance, severe enough to filter down to the physical level and distort the pattern of the manifest, physical body? Prolonged, energetic disturbances of the flow of the meridian causes distortions of the physical body and expresses itself possibly in postures, in habits or even in illness? And yet the conscious energy itself, the Movement of Life, is blameless; it is in the nature of itself that distortion happens.

Pure consciousness is always blameless. Man is always good, always divine, yet he suffers, or as Chokamela, a poet saint of Maharashtra (ca 1250-1350 AC) says:

"A sugar cane may be crooked, yet its juice is not. A bow may be curved, and yet the arrow is not. A river may be winding, and yet its water is not. So also Choka may be a pariah, and yet his heart is pure" [9].

The Movement of Life, life-energy is value free. Nothing last long enough to merit identifying with it, to get attached and bear its pain, for the hurt comes and goes, joy comes and goes, life is the ONE in innumerable manifestations. Oh, to keep that awareness every moment of my life, then I could be free. The One is constant, is eternal, the manifestations are not! The divine is what is in all of us, the human part makes us unique. The divine energy itself is always, yet it's unique patterns are in constant movement, therefore we call it the Movement of Life. It flows in and through the *chakras*, it flows in the meridians, it manifests itself as bones, tissue, organs and blood. I propose it also manifests as posture, gesture, habitual body language and even more etheric, as character, behaviour patterns and feelings, and on a higher level of frequencies, as spiritual attitudes and extra sensory perceptions.

Meridians (and *nadis*) as well as *chakras* can be described as channels and doors connecting various energy fields from the gross physical to the subtlest, for mutual benefit.

For just this task the Chinese have discovered 12 channels for our "bio-energy"; they called them meridians. The older Indian cousins too recognised 12 such channels and called them nadis, but they also recognise hundreds more subtle channels. Both traditions connect these channels each to a hollow or solid organ of the body. Both cultures use needle-treatment as well as massage to balance these. In recent times this use was brought to the attention of the West from China (under the communist regime). Consequently a lot of practices and terms in common use today are linked to Chinese, or rather Taoist terms and traditions.

For example, the 12 meridians are grouped together in a brother or sister relationship, which is based on the Taoist Chinese principle of *Yin* and *Yang*, their functions are complimentary. The *Yin* meridian and the *Yin* Organ are in Traditional Chinese Medicine (TCM) called the *Zang* organs, 'solid organs' or visceras; viscera because they are said to contain the pure essence of food or *Gu-Ki*. They are also called 'core-organs' or respectively 'core-meridians' because they lie deeper in the body and deal with deeper more refined energy processes. The pure essence of these *Zang* Organs are difficult to replace.

The *Yang* organs are called in TCM '*Fu*-Organs' or 'Hollow-Organs', their function is more that of a 'work-shop' processing grosser matter then passing on the refined essence to the partners. The *Yang* Meridians protect and support the *Yin* Organs and meridians therefore they lie closer to the surface creating a conductive internal environment in which the latter can operate.

In TCM the organs have a wider role than in Western medicine; a whole range of physiological and psychological processes is covered by referring to these organs, and they operate in tune with moving energy fields rather than defined specific 'things'. Thus in future, when referring to the TCM concept of an organ, I will talk of Organ-Networks, and use the word organ only when referring to the Western anatomical 'thing'. This is in accordance with the concepts of Buddhist, Ayurvedic and Tibetan medicine. for example, the Heart which represents the Element Fire, is not identified with the organ as such, but with the fire of inspiration, the psychic fire, the fire of religious devotion, the intuitive mind etc.

The Movement of Life in the Meridians

In order to prevent confusion I have to clarify yet another concept that roots in TCM. The Life-Energy or Movement of Life that we have talked about so far is called *Qi* (Japanese *Ki*). It is globally described as "that what makes things happen *in* energies and energies that makes things happen", or even "energies in which things happen". Thus this energy of life has a wide open meaning, it is fluidity often eludes the Western mind. Within the human body, *Ki* is what makes us alive, be it derived from food or air, or congenital. It is seen in TCM as manifest in three ways, in Blood (carrying nutrients, thus governing the material form of the body), in moisture (referring to everything connected to fluid from generating, distributing to storing it) and *Qi*. In this specialised sense, a substance that is invisible. Qi is none the less as real as that which manifests as movement and activity. These three work together, interdependent, co-generative and mutually regulating as one *Qi*, the gross and the refined substances and processes of body and soul[10]. For us Westerners it is a difficult idea to grasp that the particle could be the same as the whole - both called *Qi*, yet in the holographic image of life it makes sense, the part contains the whole picture.

The meridians now can be described as rivers that provide the human with a three-fold energy through different levels of the Organ-Network. Moving through the meridians, this energy follows a particular order, linked to a life cycle for the basic principles of life.

> The flow starts with the Lung Meridian (LU) and goes in succession through the Large Intestine (LI), Stomach (ST), Spleen (SP), Heart (HT), Small Intestine (Si), Bladder (BL), Kidney (Ki), Heart Constrictor (HC), Triple Heater (TH), Gallbladder (GB) and Liver Meridians (LV). One cycle of energy is complete when energy from the Liver Meridian returns to the Lung Meridian, where the respiration is adjusted according to the state of all the other meridians and organs and then the cycle is repeated with that modification.

51

Life Cycle: CV & GV.

There are two original meridians, called the Conception Vessel (CV) and the Governing Vessel (GV), considered to be the first source of energy for forming the cell. On the grown body they run central to the front and back respectively. They form the core of our energy system and act as regulators to the overall body. They affect energy at a deep constitutional level. They join the two halves of the body. They help create forms through which *Ki* can flow. They are *Ki* reservoirs and *Ki* regulators. They are a source of *Ki*.

<u>CV</u>. *Ki* reservoir of *Yin* energy and regulates all *Yin* energies of the body. Also called, the 'central channel' or 'the spiritual channel' or 'Great Mother Flow' and the sea of all *Yin* Meridians.

<u>GV</u>. *Ki* reservoir of *Yang* energy, regulates all *Yang* energies of the body. Also called 'great father flow' and the sea of all *Yang* Meridians.

Life Cycle: LU & LI.

First the individual cell, as well as the body must define itself by creating boundaries between itself and the external world, and learn to cope with and adapt to this external world. An organism does this through the process of exchange and elimination. These are the functions of Lung and Large Intestine [11].

<u>LU</u>. Location: Along the trachea, down and along the clavicle, along the inside of the arm down to the thumb, to end in a point on the nail-bed of the thumb; it goes down, in addition, from the hollow underneath the clavicle down one side of the chest through the belly it resurfaces along the inside back of the legs down to the sole of the foot.

LU "takes the vital *Ki* energy (basic life force) from the outside world into the body through the in-breath (inhalation) and refines it by eliminating unnecessary substances through the out-breath (exhalation) before distributing the *Ki* around the body. Our lungs communicate between the inner and outer atmospheres and therefore constitutes a key organ of our existence"[11].

LI. Location: Starting at the nail-bed of the index finger it runs on the outside of the arm, across the shoulders; along the throat to the nostrils. And again on the outside edge of the back of the legs to the sole of the foot, ending on the ball of the foot.

LI "aids the Lung and functions to process and eliminate food substances taken into the body, thereby eliminating stagnation of Ki energy". It is the "Dustbin Collector", i.e. this organ forms, stores and eliminates the waste (faeces). In Chinese medicine it is called "Official of Transmission", i.e. it carries out the will of the Lungs by expressing this vital relation of exchange and elimination with the external environment in a practical way, i.e. by processing the grosser materials"[11].

Life Cycle: ST & SP

"Next the cell (as the body) in order to keep going, must maintain and reproduce life. So the ingestion, digestion and assimilation of food taken from the environment is a necessity if the organism is to grow and sustain life. Stomach and Spleen control the body's intake of nourishment"[11].

ST. Location: Starts underneath the eye, runs central through each side of the face along the front of the body (bilaterally) and parallel to the mid-line of the body, along outside edge of the chin and ends in the second toe on the outside edge of the nail-bed.

ST "relates to the intake of food, receiving nourishment through eating, integrating it through exercising and bringing it to fruition through the production of body heat plus reproduction for women. It takes the energy from the food for the spleen to distribute. It is related to the entire upper digestive tract, from the lips through the oral cavity, oesophagus, stomach, duodenum to the jejunum. ST controls appetite, lactation, and ovaries to some extent, as well as the menstrual cycle"[11].

SP. Location: The Spleen Meridian begins on the big toe and runs up the inside of the legs, along the front of the body, then, at the level of the arm. It runs down the inside of the arm to the inside of the index finger, and a branch runs off across the clavicle into the head ending above the temple.

SP "relates to the breaking down of food through digestive juices and the distribution of food as energy. It relates also to reproductive glands (breasts and ovaries). Since the spleen distributes the energy obtained from food through the body, the other organs depend on it for life"[11].

Life Cycle: HT & Si:

At the same time as an organism forms a boundary between itself and the outside world, it must form a centre for itself. Under the control of the heart with its integrating function, digested food is converted into useable energy (small intestine). Heart and Small Intestine have to do with 'integration' and 'conversion'.

HT: Location: The meridian runs from the centre of the armpit, along the inner arm down to the inside edge on the nail-bed of the little finger. It also runs from the armpit across to the sternum, bilaterally and down it. It runs through the belly and surfaces again in the inside of the leg, in the knee, along the calf and between the ankle and the heel to end at the sole of the foot circumventing the ball of the heel.

Heart has to do with the ability to rule. It represents compassion and therefore governs emotions and spirit as well as blood circulation. It carries warmth, oxygen and nutrients throughout the body. It functions to assimilate and integrate by receiving stimulus from the outside via the brain and five senses and adapts this to the body's internal environment. It is the 'Supreme Controller'.

Si. Location: it starts at the outside edge of the little finger, bilateral; along the outside of the arm and shoulder and up the neck to end in a point just in front of the middle of the ear. It also branches off at the neck through the middle of the shoulder blades down to the middle of each side of the back, into the buttocks, through the pelvis surfacing again in the middle of the inside leg, down across the middle of the ankle to the ball of the heel.

Si "functions to receive, digest and assimilate nourishment. It sorts out and extracts the good from what we ingest. It is the 'separator of the pure from the impure' (physically and mentally). It is also related to the function of the ovaries and maintenance of menstrual regularity. It also aids the Heart Meridian by keeping *Ki* down in the *hara* area to maintain calmness and composure. Shock, anger, anguish can cause blood stagnation in the lower abdomen"[11].

Life Cycle: BL & Ki.

Next in the cycle are the Bladder and Kidney Meridians, a further system to refine digested materials. Together they perform the function of supplying vital energy and of purifying all bodily fluids.

BL: Location: This meridian runs the whole length of the body. It starts bilaterally in the inside corner of the eye, over the top of the head, either side of the spine, down the back of the legs to the outside of the foot and ends on the nail-bed of the little toe.

BL "relates to the autonomic nervous system (close to the spine) through to the pituitary gland. It controls the reproductive functions and the uterus as well as urinary organs, which collect and excrete waste products after the purification of body fluids. It co-operates with the kidney hormone system.

The bladder is the seat (storehouse) of the emotions. If it is not functioning well, then the rest of system stressed"[11].

Ki: Location: Starting in the centre of the sole of the foot, this meridian runs along the inside of the foot to the ankle. Then it runs on the inside up to the knee, along the thigh to the pelvis, up along the chest (two thirds from the outside on each half of the body) to the clavicle. A branch goes off along the inside of the arm ending in the palm on the pad of the little finger.

Ki "filters the blood, keeping the blood and the body clean and in balance. The water and the acid-base balance are maintained by the kidneys. Kidneys regulate (detoxify and purify) bodily fluids and the final elimination of waste through the urine. In the Chinese system, the kidneys are seen as storing the energy of the life force (*Ki*) itself. The kidneys are ancestral energy and if chronic illness is present, one should look at the kidney energy. It tells us of the past. Willpower is seen as coming from the kidneys. Strong kidneys give us the ability to adapt to stress. Likewise, stress shows in the kidneys"[11].

Life Cycle: HC & TH:

Next in the cycle: Heart Constrictor and Triple Heater carry out the will of the Heart Meridian by transporting the refined substances throughout the body to nourish and protect it. So, they are involved in circulation and protection. HC and TH circulate nourishing *Ki* and protective *Ki* to central and peripheral areas of the body.

HC: Location: It starts just beside the nipple, bilaterally, along the arm over the centre, inside of the palm, ending in the inside nail-bed of the middle finger. Also from the nipple edge a half moon shape goes to the sternum, bilaterally up to the throat and unilaterally down to the end of the sternum; it surfaces again on the inside legs and runs down more or less centrally to the side of the foot.

HC "is a supplementary function to HT. It protects the heart and regulates the blood flow, heat and nourishment throughout the body (i.e. vascular system, arteries, veins, aorta and central circulatory function of HT). The Heart Constrictor intercepts blows of stress, pain and traumas as well as information that could harm the heart; likewise the heart gives messages via HC. If the HC breaks down, then the HT gets the blows and eventually there is heart trouble"[11].

TH: Location: Starts on the outside edge of the nail-bed of the ring finger, goes along the outside of the arm through the elbow, up one of the shoulders into the neck, behind the ears and ends beside the eyebrow. At shoulder level a branch also goes down the outside edge of the back, then along the ridge of the pelvis and thigh, down the outside of the leg into the middle toe (third toe).

TH "has a supplementary function to the Small Intestine. It acts to maintain the proper temperature and warmth. It controls the peripheral circulation (sends heat to extremities) and the lymphatic system. It governs the immune system. The body is divided into three areas, each with its own ' heater' or *'chou'* centres of metabolic activity: located at: 1) mid chest, and relates to HT and LU; 2) at solar plexus and relates to ST, SP,GB, LV. and 3) at umbilical area and relates to LI, BL, KI and SI.

Their job is to produce heat and energy for the body through respiration, digestion and elimination respectively. Each area should be of equal warmth. The TH encompasses the whole body's central heating system. In this way, TH corresponds to all organs and, according to Chinese medicine, should be considered in all illness".

Life Cycle: GB & LV

Last in the cycle are the Gall Bladder and Liver Meridians. These meridians store the refined substances (nutrients) and release them for use for physical energy. They keep the body active and vigorous.

GB: Location: Starts at the outside point of the eyes, wriggles along behind the ear, then down the neck, around the shoulder blades curving right to the side of the body, going along the body and leg down "the trouser seam", through the ankle to the fourth toe.

GB "distributes nutrients and Ki around the body. It balances total energy through aid of internal hormones and digestive enzymes (saliva, bile, pancreatic juices and intestinal enzymes). It is related to decision making; decides courses of action such as which part of the body needs the energy"[11].

LV: Location: starts at the outside edge of the big toe, runs along the frontal inside of the leg up to the groin. It surfaces on the outside of the chest and goes up to the neck. At arm level a branch goes off along the inside of the arm ending on the palm side, up at the top of the ring finger.

"While life itself depends on our lungs, heart and circulation to bring oxygen, warmth and nutrients to all the cells of the body, the liver provides essential support to all these processes. It stores nutrients and energy for physical activity. It is involved in the formation and breakdown of blood and filters toxins from the blood. Its job is to keep the body full of vigour. It is the planner of how the vital energy of the body is to be used, while the GB is the decision maker"[11].

Life Cycle: LU:

And so the cycle begins again.

General: Physical problems, begin with imbalances in the supply of KI along the meridians to the cells of the body and eventually an organ is held responsible and it begins to give trouble. This situation requires the whole body to rally and help bring about balance again so a particular organ is no longer straining in its function.

*****

If we drew a stick man with his arms raised and legs spread wide, it would appear quite naturally that the body forms two triangles. The first is formed by the lower abdomen and both legs and the distance between the parted legs. Where the waist is another inverted triangle rests, seemingly on the tip of the first one. The navel could be the point of contact. The arms raised above the head form the sides of the second triangle. The base is the distance between the hands. The area where both triangles meet, according to such diverse people as Michelangelo and C.G. Jung, is the point of balance, "the centre of man"[12]. This centre is what is in the Indian tradition is called 'the heart of Shiva', and described as from just below the navel to the sternum, flanked by the base *chakra* (*muladhara*) and the heart *chakra*. The Japanese call this the *hara*. *Hara* does not only describe an area of the body but a quality of having strength, energy and focus. It is used by the warriors of the East to centre and build up power from which to draw strength in combat. In the *hara*, just below the navel, is a centre point called the *tantien*; in the martial arts all actions come from here. This power point and area is believed to be the source of intention, our intention to manifest, be it behaviour, thought, energy or even the auric fields. Some imagine from here a line runs up beyond our head to a point from where we connect to the godhead and descending down deep into the core of the earth to ground us[13].

Furthermore within the area of the *hara*, on a deep level some esoteric anatomy believes, exists a point just above the navel called the 'Core Star' or the seat of individual divine essence. The eternal light of existence that is "both the individual God within us and the universal God at the same time"[14].

The significance of this area we call *hara* is recognised in many cultures. Do you remember seeing pictures of Chinese, Japanese or even medieval Christian sculptures and paintings with gods, monks and saints which have huge exaggerated

Chapter 2

bellies? This is a symbol for 'a strong centre-of-man', something akin to heightened energy.

Let's take a few minutes to see how this relates to our lives. We, certainly in the West, have an idea of how people ought to look and dress. Our ideal is obvious when we open any magazine. The male as well as the female ideal figure is basically viewed as wide shouldered or with a big chest and a slim waist and hip area; the belly is definitely to be small and tight. Most fashion and most exercise programmes aim at such a figure. If the belly is the energy centre it means we voluntarily restrict our life-energy! Fashion dictates that we literally cut our life-energy off, with tight belts, trousers etc., thus encouraging this self-mutilation. Even in loose clothing (which is often modelled on eastern fashions), the underlying lines are shown as slim and tight, to emphasise the 'flow of the garment'.

Why is this? I am sure there are several reasons, such as the association of a 'fat belly' with certain lifestyles, or with loss of elasticity of body and mind. But there is also an underlying attitude of control; if we can control ourselves in this way willingly, then we can also be more easily controlled by others for the same reason, e.g. being controlled by the fashion industry, politicians, etc. We literally hand them over our life-energy, we empower them, instead of ourselves, why? Have we forgotten that we are not separate of the rest of the universe, but the same? In any which way we look we are interdependent with the rest of the world. We could not exists alone. Somehow we know we belong with all others. Yet we live in a society and a time where 'individualism' is the highest god. The whole of Western society is built on the notion of the big 'I', and 'mine' and how 'I differ from you', so that our deep knowing is pushed back, and our longing to return to the All can only be fulfilled by identifying, by following anybody who promises 'a belonging to a group'. We willingly identify with false images, with 'maya', with false ideals, dismembering ourselves to belong to powerful others. We restrict our belly, our central collecting area of Life-Energy to belong to the 'followers of fashion'.

But let us go back to the meridians. The centre, belly or *hara* is an area of special significance to the meridians. Each meridian has an area of concentrated energy within this location. This area is not only representative of the energy-state of the meridian itself, but also the organ-network associated with it. A strong belly (a strong *hara*, or energy centre represents a strong healthy meridian system, and well functioning organs). It seems natural then that this area is used in diagnosis - but this is not its only function. We have seen earlier, that the energy fields are influenced by other energy fields. To touch, in diagnosis, then simultaneously alters the energy -state. To touch the centre of man is then synonymous with changing the energy -state of the area. To touch, for example, the area for the bladder meridian in the belly influences the energy anywhere in the flow of that meridian. In this case, for example, it could influence a pain in the back of the legs! Moreover because of the inter-relatedness of the meridian system, touching one here, changes the energy state of the entire body. Similarly working in this area can quieten the whole energy system. The importance of this area is the reason why meditators focus on the belly. They try to still the waves of activity. Trying to reach a state of rest, a point of stillness. Stillness, rest or peace, is, as we have seen earlier, a prerequisite for creativity, according to the triadic rhythm of life: stillness, activity and dissolution.

Out of the centre of stillness, the meridians rise to activity and stretch out, filling the body with energy and then flow out even further beyond the physical body reaching into the energy field around us characterised by five elements. In turn energy fields of the environment reach inside us, affecting the nature of the meridians. In this way these five elements give their qualities to the meridians. It is a living, breathing interchange from outside the body at large, to inside, down to the smallest component, and back again. To gain understanding of the meridians as they go about their work of being and becoming

Chapter 2

we have to focus on the 'Five Elements'. They can be seen as the colours of our being; the character of the picture or the 'inner nature of the meridian'.

But not before we realise that our understanding has its limits.

> "Cottleston, Cottleston, Cottleston Pie,
> A fly can't bird, but a bird can fly.
> Ask me a riddle and I reply
> Cottleston, Cottleston, Cottleston Pie.
> Cottleston, Cottleston, Cottleston Pie,
> A fish can't whistle and neither can I.
> Ask me a riddle and I reply,
> Cottleston, Cottleston, Cottleston Pie.
> Cottleston, Cottleston, Cottleston Pie,
> Why does a chicken, I don't know why ?
> Ask me a riddle and I reply,
> Cottleston, Cottleston, Cottleston Pie".

...A fly can't bird, but a bird can fly, very simple, it's obvious isn't it? And yet, you'd be surprised how many people violate this simple principle, every day of their lives, and ignore the clear reality that things are as they are...

> "Tell them about Cottleston Pie, - what it means",
> whispered Pooh...
> "Pooh wants to know that the words Cottleston Pie are a way of saying 'Inner Nature'"...
> Ask me a riddle and I reply,
> "Inner Nature" - "Hmm"
> "Cottleston Pie sounds better", said Pooh
> "Well how about this, Pooh?"
> Ask me a riddle and I reply...
> "Things are as they are"
> "Better... But it still doesn't rhyme"
> "All right , how is this?"
> Ask me a riddle and I reply...
> "Cottleston, Cottleston, Cottleston Pie"
> "Just right" said Pooh [15].

PART II

THE MOVEMENT OF LIFE AND THE FIVE ELEMENTS

The Energy of Life in us, and the world around us is constantly changing; thus we call it the Movement of Life. It changes from one season to the next, from one physical state to the next, from day to night and night to day, from fashion to fashion, from health to illness. It changes from fortune to misfortune, from love to hate, from anger to joy, from aggression to peace, from growth to decay, from manifestation to dissolution and so on, *ad infinitum*. Yet from time immemorial man has tried not only to understand this energy, but to describe and categorise it, in order to gain knowledge with which he can work.

One such way to describe the flow of energy are the Five Elements, or five fundamental processes (some cultures limit it to four), agents, movements or powers. But despite classifying Life into these five forces one has to be aware that nothing is static and that even in each phase, each element, there again are the same five characteristics. It is like a hologram where each particle contains the whole picture. This idea suggests, whether we look at the rotation of the planets, the growth of your fingernail, the explosion of a volcano or the working of an ants colony; the digestive process of our stomachs, the growth of a tree, the emotional make up of my daughter or my career - all reflect each and every part of the whole of nature. All are following and being guided by those five phases or elements. They serve as a map or blueprint, "that charts the course of process, a guide for comprehending our unfolding"[1].

For instance as the year goes through the seasons of spring, summer, late summer, autumn and winter, so the human being goes through cycles in their life. It begins with birth followed by adolescence as a student and years of establishing a family or job. Then the years of collecting the fruits of our labours follow and are finally succeeded by the phase of retirement and death. Similarly, what is true for the stages of life is true for the emotional and personal characteristics as well as the physical workings of the body. Even buying a house or any other mundane business follows the same pattern corresponding to the Five Elements. To understand the elements helps us to understand the nature of all things, including the nature of ourselves be it in health or illness. Furthermore it helps the practitioner and therapist to understand their patients needs.

If we look at the Movement of Life at a glance we see Space (or Wood as TCM calls it) representing the phase of expansion, the outward movement, which then culminates in the phase of Fire, which spreads the energy on the surface. At its furthest point we encounter Metal (Air), the phase of contraction, the inward movement towards the core, it culminates in Water which confirms and strengthens the inner, site of germination and creation. Earth, is the one in the centre that stabilises us, the point of balance around which activity takes place. It is the axis, or churning stick in the Indian creation myth. At the centre is the origin of all abundance.

All these states are represented in the body, mind and soul and discord manifests itself in the physical form in organs as illness, in the mind as fixations, blocks, character traits, and in the soul as distress and anguish (*karma*)- or bliss (*ananda*).

Before we look at the elements individually, here is a word of caution. We must remember the intention of the sages of old to understand the holographic concept of nature in constant movement and not consider the elements as a box in which to put a person or event. A person can be, for example, an apprentice learning a new trade - in the Wood-phase of his life. His most apparent character trait might be his humour; all his life he managed to look at things with a pinch of laughter thus he probably has a dominant Fire Element.

Yet as he is at present, going through a patch of fear and anxiety with the approach of his final exam and he is filled with fear. Will he pass or not, thus temporarily his Water

Element is strong and overriding the others. He has a strong bond to his hometown and likes to be with his large family, - e.g. he has, a well developed Earth Element. Unfortunately at present he suffers from constipation. His Metal Element has become blocked by sitting for so many hours of studying, being hunched over his books, not moving, not breathing properly and overriding all elimination processes (effectively blocking them) with acquisition of knowledge.

PART II

Chapter Three

Invocation of Earth

I am Woman
I and the Goddess are one
I am the mother of all that exists
I walk in tune with the universe.

My head -	is Saraswati, delivering all from ignorance.
My mouth -	is the mouth of Kali, drinking the blood of those who dishonour me.
My eyes -	are the jewels you find in the diamond mines of South Africa.
My nose -	is disgusted by the stench of human sacrifice, be it on the slabs of a stone altar, the computer of a business tycoon or the sweat shops of the Third World.
My cheeks -	are those of a young girl meeting her first lover amongst cherry blossoms in Nara.
My ears -	are tired of hearing your cries of "more, more", are you deaf to the sound of enough"; have your drums lost the memory of the rhythm of gratitude?
My hair -	is the cornfields, swaying in the vast grain-belts of America and Russia.
My throat -	gets irritated by the acid rain you pour down my waters; do you want me to treat you with the same disdain?
My chest -	is heaving with sympathy and compassion, bringing forth plants to heal, medicine for you who have lost the vision to inherit me.
My lungs -	are the forests of the world, be aware how you treat them, unless you want to suffocate.
My heart -	is the molten core of the planet, an incalculable power linked only to the Grandfather Sun, who gives light, life or death and purification.

Yours is the choice.

Chapter 3

My veins -	are the rivers of five continents, through them pulses the water of life.
My liver -	and kidneys are the beds of sandstone and lime that filter the water, so I can sustain you with clear, clean blood.
My stomach -	is wherever death occurs, for I digest and transform manure into the sweetest smelling rose, the most succulent peach.
My guts -	are the sewers of every civilisation, from the ancient Mohenjo Daro in the Indus Valley, to the favelas of modern Rio de Janeiro.
My faeces -	are the opals, golden nuggets and other treasures, you grovel for in the dirt.
My spine -	is the Himalayas, my bones, the mountains of the continents and oceans; they are your strength, they support me and in turn fortify you.
My breasts -	are the breasts of every woman that was ever born providing nourishment for all creatures, nurturing without judgement, providing for the weakest cub, the most crooked tree, generous, giving, none is considered unworthy I provide for all, it is you who have lost the ability to share in flood or drought, how dare you treat each other with such shameless disdain?
My pelvis -	is the valley of the Tansa River, where the Lingam meets the Yoni, where Shiva meets Shakti, or where earth meets sky.
My womb -	is more vast than the surface of this planet, for every inch brings forth life, is sacred space to be honoured in my name. Even what seems dead to you, the soggy swamps or dry dusty deserts, support uncountable colonies of microbic life, only extreme heat or water makes me sterile.
My vulva -	is the rift valley in central Africa, from where man originated, on the banks of Lake Turkana.
My skin -	did you not realise that my skin covers all of this planet? Then why do you stab out a burning cigarette on your mothers skin, or cover more

The Element Earth

	and more of it with tarmac, is nothing sacred to you?
My arms -	reach out to each starving child, to offer rest in my heart.
My hands -	the hands of Lakshmi, shower grace and blessings on to everyone, they caress each creature with equal love and tenderness, even those that are too blind to see.
My thighs -	are the thighs of each grandmother that rocks a child on her lap, secure and immovable like a mountain.
My calves -	are the vital support and strength of Durga, holding up right dharma in giving to those less fortunate than yourselves.
My feet -	are tapping out the rhythm of life, the animation of all creatures, decorated with bells creating the original sound.
The soles -	of my feet are carved with the cave paintings of the first people, their symbols are dear to me, for they knew the earth was sacred and painted with its dust.
My toes -	are the islands in the sea, decorated with jewels of shells and flowers.
My joy -	is in the first smile of a baby.
My wrath -	is in the rumble of an earthquake.
My smile -	is like the dawn.
My tears -	are like the ocean.
My pain -	is your pain.

My memory - is long, many thousands of years. So be aware of
the hurt you inflict on me,
what waste you bury in me,
what suffering you cause in my name, for in...

My revenge - I am Woman
I and the Goddess are one
I am the mother of all that exists
I walk in tune with the universe.

Character of Earth

Earth, as the centre of gravity has been in the minds of people since the dawn of time. Every civilisation generated their own myths and stories about this source, this stable, seemingly immovable ground, that with the "kiss of rain" turns into a fertile field, abundantly giving life to all that grows. Earth stood in the centre, with the sky above, the fire of the sun warming it and the water beneath. Water rising into the sky and then coming down to fertilising earth, a union like that of man and woman.

In more than one way primitive man experienced his life as totally dependent on what earth gave him. He relied on the earth for all he needed much as some tribal people still do today.

Several years ago I spent some time with the Igorots of the Philippines, a mountain tribe that still lived similar to the Stone-age (doubtless that has changed since then). Then, they lived in long-houses built with sticks and grass that the plains had provided; the foundations and supports for the house structure were young tree trunks, slowly cut down with sharp flint-stones found in the mountain streams. Their furniture was well chosen stones, some felt even soft to the touch as for generations people had slept on them as beds, their body grease polishing them. Their cooking utensils were all of clay; their clothes a rough matting of woven grass. They made fire by hitting special stones and catching the spark with dry fluff. Their cattle - "wild pigs" were kept in holes in the ground; it was much easier to dig a hole than to build a fence. Their crops were a kind of wild rice and beans, planted in terraces on the mountain slopes. For threshing they used sticks and a grass mat; two stones ground the grain to flour. Apparently everything they needed was provided by "mother" earth. Earth was revered as a mother with several daughters; the behaviour of the different daughters was responsible for the changes in seasons, day and night, human fortune or mishap. The "mother" was the stabilising, balancing centre - not unlike in most other societies. Even in modern societies the mother is, (often) still the centre point for the family; even though the times where the family actually gathers around the mother physically may be (in modern Western civilisations) limited to feasts such as birthdays, Christmas etc. Could it be that our society has so much problems such as criminality, pollution, political instability and so on because it has lost its focus on the mother and/or the earth?

The earth is the ground on which we stand, it is the base, the root, it imparts stability, it locates us in space. We have no difficulty in accepting that plants and trees need to be firmly rooted in the ground or the wind and weather will kill them; - why is it so difficult to accept that people need a similar grounding stability?

The earth has many textures, many different features. How many landscapes are there? What variety of vistas, of textures has she got, each looking different from the next? In places she has a loose surface of gravel and sand from where a weed is easily pulled up; in some others she has the most waterlogged swamps where only specially adapted life can exist. In some she has heavy clay soil, rich in minerals that holds things firmly in their place and some have wonderful rich fertile soil where much can grow. When earth is too porous it cannot hold anything, it erodes quickly; if it is too dense it will hold things so tight they will get stuck, unable to move and will be throttled.

We can choose the ground we stand on (in more than one ways) and there is an abundance of places that could nourish our life. From the Himalayas to the Andes, from the African plains to the fjords of Norway, from the Siberian tundra to the tropical island; we can choose to grow in crevices, shallows or on mountain slopes. We can live on plains, flatlands and open spaces; everywhere we will find people, tribes, nations that grow food in fields, forests or paddies. All people live from the fruit of the earth in one way or another, and so do all plants and animals; earth provides for all, there is no other source than her. And once we have lived, earth takes us back! All- good and bad, beautiful and ugly, she does not judge, her generosity takes all, gives all.

> "Every part of this country is sacred to my people...
> has been hallowed by some fond memory or sad
> experience of my tribe...
> the very dust under your feet... is the ashes
> of our ancestors, and our bare feet are
> conscious of the sympathetic touch,
> for the soil is rich
> with the life of our kindred"[2].

The earth re-integrates what has existed, purifies and assimilates it to be re-used. Yes the earth is the first, best and last re-cycling 'plant'. In literature it is described as the womb and the grave; as the beginning and the end; as life and death; as death and rebirth.

Not so long ago I sat in a Cornish Fogou to meditate. A Fogou is a prehistoric earth tunnel with one or two chambers, built into and fortified by granite boulders. It reputedly was used for ceremonies, healing or simply as a shelter in times of tribal fighting. To sit in the bowels of the earth, as in a womb put me into touch with the potentiality of earth. There, it is still, there is apparently nothing - yet a feeling of potency, a fullness that can only be experienced, not described.

Later the same day I went to a Cornish "Holy well", that for equally long, has been a sacred place. Here from the opening of the earth a different energy emanated. There was lightness, quickness, giving. No wonder these springs were considered to give healing and grant wishes, then as today. At the well earth was giving "things" out at such a fast rate! No more stillness, just profuse giving, infinitely generous, gracious and sparkling, - and the strange fact is that these holy wells are not water gushing forth, not a spring in that sense, but more still, crystal pools, - thus the feeling of gushing forth "comes from a different plane". Both these experiences characterise earth:

there is the quiet, resting centre - and the coming forth, the source of everything; the potential and the action.

To summarise, earth is the potential and source of everything; it is rich and plentiful. It shares its riches; it's generous; it nurtures and supports indiscriminately; it nourishes others; it is non-judgemental; giving. It synthesises opposites (life and death); it unifies, (thus makes peace); stabilises, balances. Earth is the quiet centre around which activity revolves; it is able to achieve co-operation; it is tireless in serving others; it preserves (family, society), it is compassionate and sympathetic to all in need, it re-cycles; it is strong, it holds and protects, it is a guardian.

What would a person look like, who had Earth as their dominant, influencing Element? She may be a housewife and mother, but not necessarily so. She may be a teacher, a diplomat or in any serving job. If not, she will certainly be involved in helping others in some way, even if on a voluntary basis and in some kind of charity...or two...or three! She might be somebody spending a lot of time organising jumble sales, baking cakes for school fairs etc. She holds her family together with a practical, down to earth, intelligence, circling around their needs and the needs of others, to the extent that she might forget her own needs, having difficulty in saying 'no' to the demands of others.

She might be fleshy and strongly built, with solid hips and thighs, her feet either firmly on the ground, or if in an unbalanced state, she might have difficulties putting her feet on the ground. Her feet and hands seem small. Her heaviness does not stop her from being quick and efficient, accomplishing her tasks with gusto. She is a patient listener who makes people comfortable, but is not somebody who hides her own feelings either. Her home is very important to her, as is family and where she lives, her surroundings are warm and cosy.

She is protective towards her family and an extended network of friends. Being needed by them makes her feel good, makes her feel useful to the extent that she can be completely absorbed in others. Her need to fulfil others can leave her own self, feeling empty and unfulfilled. She mistakes this emptiness for hunger, cravings for food and eating become a "must". Being 'full' slows her metabolism down, food remains undigested, inflating her abdomen with stagnant energy, fluid and gas. Her remedy is to eat more, for the body does not get the energy from the undigested food. This extra physical weight, as well as the extra emotional weight taken on from other peoples problems, increase her physical and emotional weight, to her own detriment resulting in sluggishness and tiredness. In the extreme she feels "stuck". She might have benevolent lumps of one sort and another in her tissue, since "disease is located within the flesh"[3]. And since the Earth Element covers feeding others - mammary glands might especially be affected, or it might lead to fibroids, especially in the womb, or other forms of fibrosis.

If the environment is generous and without too much change, with lots of social tasks to fulfil, she will be happy and have a stabilising effect on the world around her, keeping her tendency to overcompensate well at bay. Her life is like a play: she supports the players providing nourishment, physically and mentally, thus setting the tone, ensuring that the play of the world can continue and that every other player can do their part.

Associations to the Earth Meridians

The two meridians that are connected with the element Earth are the Stomach meridian (*Yang*) and the Spleen meridian (*Yin*). The meridians are not to be understood as representative of those organs, or directly linked to them, but are much more widely understood. The concept includes an Organ-network relating to the physiological as well as psychological energy fields, connecting thus, body, mind and soul. We have to guard against using the Chinese concept as boxes in which to put "things" but rather imagine them as fluid concepts.

At this point it is interesting to add that the 12th century medic and mystic Hildegard von Bingen, worked with a very similar scheme. All illness is based on distortions of the elements. She described illness and cures in great detail and with an understanding and insight we otherwise only know from eastern traditions. To her (in addition to what we mentioned before) the earth has also the capacity to be cool in summer, especially in her depth so as to protect the growing roots from withering in the heat. Furthermore the earth is warm in winter to keep potential seeds from being destroyed by cold. So earth balances and protects in order to bring "Life's essence to the light".

She also describes Earth as supportive; the hard baked earth or even frozen earth, carries enormous weight. She also has earth linked intrinsically to Fire and Water; and with it the support of growth is almost like a covenant that God has with the world.

As for the interdependence of the elements, she says "would the earth not fulfil its task of providing 'growing', there would be no air; if the water would not be softening and taming the earth... and the earth not taming the water, and lead it into the right pathways, the water could not have its mirror-like quality that points to the depths... The dew is a symbol for right mixture of fire and air, bringing the right condition for abundant ripening of fruit, fulfilled in the fire of the sun. The hardness of one element supports the softness of another, and the softness of one soothes the hardness of the other, in such mutual benefit the elements can exist in harmony and balance..." Furthermore she connects the earth to the conditions within the body and its health and illness. Just like in the Chinese system she links the stomach, the flesh, sexual organs and fertility, the mouth and all forms of ingestion and other similar concepts to earth[4].

Ayurveda associates the earth (*Prithvi*) with the state of *Kapha*, one of the three 'states of being'. *Kapha* is associated with stability, allowing growth, heaviness, as well as congestion and lack of flow; it specially relates to those states of the organs that result from accumulated mucus which stops the flow (for Earth and Water mix). It is linked directly to the stomach, and also to the spleen. The latter extends into a second state of being, called *Pitta* that focuses on blood supply to the organs.[5]

Buddhist traditions, such as the Tibetan medicine, see earth in even a closer relationship with water than the above two approaches, thus affecting kidney and bladder, sexual organs etc. as well as the traditional stomach and spleen. More emphasis is placed on the psychological and mental aspects. Such attitudes as fear, jealousy, frigidity etc. on one hand and sacred actions and secret offerings on the other hand are connected to Earth[6].

We will primarily follow the Chinese/Japanese concepts, because they are well recognised and practised in the West. But first we will look at traditional Western anatomy of the stomach and spleen, and their function for they reveal their own intrinsic truth.

1) <u>The Stomach</u> is a part of the alimentary tract, which is a long tube through which food passes; it commences with the mouth and ends with the anus. The stomach has the shape of a 'J' and is a widened part of the digestive track lying in the abdominal cavity, in front of the left lobe of the liver. One end of it is a continuation from the oesophagus and it ends in the duodenum, which is part of the small intestines. The stomach has a valve at either end, and a kind of 'head-space' on the top, above the entrance from the oesophagus. It is lined with four layers of tissue and is protected by the fatty skin of the peritoneum.

When we have eaten something, the food accumulates in the stomach, the "desert" remains in the widened 'head-space'. The food is mixed with gastric juices that are secreted by special glands, (mineral salts, mucus and water, hydrochloric acid, 'intrinsic factor' and enzymes). The muscles contract in a constant churning movement that breaks the food down and mixes it with gastric juices. The juices liquidise the food and the acid kills microbes and prepares the food for digestion by pepsin. Pepsin begins the digestion of proteins by breaking them up into smaller molecules. Intrinsic factor helps with the absorption of Vitamin B12. Mucus prevents the acid from destroying the stomach itself. After the food is sufficiently liquid and broken down it is passed on to the duodenum.

The stomach then, seems to have a slightly different task from what is commonly believed. It does digest food (in the sense of absorbing it and making it available to the body) but only to a limited extent. Its main functions are to act as a temporary reservoir for food and allowing the food to be prepared by breaking it up physically, e.g. into small and liquid particles and starting the chemical process of dissolving it into nutrients, and moving the matter, called 'chyme' onward.

2) The Spleen is part of the lymphatic system. It is formed (in part) by lymphatic tissue and lies in the abdominal cavity, in between the fundus and the diaphragm. It is slightly oval shaped and is enclosed in an elastic capsule which consists of spleenic pulp, e.g. lymphocytes and macrophages. Blood flows through the spleen. After their life span of approximately 120 days, red blood cells, formed in the bone marrow, get broken down mainly in the spleen, but also in bone marrow as well as in the liver. The broken down products of the spleen are passed to the liver. Other cellular material and microbes are ingested and killed in the spleen (phagocytosis). The spleen also provides many lymphocytes (B- and T- lymphocytes) needed for immune reactions.

The task of the spleen can thus be summarised as a cleansing and protecting agent fundamental to blood, its function and healthy distribution. The spleen's role is thus one of support, transformation and protection.

The Nei Ching, the ancient Classic on Medicine by the Yellow Emperor, talks about the spleen as "the solitary organ, (that) can irrigate the four others that are nearby", (meaning the liver, heart, lungs and kidneys). It is easy to see why the spleen is described as the supporting agent of the major body organs. These organs "receive the impact of the life-giving force from those who generate them and they pass it on to those which they subjugate, their force of life is bestowed upon those who they beget; they are in communication with one another and influence one another"[7]. If one is well and healthy it helps the others, if one is ill it will also affect the others. So the spleen is seen as being in the centre of the bodies functions, as well as in the centre of the Earth. It is interesting to note that the diagnostic area location for the Spleen occupies the central position of the *Hara* (the belly), the area around the navel. The Nei Ching talks about the Stomach meridian as the "official of the public granaries (that also) grants the five tastes"[8]. Food is not just gathered and redistributed in the stomach, but the condition of the "food-silo", as well as the contents of the food, determine how long the food remains in the stomach. This can vary from twenty minutes with fruit or juice, to two hours for carbohydrates or for complex mixtures and in extreme conditions, up to eight and twelve hours. So food can sit a long time in the stomach sometimes creating nausea and tension. A resistance to pass through, a holding on to food (or emotions) signifies a holding on to reality, attempting to prevent absorption, inevitable moves or change.

From this description of the organs and their function it is easy to abstract some characteristics.

- For the Stomach we could mention: receiving, accumulating, mixing, grinding up, preparing stuff for others, absorbing bits (but not all), holding, constant activity, protecting, passing on to others, giving.

- For the Spleen we could mention: being essential support, being of service, breaking down matter, 'killing unwanted' stuff, protection, passing on to others, giving, a central task.

Similar functions reveal why these two organs are sisters and seen as a pair. Glancing back to the summary of the earth-characteristics similar attributes for all can be found. They are involved in:

- receiving and accumulating,
- some sort of preparation, synthesising and transforming,
- holding and supporting,
- constant, tireless activity,
- nurturing and sharing,
- passing on to others and giving,
- support and more support,
- some absorption,
- protection and more protection.

By observing one, the Chinese Sages of old connected it to the other and established that stomach and spleen are truly linked with the earth. They are the personal link of each person with the energy field of Earth. They are our own intrinsic Earth.

To be of this earth, even made from earth, as the description from Genesis in the Bible has it, does not surprise anymore. We recognise that our relationship with the earth is a necessary part of self-awareness. It is a sacred duty of each person and a responsibility among the society of 'Earth-lings'. Ideally we all would be well centred, (grounded) in ourselves, as well as open and participating, receptive and willing to digest the world outside us. But what if this relationship is ailing?

Obviously all processes of ingesting will be affected and this has far reaching consequences, because we take in air and 'digest it' as well. We take in rest (sleeping patterns); we take in movement (bodily co-ordination); we take in thoughts and ideas (brain activity); we take in sensory impressions (emotions); we take in seeds (female reproductive cycle); indeed it seems that the *taking in* is central to just about all human activity. Consequently ailments, that derive from malfunctioning of this process of 'taking –in' are also far reaching and range from obesity, stomach ulcers, colds and nasal congestion, to too much thinking and worrying over details, forgetfulness and restlessness. They include being easily tired and yawning a lot, as well as a malfunctioning of the female organs and reproductive glands. It includes the inability to assimilate new ideas as much as the hardening of the arteries due to stress (for the stomach has a link with the Hypothalamus - endocrine glands-). All these and more, are linked to the Earth Element.

Our language often mirrors such importance in proverbial sayings such as:

A person "loses the earth from under his feet", when they display signs of nervousness, instability and emotional imbalance.

A person may feel "uprooted" when they feel excluded, lonely or homeless.

A person described as "ego-centric" is one that pleads to re-define their centre; they have lost their stabilising earth.

A sterile person, be it because of difficulties to conceive or because of lack of ideas, is described as "infertile", their earth is "infertile", no seed can grow. A woman that is infertile is described as "barren" as is the soil, the landscape of a desert plain.

People and tribes in all ages from Aboriginals of Australia to Zulus of South Africa, Indians of America, the Sudanese in Central Africa, or the Serbs, Croats, Bosnians and Kossovo Albanians in Europe fight for the "Earth" they live on. If their earth is taken from them, they wither and die. As the tree and anything living needs a healthy earth, in order to grow, mature and even to die, so as people we need the Earth as a central, stabilising and nourishing "Organ", in order to grow, mature and thrive.

> Children of the one earth, you and I,
> Listening to the drum of our mothers heartbeat,
> What long walk we have to dream'

What pain we have to suffer,
Until the song of our own drum
Tunes into the rhythm of her soul,
Until we realise, that the beat we seek
Is the song we are.
Is the song she is.

The Cycle

The Chinese believed in something, we could call a "body-clock" or body rhythm. The five Elements and their meridians have a designated time of optimal and minimal work. Stomach and spleen are at their best, working most beneficially, between seven and eleven a.m. It means that this is the optimal time for digestion and assimilation. Why this is, is obvious if we recall that breakfast used to be the main meal of the day, and for many it still is (for some, like Tibetan monks, it is the only one). On the other hand twelve hours later between seven and eleven p.m. is the time of slackest digestion. An imbalance of Earth is indicated if this peak time turns out to be a time, when a person does not like to eat. If a person habitually does not eat breakfast, he/she constantly injures the Earth Element. A person with the main characteristics of the Element Earth (balanced) might feel especially fit and willing to eat and do things in the early morning, and conversely feel that a late evening meal is making them feel sluggish, heavy and even give them indigestion. Of course in general this is true for all of us. We all have this body rhythm, but it is especially significant for someone where the whole personality is dominated by Earth tendencies.

This realisation can have far reaching consequences. Some diets, like the 'Hay Diet' or 'Fit - for - Life - diet' advocate no breakfast, or to eat just fruit. According to the Element theory this does not make sense. Furthermore, in some countries, especially the Mediterranean countries, the main meal is in the evening when the family is re-united after a day's work. So far so good, but, according to the 'body-clock-theory' this is inappropriate. The old English custom of a hearty breakfast and a small meal at supper-time (five o'clock) seems to fit well, if not for <u>what</u> is eaten, surely for <u>when</u> it is eaten. It is interesting to re-call, that farmers (people close to the earth) of nearly all continents seem to adhere to this internal body-clock quite naturally for their mealtimes. Disregard or misuse of these eating times, can result simply in lack of energy and stamina because the stomach is unable to digest and prepare the food adequately for the body to use its energy. Although one might have eaten a good meal, or even a big meal - the food just lies in the stomach, heavy and unused. Unprocessed food does not only deteriorate and gives no energy, but it rots.

TCM pays great respect to these times, stomach medicine would be administered, or acupuncture points treated at these times with greater success. If the Stomach energy needs balancing, no matter in what therapy, better results are achieved early in the morning, in Earth-time.

The Season linked to the Earth Element is late summer, the three months of summer "proper". It is the time in the middle of the year, when abundant green colour lingers yet a hint of autumn already beckons. It is the central focus of all the seasons. The late summer is the time where all things seem to culminate; there is frantic activity in the insect world, changes happen fast. The berries, that seem to have only just flowered, suddenly change colour and are ripe to eat. It is a time when we can harvest the first fruit and vegetables, potatoes, the *Pomme-de-terre*, the apple of the earth. Vegetables sown in spring might have been germinating but seemingly doing little for weeks or even months, then in summer the seedlings suddenly grow. We can almost watch them mature.

This time of abundant growth and ripening, we also meet in people. The early summer of life is that of marriage and founding a family, yet late summer sees the children grow into adults, sees the fruit of ones professional life mature. In the East people are conscious of the association between a stage of life and the seasons. With summer the concluding part of family life and duties towards society have to be fulfilled -

after that the person changes into a "forest-dweller". The summer is the time to enjoy the richness of life and a stage of vigorous activity. But as the "Summer of Life" glides into the autumn the time for taking stock has also arrived, where do we go from here? The mid-life crisis approaches, confirming what already is or suggesting a turning point in life. Whatever takes place in this season happens with vigour. This makes our connection to the earth specially important so that change does not toss us into chaos and a whirlpool of emotions. The menopause and all the associated symptoms in women, with their cycle of one kind of fertility coming to an end, often is accompanied by imbalances in the Earth Element.

Similarly many illnesses to do with female hormones, infertility, the womb, ovaries or testicles might be connected to an imbalance in the Earth Element. If people are drifting through mid-life like a rudderless ship they obviously have an imbalance in their Earth Element; when people start many different things so that they never get to see the fruition of any of their labours, it points to an Earth imbalance in their life. If someone does 'this and that', like the dance of a busy bee, they might have an imbalance in their Earth Element.

The Direction associated with Earth is the centre. The centre is the still point that holds all potential and that very first inclination to move out. The centre is described in Tibetan Buddhism describe as "Ground Luminosity". It is that part of the divine that is the Source of everything, associated with potent stillness; it is the ground Christian tradition describes as "the Father". It is the potential that holds all for the Hindu; and the centre is more! In the centre that first stirring happens. The potential has to recognise its wish to create. This first awareness of itself, is the falling of the "Veil of Shiva" where the original starts to separate out into the new – it leads to a new creation. It is that very first stirring, initial movement outwards, that first sound of OM, of creation; the first drumbeat that starts the rhythm of the *dharma*, it is the first movement of *Spanda*, the wave of creation, the first stirring of

Life. Some talk about and indeed celebrate this time as the advent – yes, the advent of the birth of the Christ.

Every tradition has its own way of expressing this initial realisation. It is a messenger of the coming. This opening, this herald of abundance that we feel has always been connected to the heart, a pure, original love, which is nothing more nothing less than abundant freely giving positive energy. It is in this context, interesting to note, that the contact point (alarm point) for the Earth energy is in the diagnostic area of the Heart, in the *Hara*; the centre. This centre of man's gravity holds two more power points (used in various systems of Marshall- art, and complimentary medicine) the *tan tien* and the 'Core Star'[9]. Both are believed to carry the 'Core of our Essence' and both lie in the diagnostic area of the Spleen, within the belly of man. Injury to this centre, be it to the organ of the Spleen itself, or to those two points, will result in serious damage to life and even death, because they represent body, mind and spirit. This is familiar from the famous word *hara-kiri*, meaning splitting of the belly (stomach and area below the navel) this fatal incision is made because the belly is considered the seat of Life. "H*ara*" implies for the Japanese all that is considered essential to man's character and destiny. "*Hara* is the centre of the human body..., it is at the same time the centre in a spiritual sense, or to be more accurate, a nature-given spiritual sense" [10].

Society too is represented by the Elements. Within it each Element has a place. It is just as detrimental to the individual itself to neglect that centre, as the one in his body. If he neglects what is central to his life, be it health, family, friends, job, values or any of his basic needs, it will affect his life negatively. If the centre is his divine core and he neglects to acknowledge or to live according to it, it will affect his life too. He will feel cut loose, uprooted, at odds, restless, frustrated, a strange unearthly loneliness, a lacking, a craving but for what? He will be searching, always searching to fill his void centre with substitutes, e.g. overwork, thinking too much and worrying too much, or – feel a craving for snacks and sweets, affection or sex and even turn to addictions such as alcohol and drugs. If we look at social problems of our western society, we might find it indicative of a neglected Earth; our spiritual sense of belonging has been neglected.

The Climate related to Earth is humidity/dampness. Dampness stems from accumulation of moisture, it arises from a build up of fluids, it makes the person feel full and heavy, it causes stagnation, nothing is moving, and thus it affects the circulation. At its roots dampness and the resulting contentedness can be beneficial as it gives a sense of stillness and peace. In nature we come across this especially in late summer. Yet when it is too damp, the air is still and the atmosphere is heavy. This condition corresponds in the body showing accumulation of phlegm, abundant mucus, water retention especially in the abdomen or the joints and extremities. Oily skin and/or sticky perspiring hands and skin. These lead to heaviness in the head, a dull feeling and general lethargy. Usually the dampness is accompanied by, either heat, cold or wind. If it appears together with cold there is restricted circulation, stiffness and soreness of muscles and fatigue. When it is accompanied by heat it expresses itself in illnesses such as herpes, shingles, jaundice, bronchitis, cystitis and any amount of red, raised puss filled sores, such as abscesses, ulcers, mouth ulcers. When it appears in conjunction with wind, it produces swellings that migrate, such as hives, swollen lymph-nodes, wind in the stomach, sores and ulcers. In extreme cases, it creates obstructions that can cause seizures, strokes, vertigo, fuzziness and psychosomatic states like clumsiness, lack of co-ordination and such like.

The ultimate dampness, the ultimate waterlogged Earth, of course is a swamp, which cuts off nearly all life because neither breathing nor movement is possible and death results.

The reverse of dampness of course is dryness. Imbalance happens between these two poles. Too much dryness causes just as much hazards. If cell lack moisture they literally dry up and shrivel and illness result. States such as anorexia develop where mind and body waste away.

Tissues or Parts of the body associated with Earth are the flesh, e.g. muscles, lips, collagen and fat. Flesh signifies and describes the body mass, that which gives the body its gestalt. Not only the mass is relevant here but also its condition. Its elasticity and temperature can tell us about the owner; healthy flesh feels full without being tense, tight without being overburdened, bouncy but not repellent. Illnesses such as muscular dystrophy and other wasting diseases are linked to an imbalance in the Earth Element. The person lacks nourishment on whatever gross or subtle level to the cells and furthermore might lack that vital relationship with the centre of being.

Muscles are said to correspond to the mental energy and it is frequently that we find knots, e.g. in the shoulders as manifestations of such energy. Tight muscles in the upper back are said, "to be loaded with rage that was initially aimed at ourselves but then gets projected outwards towards others. This can be seen in what is known as the 'dowager's hump', a formation of soft tissue that builds in the upper back, most often in older women... a collection of angry and resentful thoughts... connected with frustration and irritation in not doing what we really want to do, with thwarted ambition or achievement"[11]. Another quite common manifestation connected to gathering and hardening of mental patterns is fibroids, or fibrosis. Suppressed feelings of femininity, sexuality and motherhood; unexpressed guilt, confusion in what we want to do, how to live, past hurt..., all these can be manifested in the flesh. Tight muscles in the legs and thighs might be related to not liking "where we are going", dissatisfaction or disorientation about the direction in life we are taking at that moment in time.

The Sense organ connected to the Earth is the mouth and the sense is that of taste. The mouth as the sense organ is hardly surprising since it is the start of the alimentary track. It's a gate, where we take in and reject physical and emotional energy. Through it we receive food and drink, but we also breathe through the mouth. Food and air are life sustaining raw energies needed for a healthy organism; they enter here. Many illnesses and our general state of well being are influenced by the sort of food we take into our bodies. Beyond this, the mouth has an additional function, especially in young children, they recognise, feel and experience their world through the mouth. The first experience is the breast of the mother, yet for a long time after toys and any other tangible objects are put into the mouth, either in order to recognise shape or texture or for emotional satisfaction. This acts as a reminder of that first experience of nourishment, of "earth providing". The intention to go back to that original experience has stimulated countless ideas around the topic of "oral gratification", including such mundane issues as smoking and chewing gum.

The mouth is vital to communication. With the mouth we express our thoughts and feelings, just the way the lip is moved - (or dropped -) by my daughter lets me read a whole array of states of emotions! The mouth is also used to get rid of things and feelings as in spitting, vomiting etc. Many illnesses effect the mouth with ulcers, swollen gums, throat diseases, roughness, blistering etc. Difficulties with or illnesses of the mouth can be related to not wanting to taste or swallow or digest the reality we live in, the feelings and thoughts with which we are presented. The same can be said for likes and dislikes of textures and flavours, be they concrete or abstract.

The Orifice related to the Element Earth is also the mouth.

The Fluid associated with the Earth energy is that of saliva. Saliva is part of the digestive process. Food is cut up and mixed with moisture in the mouth for easy swallowing. Similarly emotional upset or issues our body does not want to digest become "hard to swallow", they are "dry facts", they are "unpalatable"; our body, mind, soul entity refuses to moisten them with saliva in preparation for taking them into the body. If a person suffers from too much or too little production of saliva, or complains about other difficulties in swallowing, it is obviously prudent to look at the Earth Element for imbalances. I remember my daughter complaining about meat always being too dry, her mouth simply did not produce the same amount of saliva say for roast beef as it did for dry bread or crisps etc. and that was even when the meat was accompanied by gravy!

The External Physical Manifestation of Earth is the flesh, thus see also under 'tissues, parts of the body.

The Colour is yellow. Since thousands of years of Chinese medicine has taken the colour as an important tool for diagnosing and healing. It does not of course, relate to the genetic colour of the skin, but refers to subtle nuance, recognisably different, from that person's normal colouring. In this case an imbalance of the Earth Element will produce a yellowish hue. The Nei Ching says: "When their colour is yellow like oranges, they are without life"[12]. Furthermore a person that chooses to dress pre-dominantly in yellow (or conversely dislikes yellow) shows characteristics of the Earth Element. One might well ask why? Colours vibrate at certain frequencies (see list of *chakras* -). A person who either desires or dislikes a colour, expresses attraction (need) or dislike (overproduction) of that frequency.

Why would Earth related Organ-networks attract yellow? Yellow could to be connected to the Spleen, the colour of bilirubin an iron by-products of the spleen's breakdown of cells and blood. But how does it relate to the Earth? The answer is simple, one of the most common minerals in the earth is iron and iron appears naturally in three different colours, yellow, red and black. We are familiar with the rusty red of many soils e.g. the soil of the County of Devon in England, the centre of Australia and many parts of Africa, but we may not be so familiar with yellow except when we go to China. Taking a boat trip in the South China Sea suddenly reveals the mystery. The Yellow River so called because it is filled with yellow mud from 'up-country', spills into the sea with gusto. The earth in large parts of China is yellow due to the presence of yellow iron oxide. Parts of the Himalayas and especially the mountains of Tibet are described as yellow, even as "lemon yellow"[13]! Looking at the *chakras* and other traditions of colour interpretations, another interesting link can be "unearthed".

The Element Earth

Yellow is the colour of the third *chakra*, the one that covers the *hara*, and is described as relating to the mental body and mental energies. We have seen earlier that blocked mental energy leads to diseases of the flesh -e.g. to illnesses of the Earth Element.

Yellow in Tibetan medicine is linked to the second *navel chakra* and the colour of the healing Buddha image of Ratnasambhava. He is said to grant purification of pride and miserliness, give generosity, and have the wisdom of equanimity.

The Smell connected to Earth is a sweet fragrance. The Nei Ching says: "Humidity is created by the centre. Humidity nourishes the earth and the earth produces sweet flowers. The sweet flavour nourishes the stomach, the stomach strengthens the flesh"[14].

The Smell or odour is not just meant as something a person with a dominant Earth tendency (in future referred to as an Earth-person) likes or dislikes but, because of the condition of the organ network, the person actually 'takes on', these odours. Their skin smells in a certain way and thus the smell becomes a diagnostic tool. A strong fragrant emanating smell from a person, or even a sickly sweet smell that reminds one of well rotted manure, indicates an imbalance in the Earth Element.

The smell of a fragrant tree carries far, in the same vein the actions of the Earth-Person can carry far. One of the main characteristics of an Earth-Person is giving, abundantly giving with compassion. The "smell" of such a person can carry far their "charitable deeds" can involve world-wide actions.

Unfortunately we do not always act so true to our character or with such conviction, with such truth to our Earth-nature. We misuse our senses in a literal and metaphorical sense. In fact what have we not done with them:

89

Our eyes steel someone's husband
Our eyes create illusions that we can sell
Our ears listen to all sorts of gossip and slander
Our ears cut off the sound of ocean waves
Our nose interferes in anything and all
Our nose tempts and beguiles even ourselves
Our tongue blames and accuses
Our tongue tastes the sweat of the workers
Our skin pretends and hides
Our skin separates and denies

To satisfy our senses we become their slaves and risk honesty, honour, family, commitment, dignity, wisdom, even our lives.

The Taste related to Earth is sweet. The Nei Ching says: "If people pay attention to the five flavours and mix them well, their bones will remain straight, their muscle will remain tender and young, their pores will be fine in texture, and consequently, their breath and bones will be filled with the essence of life"[15]. Each taste is linked to one of the Elements and helps to balance them, excessive consumption of one, on the other hand, damages the related organ network. Thus a longing or even a craving for sweets, cakes, sugary dishes, points towards the Spleen. Spleen and pancreas, even in Western medicine, are linked to such illnesses as diabetes, hypoglycaemia etc, for their part in the sugar metabolism.

This does not mean that anybody liking sweets has such an illness, but the taste guides us to investigate for an imbalance in the energy field of the related Element; this applies to likes just as much as dislikes.

Yet in another way we are pointed to the Earth as the Centre. The stomach is thought of as the seat of all the five tastes.

The Grain associated with the Earth is millet.

The Fruit is the apricot.

The Meat is beef.

The Vegetable is the shallot.

These foods are a guide to a balanced diet. Each individual has different needs that are combinations of the foods of the Elements, which are best and personal to their balanced state of health. It may support the general harmony of the body to eat more or less of any of these if the Earth Element is showing signs of an imbalance. Why are these foods specially recommended or linked to the Earth?

The fruit and vegetable might be chosen as much for their mineral content as for their colour or growth habit; their round shape could also be significant in remembering the earth; the latter could also apply to millet. Millet being a complex carbohydrate is easy to digest and is very nourishing. But beef? Some texts translate the Chinese symbol as being the 'Ox' or 'Bull'. In Chinese the animal symbol for the bull or ox is described as a strong, hard working, down to earth animal, he is described as a family type, complacent until challenged; helpful and of service to man[16]. Strangely enough these characteristics all can be attributed to Earth. Yet I venture to say there might be an older reason here. As we said before, behind the Chinese tradition, stands the ancient Indian lore. In India the cow plays a *central* role, because it provides the village with its basics. It gives food (milk) tools (bones) fuel (dung), cloth and shelter (hides) strength (working animal). Originally possibly the cow was attributed to Earth, due to its central and vital role, the fact that in the Chinese mentality it was grouped with food- seems, in cultural terms, ironic.

The Emotion attributed to Earth is sympathy. Sympathy for others surely includes compassion and non-judgemental love. Sympathy surely also extends to compassion and love of oneself.

Sympathy and compassion arise from understanding; a knowing that stems from our connection to the earth. If I am a child of this earth then you must be too. If my physical and emotional being roots in the earth, then yours must also. If I am a child of the divine (Earth), then so must you. Out of the understanding of myself, comes the recognition that you are my brother, my sister, that you are indeed no different from me, that there is only one brotherhood of man. With this I can recognise the physical, material and psychological suffering that is yours. I can put myself inside your skin; I can "step into your shoes" and feel your suffering. This goes far beyond shallow observation of that poor person who has ill fortune; into "com-passion", a "suffering with" that person, as though their mishap is happening to me. With that recognition I know how to help. This centrally orientated empathy, rising from the Earth, rising from the stillness of the belly, is by nature not dependent on the other person being loveable; it is by nature non-judgemental. In a manner of speaking we are helping "ourselves".

The same can be said for the hurt we ourselves experience by others and the compassion and sympathy we need towards ourselves. If we re-connect with that centre, the Earth, we are able to realise that the person who hurt us (or the circumstances, which hurt us) is merely existing as another fruit of the Earth, no different from ourselves. Slowly an understanding rises of our link in suffering -, bitterness will vanish and make place for reconciliation.

The same road leads to self-acceptance, self-love and sympathy towards oneself. Out of the reconciliation with the self, abundant growth of talents, ideas and feelings will blossom. A person, who has lost the ability to empathise or feel compassion towards him/herself is uprooted and segregated from his original nature, cut off from the source of love. This is an imbalance in the Earth Element.

When a person who is not aware of his brother's and sister's suffering often can not "stomach" being in the presence of the poor, hungry, dirty or sick; such person has lost the connection to the centre of being. They are likely to show symptoms of nausea. As we hear people say, "to see these people makes me sick".

On the other hand people who are constantly "fussing over" others for the slightest mishap, a mother who keeps her child so "tight to her heart" that the child cannot flourish; also shows an imbalance in the Earth Element. They are over-indulging in just the same link; they identify completely with the other and forget that "although we are the same essence, we are not the same in our patterns"; that we are all children of the earth but not "identical twins". They have lost trust in life, the centre of being and "they worry themselves sick" over others. Often they are holding "things" too long in the stomach, too tight in their arms; they suffocate "things" and give the "stomach" no chance of churning the food over in order to pass it on to the next stage. The food then rots.

The Expression associated with the Earth is singing. The expression, the tone of voice, the underlying sound of a voice is a subtle indication of an imbalance. We might hear an underlying, monotonous or melodic ring to a voice, a soft whining sound or even a continuing sing-song. As with the colour, this refers to changes to the normal voice of that person. It is the quality of the voice that one is looking for not so much whether the person likes to sing or not.

The beginning of life, the source of life is the Earth. In the East the beginning of creation is understood as sound, Nada. The original sound, OM, arises in the person from deep inside the belly, rises from the Earth within man. Distortions like sound rising high from the throat, or from the vocal chords point, to an imbalance in the Earth energy. The same is true for what is described as quavering or quirking, or even a trembling within the voice box.

The Sound attributed to the Element Earth is belching. Belching is directly linked to the digestive process and is connected to the ability of the stomach to pass things on. If food lies in the stomach beyond a reasonable time, a process of rotting starts which releasing gas. This then needs to escape. Belching indicates that the food has been kept too long. Similarly ideas, patterns of behaviour, attitudes and arguments can be held too long, despite the fact that they are ripe for letting go. The fruit of the tree needs to be harvested, otherwise it rots, the corn needs to be harvested or it will "blacken". Belching thus becomes an indication of an imbalance in the dharma of " passing on".

The Manner in times of excitement or change is that of stubbornness. This category relates to the reaction to unusual demands. Earth people hold on to what they've got; hold to ideas and opinions with unrivalled stubbornness. As in the above category, stubbornness is a sign of holding on beyond reasonable time or circumstances. On the other hand, if a person has the habit of changing their mind quickly and cannot hold on to an idea, argument or feeling, then their Earth Element might be out of balance. The person is not able to profit, to harvest their "investment! Nothing will bear fruit because they switch too quickly from one idea to the next, like dust in the dry deserts of the earth, where nothing can take root.

The Attitude associated with the Earth, is "catching food in hand". It is easy to see the Earth person just catching, snatching a bite to eat, for the time spent sitting down and having a meal is wasted time for them, since there is yet another village fete or another charity concert to go to. Meanwhile they are paying too little or no attention to the needs of their own body. Yet food is important to them, they like eating and need the food and rather than doing without it they are constantly nibbling. If there is an Earth imbalance, one is plagued by a constant feeling of the emptiness in the centre. Quite inappropriately so one tries to fill that whole with food.

The Movement of the Energy is one of holding and embracing.

The holding and embracing is an expression of the centrifugal power of earth, of being at the centre; holding giving each what they need. Some people are desperate to hold things – they are desperate in their need to embrace others for the lack of being embraced themselves. They are in fear of falling apart of not getting what they need. Giving out too much however, depletes the person and leads to imbalances.

The Quality ascribed to Earth, is that of being "intellectual". If we consider the qualities of holding, accumulating and digesting or transforming by the Earth and her related meridians, then we will understand why. Intellectual activity is where the brain accumulates, holds and digests facts and transforms them into knowledge. When the heart and soul are also partaking in this process, facts and experience are transformed into wisdom. One could say that when facts and experiences are only partly digested and remain in the realm of the brain only. This we commonly call intellectualism, and as such, like all half-digested ideas, it indicates an imbalance in the Earth Element. On the other hand, when experiences and facts are not assimilated and digested by the brain, but only felt and understood intuitively with the heart, we encounter knowledge commonly understand as common sense. If experiences and facts are only linked to the spiritual or soul-level, then understanding becomes unreal, up in the clouds, ungrounded, and can easily be considered or classified as insane. All true masters and teachers therefore place great emphasis on studying the scriptures as a grounding activity. To be whole, to be balanced in the Earth Element, we need all three - body, mind and soul, or brain, heart and spirit, then we can gain supreme knowledge. An imbalance in this triadic rhythm shows an imbalance in the Earth and leads to the quality of "mere intellectualism".

I was brought up by a refugee family, with the belief, that you have to study hard, what is in your head 'no-one' can take away. It took me decades to see that this is the view of uprooted, unearthed people, making an understandable virtue of a hard-learned lesson. I am grateful and feel fortunate to have the opportunity to begin to see otherwise.

The Activity associated with Earth is, absorbing. Absorbing is a characteristic of the earth, she absorbs rain in order to gather humidity needed for growth, but she also absorbs matter, effluent, poison etc.; decomposes it, and assimilates it as harmless substances so that life can go on. The stomach, similarly, has as one of its functions the absorption of certain minerals, vitamins and nutrients. The mind absorbs knowledge, the soul absorbs pure energy. Absorption is the ability to make something part of itself. An inability to absorb, be it knowledge, nutrients or experiences and make them ones own points, to an imbalance in Earth.

The Condition is one of poise. The image arises of planet earth poised in the universe, full, majestic, being-without challenge, without purpose; its path and its purpose are the same; it just is. It seems held by invisible strings of luminous energy. Just like the planet earth, a person has poise, can stand on their own, stable in their centre; straight; almost proud, yet neither stiff, nor aloof. A person who is secure and balanced at their centre of gravity will, like a child easily return to their centre when knocked off balance. That person acts like an island around which others move. By contrast a person, who has lost their centre, their connection to the Earth, has no poise, has no stance, no weight and is easily pushed over. Poise needs trust and knowing that all is well; needs a link of equal support to inside (belly) and outside (environment). It reminds me of a stalk of grain dancing in the wind, wafting elegantly like a prima ballerina, - or indeed a whole field of grain, a field of plenty, poised in late summer, ready to be harvested to fulfil its duty, its *dharma*.

> "Field of Plenty,
> Abundance for all
> No hunger
> No more pain

Great mystery holds
Earth's children dear
And feeds them with
Eternal flame.

Children of Earth, trust again!
Be grateful and give praise!
The field of plenty will remain
To sustain us all our days"[17].

Qualities/ Steps in Sadhana. Breaking away a bit from the traditional associations, I would like to add a category here. In my understanding the spiritual aspect of the body-mind- soul undergoes a path of development. This expresses itself like all other aspects of life in the elements. The spiritual path is called *Sadhana* in Sanskrit. I propose that here too Earth has its distinct character.

Earth refers to the manifestation of spirit in matter and the mind. It refers to our identification with the body, the first phase of becoming conscious of who we are. We identify with the body. "I am body". Some go no further; some become aware that the body is manifest life-force, the most solid of the states of subtle energy. The body is seen as God, Spirit, Life - incarnate; this is the end (or the beginning of the line). The bug stops here, all is worked out on this level. God, the word has, for example become physical man in Jesus.

Indian philosophy recognises four different stages of consciousness. We traverse these as we develop as human beings into our fullest potential. They are the waking consciousness, the dream consciousness, the deep sleep consciousness and the turya state, the state beyond. The Earth Element belongs to the waking consciousness. When we are awake, what we perceive of the world is what we deem real.

The Relationship of the Earth to the other Elements is from the centre. One model of these relationships is called the cosmological cycle. There the Fire Element is seen at the top of an axis, the Water Element at its opposite end, with either energy reaching out to one another. The Earth energy is in the middle with Wood and Metal on either side of it. But in time, the Earth came to represent a stage of transition between summer and autumn, late summer: between noon and dusk, late afternoon. So, Earth was placed schematically along a circular continuum between Fire and Metal. This model has become the one conventionally used in many complementary medicines. It is also called the *Shen-Ko* Cycle. It shows the co-operation and interaction between all Elements and mirrors its fluid character. The outer circle shows infinite continuity of Fire, Earth, Metal, Water and Wood. It symbolises there is no beginning or end to the cyclic relationship. Within the circle is a star. Each line portrays a controlling flow of energy, from one Element to another, just like an arrow aimed at an Element; thus revealing a pattern of controlling as well as being controlled by. In this way Fire controls Metal; Earth controls Water, Metal controls Wood, Water controls Fire, Wood controls Earth.

Talking about the *Shen Ko Circle s*ome start with the Wood-Element, as it relates to the beginning of the year and speaks of rising *Yang* energy. Some start with Fire, for Fire is the inspiration of things, as Wataru Ohashi says, "The process (is) beginning with the original inspiration, the world of ideas"[18]. Then it manifests in the Earth.

Although the Cosmological Cycle and the Chen Ko Cycle are the most popular ones, they are not the only ones. Aryuveda uses several models describing the relationship between the Elements: The Wheel of Creation, The Wheel of Destruction, The Wheel of Control, The Wheel of Support. The latter two we recognise as similar to the above-mentioned *Chen-Ko* Cycle. The Wheel of Destruction (*Vinasha chakra*) sets the Elements in the same order, but the spokes or arrows of the five-sides star are point in the opposite direction from the *Chen-Ko* Cycle; thus Earth destroys Wood (Ether) which in turn destroys (Air/Wind)/ Metal. The latter destroys Fire (Wind fans, but it also blows the Fire out). Fire in turn, dries up Water and the latter washes away Earth.

Why the difference between controlling and destruction? I can only think that the reason lies in the amount of force. Once too much force is used, the pendulum swings and it annihilates. Amongst the different wheels, the most interesting is the Wheel of Creation, which follows a different Path altogether. A source of Prana (outside the circle) is imagined which then becomes Ether (Space, Wood) and creates out of itself Wind (Air) Movement. Out of Air, Fire is created (lightning?). Where there is Air and Fire, chemically speaking, Water molecules are made thus Water is the next in line. Out of that 'liquid' state, Earth is created, by solidifying matter. From here a direct link feeds back to Space/Ether and closes the link.

This seems interesting on two accounts. Firstly the more subtle energy, which precedes manifestation of the Five Elements is included. Secondly it incorporates the original notions of Space and Air, (Space and Movement of the Vedic Tradition) and thirdly this system appears to adhere to today's scientific ideas and/or it shows "how *Prana* develops from pure energy into the most physical of its forms in the body"[19]. This approach is shared by Tibetan Buddhism and mirrored in the allocation of the *chakras* to the body[20]. The lowest step of this ladder, or rather the "end of the circle", is Earth, the beginning - or the end.

The Earth is described as the mother of all that lives, I think this is a good point to enter the circle, and I will follow the *Shen-Ko* cycle from there, since it is not only the most popular but also the widest used in complementary medicine. According to this model, Earth <u>gives birth to Metal</u>, and several links have already hinted at this; the earth contains rocks and minerals, in fact, it is made of them. Yet she - like a mother - gives birth to the child of her own substance, eventually lets go and the child takes on a separate existence.

In this way each Elements contains the previous to a lesser extend - like a mother and her child. This relationship is cultivated, as the mother nourishes the child. The Earth transmutes her energy to Metal. The stomach uses oxygen to digest nutrients. The meridians of Lung and Stomach are closely linked, as are those of "passing on", the Spleen and the Large Intestine.

Earth and Metal (Air) are characterised by beneficial co-existence.

The Earth <u>controls Water</u> -we can easily observe this in rivers or canals being kept in their beds by the banks of earth. Water is kept within its boundaries, restricted, prevented from flowing over and swamping everything by walls of Earth. The Earth needs to control Water to protect itself from becoming a deadly swamp; yet in order to fulfil its *dharma* of bringing forth abundant life it needs Water. Together they are fertility per se. Their relationship is characterised by measured, balanced fruitful interaction; co-operation at its best.

Earth <u>is controlled by Wood</u>. The roots of plants keep the soil in place, stop it from being eroded by either water or dryness (fire). What Earth brings forth, must be controlled, though plant life is a gift, when too much is given it exhausts and destroys. The relationship between Earth and Wood (or Space) is therefore characterised by mutual limitation and exploitation.

Finally Fire is the agent of rebirth; Fire burns matter into ashes, those very minerals that, mixed with water and aged in time, become Earth. Thus Fire gives birth to Earth; Earth is the child of Fire. Fire nourishes the Earth, replenishes its contents, purifies it and dries it when it is too wet and warms it when too cold. The relationship of Earth to Fire is one of being nurtured, protected and enriched.

And then the Circle starts again and Earth gives birth to Metal. By now we know that the Movement of Life is cyclic, yet this is justifiable only as a working hypothesis. It is more akin to a complex web of interacting fields of elemental energy on many different levels (be it body, mind, soul or - seven or more, or even twelve or more up to n-th etheric bodies). They pull and churn and feed off each other with the Earth - on any of these interacting levels, as some central, stabilising axis, or three, or twelve or n-th axes. It generates the image of a super nova. Remember a clear, deep summer night sky with many levels of stars, forever more distant. There is always one component, which is central; one that is more solid, more manifest, more practical; there is always one "Earth". It reminds me, that the belly is like the earth, the earth is like the galaxy, the galaxy, like the universe...

as above,

so below.

CHAPTER FOUR

INVOCATION OF METAL (AIR)

I am the invisible order of the cosmos
- Rita, the cosmic law and Satya - Truth

Out of me 'ritu' is born, the seasons –and
'ritual' your performances of respect,
respect for the harmonious functioning of nature.
You know the law!
You know what is needed, in your ancestral soul!

I record that knowledge
I record it in all that is ancient,
ancient like the stones and crystals,
the record holders of the earth
they store the history, that gave you birth
they store the truth you contain.

I am the breath, the blood of your vitality
I breathe the supreme force of life into you
I have unrivalled power to nurture, heal and sustain thus
honour my breath
honour breath

I am the wind you feel on your skin
I rise high and powerful to heaven where the gods reside,
I hold the gift of fragrant and sweet life rejoice, all beings, in
my generosity rejoice.

I descend as storm to the earth by the grace of the gods
tremble, all beings, before my power tremble
I, storm and thunder, the love-call of the mating dance with earth
I re-energise the Great Mother, so that life may continue,
so that the rains may feed her body.

I am the invisible order of the cosmos
Rita, the cosmic law and Satya, truth

- storms are followed by delicate stillness
- turbulence is succeeded by quiet
- chaos put into order
- abundance is succeeded by scarcity
- growth follows decay
- autumn follows summer

I am autumn, the time of farewells
- leave the clatter of accumulated riches return to your source
- leave the chatter of your monkey brain retreat into your interior, sink into your roots
- leave the exterior gloss and paint collect your resources

I am Manjushri, the Buddha that cuts away with the 'Sword of Wisdom'
- leave the frenzy of a business persona
prepare for hibernation, slow down
- leave your distractions and illusions
contract, contract into the purest substance
- leave your self-important theories and values
crystallise into 'the salt of the earth'

It is a time of farewells, for then you realise,
- that I am the fire of self-inquiry, who sees the self
- the self in constant flux;
realising

I am the invisible order of the cosmos
Rita - the cosmic law,
always accompanied by Satya-truth
- as holding is accompanied by letting go
- as ripening is accompanied by decaying
- as expanding is accompanied by contracting
until these antipodes come together,
they themselves have antipodes,
each to its own nature
each to its own truth

Thus I am truth, right action, right dharma.

The Element Metal (Air)

Each thing, animate or inanimate in the entire universe
follows its own dharma
its own 'suchness', its own truth
To find your own truth, you have to be in touch with your soul
acknowledge your soul and
do not hide,
hide behind rules, regulations and principles
preconceptions, judgements and other similar
calcified structure of armour

But - SURRENDER - to me
    me, Rita, the cosmic law
    me, Satya, the Truth.

Character of Metal (Air)

Metal, to most, must appear a strange choice as an Element. It is unfamiliar because we, in the Western world, are used to seeing Air as an element. This is due to our historical linkage with the Greek tradition where only four elements are mentioned Fire, Earth, Air and Water. This most of us know from astrological cycles. In the context of this book, I will in the main, refer to this element as Metal. It seems appropriate to stay with the original Chinese connotation because here we deal with oriental concepts of holistic medicine. Looking closer, we will find that Air and Metal have remarkable similar characteristics. This has been taken into account in the invocation. We further note that the Vedic tradition refers for this element to Truth.

For many, many years I have been a potter using earth and minerals. What seems to the eye as a stone, say a piece of granite, gets in time weathered or eroded and decomposed into its minerals, say feldspar. This is then washed down the slopes by rain and mixes, on its travels, with particles of sand, potash of vegetable origin, some organic (not quite yet decomposed) matter, natural oils, more sand and traces of other minerals, such as iron. As a result we have earth! Earth is a mixture that holds minerals and metal ores intrinsically in her. If we isolate the ore out, we are looking at metal (which befits the idea of a mother and child relationship).

True minerals and metal (which is just one form of mineral) are always inorganic and "they contain exactly those (chemical) elements to be found in every piece of matter in the solar system, from planets and moons, asteroids, comets and meteorites down to mere dust. Therefore, though formed on our planet, they are directly linked with their corresponding elements in the celestial bodies"[1]. In fact, the over one hundred Chemical Elements that are recognised today constitute all matter, including the human body and the other planets. Here we gleam a parallel between Metal and Air: both are substance seemingly found everywhere (which of course, is not true strictly so as air is probably limited to this planet).

A notable property of minerals is that they have history. One could say they bridge the gap between past and present. For example a crystal "has not been there, in that state (where the miner discovers it) forever, but over a period of millions of years (has been moved and changed by) devastating alterations of expansion and shrinkage, heat and cold", and been exposed to giant upheavals in the earth[2]. This characteristic is what leads the American Indian tradition to speak of stones, or stone people as "sacred record holders of life". Celtic mythology too ascribes stones the power to reveal sacred knowledge, which they have stored since time immemorial. In Japanese meditation practise we hear of "listening to the stones". Minerals, Metals and Stones can be said to hold earth's memory; to be calcified knowledge, to have wisdom. Calcified wisdom is dogma!

How can this relate to Air? Stale air, too holds memories, smells and feelings of what has been.

When minerals or ore is purified in intense heat, they give us the most precious substance, such as gold and diamonds. Yet often not only heat is needed for this process, but pressure, intense pressure that forces to contract. The humorous remark that a diamond is just a piece of coal is perfectly accurate. They are both the same mineral i.e. carbon, yet one has been under heat and pressure and contracted infinitely more than the other. Similarly air in our lungs changes under pressure; some oxygen is removed, the air we breathe out is condensed.

This process of distilling out and changing appearance has given the Element Metal another attribute. It distils what is good and pure from what is coarse and primitive.

As a similar process happens in the mind, through thought and speech, Metal is attributed with the aspects of defining and refining; with holding the power of discernment and the quality of seeking for the perfect form and function. On a more general note, it is said to be forever restraining, separating, purifying and reducing.

As a potter, I used to work with copper and people could never quite make sense of my explanation that a green, turquoise, light blue, pink, red, blood red, iridescent and golden looking pot, was all done with the same glaze. Through reduction (e.g. firing) that glaze displayed different states of the same mineral (of the same metal).

Crystals display the most obvious reduction and refinement; their tight structures bring such clarity that they become symbols of hardness, endurance, constancy, naked power, extreme purity and continuity of life and love.

Again we can endeavour to link this quality to Air. Pure Air cuts away at contours and makes things essentially sharp. We talk of clear, sharp skies when the air is pure and reveals the stars with precision. Painters seek out landscapes with pure air, so that the colours reflect sharp and clear for their eyes. In countries with high mountains where the air is pure, one can see different colours and a greater distance, for all hiding of impurities and dust particles have been left behind in the lowlands. Thus air too can be described as being able to refine, clarify and transform into pure essence. On the other hand Air absorbs gases, constantly new oxygen, heat, smells and fragrances and also all manner of dust and pollution. On the mental level this quality is understood as - collecting knowledge, and just as with Metal, it can refine this into pure essence, pure wisdom.

Minerals especially in the form of Crystals vibrate. Crystals have varying, but highly refined vibrations. This is used in communication systems. Ann McCaffery's world of singing crystals and singing ships[3] might still belong to the future, yet no communication system today can be imagined without metal wires, conductors, radio-crystals and microchips, even cordless telephones, wireless radios and television all need metal circuits. Communication is thus another quality associated with metal, Metal is always useful, but it's application specific, specialised not general (as for instance in Earth and Water).

Consulting the Christian mystic Hildegard von Bingen we notice that she uses the element Air instead of Metal, and sees it as the animating "enlivening" power for plants and animals alike, even extended to the stars and planets. She forges a link to water, as it both brings dew and circulating movements to all that grows. She also links it to the mind as ratio/rationality saying that Air has the quality of carrying the warmth of Fire to mans mind mentally and spiritually stimulating him. A similar stance is taken in Ayurvedic medicine where Air is linked to stimulating movement or its reverse, stagnation. Both above traditions, H. von Bingen and Ayurveda connect the large intestines to this Element for their activity is moving and expelling gases as well as matter.

Furthermore the idea of "enlivening matter" is linked to ether (Vedic) and points directly to "that which houses air", the lungs. Air, filling the lungs, breathing life into beings is *prana*, yet when it fulfils its function outside a body it is referred to as *vayu* – wind.

Vedic traditions and Buddhist medicine strongly emphasises *prana*, as the carrier of the psychic forces. "*Prana* is more than breath. It is more than the creative power of semen or the force of motor nerves, more than the faculties of thought, and intellect or will power"[4]. Breath becomes a symbol for all the forces of life. In Tibetan, the wider term *vayu* is preferred for "breath penetrates into the toes and fingertips, and rises through the hollow of the spinal column up to the brain"[5]. Air/Wind here is what moves up and presses down; it equalises and assimilates that which it penetrates. P*rana* links the outer and inner world in such a way that it creates dependency between the body, its parts, the environment and the world, the cosmos. What *prana* stands for, in all its complexity, is much too complicated to explain here in detail. Limiting it to those aspects that concern us, it is enough to mention its associations with lungs, skin, large intestines, speech, thought and (more abstract concepts like) cosmic consciousness.

Gathering the attributes of this Element, we can summarise: its inorganic, linked to all that exists (even the cosmos). It has strong links to and is an expression of the past. It can be described as transmuting, reducing, concentrating, structuring, tightening, crystallising, distilling, refining (into pure essence), restraining, purifying, clarifying, enduring, hardening, beautifying (jewels), defining, discriminating and being specific and precise. It is as well useful for conducting and communicating, especially between "inside and outside"; for taking in and letting out and it transforms the most basic to the highest.

Let us try to match these to a person who shows strong Metal characteristics. Such a person might work as a systems designer for a large international computer firm. He is well liked by his colleagues because he is well organised and methodical; he is efficient and disciplined and his analytical and critical mind ensures impeccable results. Even when there is a hardware problem he is willing to help by taking things apart and putting them together with a sense of order and purpose. As a child he might have played with a 'Meccano' set (or other technical toys). In business meetings and conferences he stands out as the keeper of standards, as the defender of principles, providing a structure for others to work with. He cuts through arguments, coming straight to the core of the problem, - or sums discussions up in a serene, unflappable manner, cutting through all ambiguity. He appears emotionally uninvolved, remaining aloof thus it is easy for him not to mix business and pleasure. He keeps his family apart from his working life, but (as in his job) he expects the family to work to schedule. He is committed to the family with integrity and reason. He has a keen eye for stark, austere beauty. He might well, as a hobby, do some abstract geometrical painting, some sculpture. He could also be found collecting antiques, crystals, fossils or the like. He dislikes all conflict and disorder, expecting life to be agreeable and sensible. Since others don't always conform or have the same high standards and principles, he judges them "unworthy" and not willing to give his principles up, he covets his own authority and expertise, withdrawing into his own company.

Since, even he himself might at times not be able to meet his own high standards, he gets disillusioned and disappointed; at this point he might resort to self-punishment or to installing order by force, sacrificing pleasure and spontaneity, even intimacy. He tightens up like a Prussian officer, a soldier with a stiff neck, a stiff spine but a barrel chest. He tends to have a tight pelvis; is rigid with suppressed emotions; pushing the chest forward as a brave front, showing the world a front that says "I am strong, I can cope - you will not succeed in getting at me".

Associations to the Metal Meridians

The two meridians or Organ-networks associated with the Metal Element are the Lung meridian (*Yin*) and the Large Intestines meridian (*Yang*). To begin with, let us look at the anatomical organs for they carry their own revelations. Yet, let us not forget that "each organ and bodily function, that makes up your body, is only a physical manifestation of a spiritual quality that was inherent in your soul when you joined the earth at your conception"[6].

The Lung is of the greatest importance to us, it is the first and last sign of the activity of Life. The lungs are the first to receive the vital energy of air, -the outside energy that soon becomes inside energy. There are two wings to our lungs, one on either side in the thoracic cavity. Each lung is cone shaped, the right lung is divided into three lobes, the left into two, to accommodate the heart. The lung is invaginated into a sac called pleura, the function of this fluid filled sac is to ensure smooth movement of the lung; like a protective punch-bag. The lungs are composed of the bronchi and smaller air passages, alveoli, connective tissue, blood vessels, lymph vessels and nerves. The actual cycle of respiration occurs about fifteen times a minute and consists of inspiration and expiration and a pause. The expansion and constriction of the chest occurs due to muscular activity, partly voluntary, partly involuntary; the main agents of this process are the intercostal muscles and the diaphragm.

When the capacity of the thoracic cavity is increased by the activity of the intercostal muscles and the diaphragm, the pressure in the pleural cavity is reduced to a considerably lower pressure than the atmosphere. The lungs are stretched and with it the pressure of the alveoli and the air passages is reduced drawing air into the lungs in an attempt to equalise the pressure. This is inspiration, when the muscles relax, the process is reversed and there is elastic recoil of the lungs resulting in expiration. The lungs and air passages are never without air; the exchange of gas is taking place across the walls of the alveolar ducts and alveoli, tiny blood vessels grouped around a cell like a bubble. The amount of air moving in and out through these 'bubbles' is about 5,25 litres per minute. Most of the inspired air, saturated with water, goes into the bubble.

Due to the tendency of gases to move from higher to lower concentrated areas, the Oxygen moves from the alveoli to the blood. The inspired air consists mostly of Nitrogen and other small amounts of gases, yet 21% is Oxygen; 16% of the expired air also is Oxygen, thus each time only a small amount of Oxygen is retained. Carbon Dioxide is originally only present in small amounts - 0.04%, on the out-breath it is 4%, so a larger amount is expired. The Oxygen enriched blood moves out of the lungs via various ducts and is collected in the pulmonary veins in order to be fed into the heart.

As mentioned before, the control of respiration is partly involuntary, partly voluntary, the latter notably when speaking, singing or during special activities. Involuntary breathing is controlled from the nerve cells in the brain stem, and are activated after a short time of holding ones breath. The control for voluntary breathing is in the cerebral cortex. There is also a process called internal or cell respiration, which relates to the exchange of Oxygen from the blood across the capillary wall into the cells.

The second organ that relates to the Element Metal is the <u>Large Intestine</u>. It is about 1.5 metres long; it begins at the end of the small intestines, or rather the caecum, and ends with the rectum and anal canal. It forms an arch around the small intestines and lies in front of the abdominal cavity. It consists of different parts (seven in all) including the ascending and the descending colon. It has the same basic four layers of tissues as all parts of the alimentary canal, with slight modifications. The arterial blood supply is mainly by mesenteric arteries; the drainage by the mesenteric veins.

The "stuff" <u>it receives is fluid.</u> Consequently one of the functions of the <u>large intestine is absorption of water</u> in order to concentrate the matter to the consistency of faeces. Mineral salts, vitamins and some drugs are also absorbed into the blood capillaries from the large intestines. They house a large number of microbes, which synthesise vitamin K and folic acid. They also contain gases, partly swallowed with food and drink, or produced by bacterial fermentation. The large intestines do not have peristalsis like other parts of the alimentary tract, but at intervals a strong wave of peristalsis sweeps along the colon, called a mass movement. It often precedes food intake by the stomach; and it forces mass into the usually empty rectum, for defecation. In an adult, the external anal sphincter is under conscious control, involving various nerves and reflexes. Repeated suppression of these reflexes or over-control may lead to constipation. The excrement still consists mainly of water, but in addition, contains large amounts of fibre, dead and live microbes, cells, fatty acids and mucus secreted by the large intestines for the purpose of lubrication.

It seems apparent that both organs, - lung and large intestines, <u>are organs of exchange</u>. The lung takes vital energy from the outside into the body and refines it, concentrates it by eliminating that which it does not need in the out-breath. It constitutes our communication with the outside atmosphere, and thus reaches to the beyond, as much as it creates an awareness of the boundaries between the external and internal world. Similarly the large intestines take stuff from the outside, prepared and processed food, collects it, concentrates it, stores it and finally disposes of the unwanted parts. They are both organs of elimination, of that which cannot be used, a most important task. What would happen to our homes, cities and society if the waste products were not removed? We would sink into rotten stinking matter and eventually die of disease and poison.

I will never forget Batavia, the old Djakarta, a former Indonesian capital where previously the Dutch had maintained an open channel sewerage system. Several years before I visited the town, the original channels had been clogged up, and given up. Now they and were of no use any more and just a stinking swamp. People used the sidewalks as toilets in order to keep their houses clean. Consequently the roads were deeply covered with human excrement. It was baked dry by the sun, but when it rained - I was walking literally ankle deep in human excrement, an experience too horrible to describe in words.

In the body - (if waste is not timely removed), it results in swelling of the body, stiffness in the shoulders, asthma, bronchitis, pains in thumbs and the chest; malicious boils and other skin diseases, headaches, mucus congestion and general symptoms of poisoning.

Since we also take the external world and experiences through our senses into our minds, a similar process is affecting our mind. What we experience, we take in, refine, assimilate and concentrate and, that which is not needed, wanted or useful needs to be released.

The energy field of the lung and large intestines thus also represent all we need to process and eliminate of our mental and emotional life. If we do not let go of outlived patterns and attitudes, if we do not let go of old hurts and emotions, our bodies will similarly congest and react with depression, melancholy, withdrawal, unrealistic expectations (because they relate to outmoded circumstances), isolation and withholding of unexpressed feelings. This results in disappointment, lack of determination, negativity and emotional poverty. Why? Because such holding on means, that we always react to already past patterns and we consequently do not live in the present. Thus self-inquiry is needed now and then to clean out old mental patterns, reflecting on ourselves to be able to recognise these old patterns and let them go. Or, as Plotinus so beautifully said:

> "Withdraw into yourself and look. And if you do not find yourself beautiful yet, act as does the creator of a statue that is to be made beautiful: he cuts away here, smoothes there, he makes this line lighter, this other purer, until a lovely face has grown upon his work. So do you also cut away all that is excessive, straighten all that is crooked, bring to light all that is overcast, labour to make all one glow of beauty and never cease chiselling your statue, until there shall shine out on you from it, the godlike splendour of virtue, until you shall see the perfect goodness established in the stainless shrine"[7].

The Cycle

The circulation of Life's energy creates the meridians Life Cycle. The time of peak activity for the Lung Meridian is the early morning, between three and five o'clock. It is interesting to note that from early times to today, spiritual teachers and masters, all have advocated that the early morning is the best time to meditate. Then the Life energy is purest. M. Simpson, the television scriptwriter talked about meditating early "in the morning because the hours before dawn are known as the brahmamuhurta, the time of the Lord. At this time of day, the mind is fresh". In Hong Kong coming home from a party, I used to be surprised to find people doing *Tai Chi Chuan* at five o'clock in the morning, but then the air is still, purer; and the time of sunrise makes for very special energy.

The optimal time of activity for the Large Intestines Meridian is from five to seven o'clock. Many people have the habit or the need for bowel emptying when they first get up in the morning. On the other hand, late afternoon, between three and five o'clock, we often feel tired and need a nap because it is the time when the lungs have their lowest time of efficiency. This is followed by the time of least activity for the large intestines, another god reason for a rest. A person who feels a lack of energy in the early morning as well as the late afternoon has most likely an imbalance in the Metal energy.

The Season for the Metal Element is the autumn, the autumn of life as well as the autumn in the cycle of the seasons. In *As You Like It* Shakespeare says:

"All the world's a stage,
And all the men and women
merely players;
They have their exits and their entrances;
And one man in his time plays many parts"[8].

In medieval times, the ages of man were divided into seven different stages, linked to seven planets. In modern times, Erik Erikson, a psychologist, designed a model of a life cycle where he sees twelve stages. In the Indian tradition, it is spoken of the four stages of the sanatana dharma, - the eternal *dharma*. There the stage of birth and student years is followed by the stage of the householder, followed by the stage of the "forest dweller", followed by the stage of the renunciate (*sannyasa*). The autumn of life is the time after the children have left home and man retires to the contemplative season of his life. Accompanied by a longing for solitude and silence and released from the obligations of family and job, the "forest dweller" can devote his time to contemplation, scriptural studies and meditation. It might be interesting to note, that medieval Christianity also mentions four stages of life. The first refers to the *common* ordinary stage of family life, the second is the *special,* people start to reflect on their why and whereabouts in life, a stage of maturity. The third stage refers to *the singular*, a stage where one is called to focus on what is essential, the inner core of being; akin to what we earlier called the autumn of life; the last stage refers to the *perfect* and points beyond death, what we call enlightened, be it in this life, or there after[9]. The stage of concentrating on what is important, is shared by all these traditions. In today's world and western society, it refers to that stage where people let go of a lot of commitment. Often they move into a smaller house since the children have now gone. They have leisure time to pursue those interests and desires that they have neglected; those that give meaning and purpose to their lives. They can concentrate on what is important to them.

It is a time when in nature most fruits are harvested, yet some still are to be reaped. Those fruits and leaves that are not, fall to the ground, where they wither and decay, there they decompose, fertilising the ground for next years growth. Likewise a person's experience and knowledge might get reflected, gathered and stored in paintings, books, letters and similar for their children to benefit from or it might just be forgotten. I am reminded of the grape harvest in my native Germany. Most grapes are harvested in August and September, yet some very special good varieties are left on the vine in order to be touched by the first frosts. This crystallises the sugar and concentrates the juice to make a special, highly appreciated, wine called *Eiswein* (Ice wine). Similarly, there is a time in life for concentrating and crystallising.

The autumn is also a time where nature, one last time, comes out with a glorious show of colour. The beauty and luminosity of a Vermont (North Eastern USA) or Canadian autumn; or the colour nuances of a Japanese mountain landscape in autumn, are beyond description. Similarly the inner riches of a person's life might be summoned up at this stage in a display of talents never seen before, they may reveal insights and visions of great beauty.

The autumn is a time for storing; the animals prepare for hibernation, either by storing food within their own bodies (bears) or storing nuts and grains (squirrels). Likewise some sort out their inner lives, some gather material wealth around them. Both prepare for scarcity, preparing for turning inward, even death. Sorting oneself out, dealing with ones problems and fears so that we are prepared for the last phase of our life. The trees and plants prepare for winter, e.g. trees, draw their sap inwards, sink into their roots, slow down their metabolism. Similar to the person, who concentrates more and more on what is essential for themselves, focusing on their true dharma; on their own 'suchness', their own truth.

People, whether young or in the life-stage of autumn, who display signs of being unable to concentrate on the important (whatever that may be for the individual), to define and delineate, or give up what is no longer needed, show an imbalance in this Element. These are necessary functions of this organ network. They govern a person's ability to identify behaviour, circumstances, relationships, life pattern and other things no longer beneficial. Time as much as energy may be wasted on petty issues, resentments or outlived habits and reactions, if they are not cleared out. Similarly people who cannot sum up or crystallise ideas, are unable to reap the fruits of hidden talents, are not able to display foresight (to plan and store for the next step in their life) display an imbalance in Metal energy. The Nei Ching says, "The three months of Fall are called the period of tranquillity of ones conduct... soul and spirit should be gathered together in order to make the breath of Fall tranquil; all this is a method for the protection of ones harvest... Those who disobey the laws of Fall will be punished with an injury of the lungs"[10].

People, who in this phase of their lives look towards the past, or want to cling to the present in order to prevent the future, show an imbalance in "letting go". People who dislike the season of autumn, who leave their fruit to rot; or have difficulty in conserving their energy, also suffer from the same imbalance and might display such physical signs as diarrhoea and constipation, or a feeling of being sick after meals, or even vomiting. Their body/mind is unwilling to gather and absorb what is nourishing to them.

The Direction of Metal is the West - or down and inward. In our society the direction of the West reminds of the setting sun - the transition phase between day and night; the dusk where images soften and contours are mellowed. This is a time of immense colour display - just like autumn and in the same colours too! This is time for preparation for the night, the time of rest and regeneration. The time of sunset is a symbol of closing down.

In the tradition of the North American Indians the West is linked to a cave, or the womb.

"The womb is a place where all ideas, as well as babies, are nurtured and given birth... the West is the 'looking within' place from where we must first understand our natures... if we understand that the spirit of all other life-forms dwells inside our bodies, we begin to understand that we can look within to feel and know the answers (we need)"[11]. The West is the direction of introspection and -the potential of the future. The cave, the womb, the time after sunset they all hold the germ of tomorrow. We were the future generation to our parents; tomorrow comes with today's sunset. The fallen fruit of this season provide the fertiliser for tomorrow's seeds. This fruit, the contents of this life, will crystallise into life's essence; this essence carries in it the germ of the future life, for that is the law of the Cosmos.

Originally the concept of medicine in the *Nei Ching* was derived from and limited to their world, geographical China. The west thus referred to as Western Provinces, and its people live on hills exposed to wind and fertile soil, thus they are described as eating "good and variegated food and. they are flourishing and fertile. Hence evil cannot injure their external bodies, and if they get disease they strike at the inner body"[12]. In a strange way, that still applies today. We in the western, so called civilised countries have ample food. We live in an environment that is affluent. Here diseases that stem from hunger or natural hardship are rare but diseases that strike at the inner body are prevalent. These are heart disease, stress related illnesses, cancer, AIDS, - also mental illness and the more unseen disease such as the destruction of the soul, the deterioration of values, morals and social standards, the increase of crime. These are in social terms "inner diseases".

These "diseases of civilisation" often result from the inability of Western man to be in touch with the laws of the Cosmos, with the inability to tune into various phases of life, or even the soul. Such introspection, such contemplation and meditation are, on the whole excluded from our societies, driven out and replaced by the analytical, secular dimension. We are distracted by images and artificial needs placed onto us by those to whom we have handed our power, political, industrial and social magnates. They have become instruments to take away our true power of self and we become slaves of other's ideas. That which can empower ourselves, introspection, self-inquiry and meditation, which tells us who we really are and what is truly valuable is - by and large neglected and thus results, for the individual as much as for society, in an imbalance of the Metal Element. This bids a strange philosophical thought: Has "the West" lost ability "to be West"; lost the meaning and willingness to live according to its own wisdom, has it lost its inherent sense of Being?

The Climate associated with the Metal Element is dryness. If we think back to the activity of the Lungs, we recall that air when reaching the lungs is actually saturated with water vapour. This enables the cells, surrounded with the alveoli, to engage in the exchange of gases. If we think back to the Large Intestines, the matter they receive is fluid and one of their major tasks is to extract water. Both organs thus are intimately connected with water. Indeed as we will see later, Metal is actually the mother of the next Element, Water. When there is a lack of water then neither the Lung nor the Large Intestines can do their job properly.

The Element Metal (Air)

As for nature en large? Organic matter finds it difficult to rot in the absence of water it just dries into dust. Both aspects show dryness as a sign of imbalance in the Metal Element, thus if somebody doesn't like dry climates, somebody has very dry skin, suffers from a constantly dry, thirsty mouth or too hard stools (constipation); they probably have such an imbalance.

Furthermore, since the Metal Element also relates to exchange with the outside world in general, dryness can show itself in other ways. We talk of an artist's creativity being "dried up"; somebody being sarcastic or having a "dry humour". After a tragedy has hit us and we have wept a lot, we feel "dry inside"; even a person as a whole who adheres to facts only, is described simply as "dry", because he lacks emotional, moist response.

The Tissues or part of the body linked to Metal is the skin. This has been described as the largest organ of our body and as the third lung. In fact the skin is both. It consists of two parts, the epidermis and the dermis. The former is the top layer that grows up from deeper layers; the uppermost always consists of dead cells that are constantly rubbed off by clothes etc. The active cells have as one of their functions the process of internal or cellular breathing.

The upper skin is the boundary between the moist environment of the living cells of the body and the dry atmosphere of the external environment. Underneath is a layer of collagen and elastic fibres, containing sweat glands, hair follicles and sebaceous glands; oily substances are produced by the latter, keeping the skin soft, pliable and waterproof. It also contains sensory nerve endings, which react by reflex action to unpleasant and painful stimuli. When the skin is intact it also provides a barrier to invading microbes. It also is the major organ of heat regulation.

It can now be understood that the skin is considered an organ that erects and protects the boundaries with the environment. In a wider sense this relates to the sense of self, the sense of ones own and others personal space. This organ network is related to keeping ones energy contained so that one does not encroach on others, and others energy does not encroach on ones own.

But not only that, the skin can also be said to symbolise a spiritual quality, that of keeping the inner and outer world defined.

> "The great Sufi Masters say;
> Whoever has the outer law without the inner reality
> has left the right way.
> Whoever has the inner reality without the outer law
> is a heretic.
> Whoever unites the two of them has realisation"[13].

To respect and love each, the outer and inner world, there has to be distinction, boundary, discrimination.

Skin is said to mirror the state of health of the Lung and in eastern and western medicine it is acknowledged that skin diseases such as eczema, scaling or other skin eruptions often accompany illnesses such as asthma, bronchitis, coughs etc. On the other hand skin diseases such as acne, dermatitis, boils and skin eruptions that appear during puberty or later in life, are seen as a way of the body getting rid of unwanted substances, just like the Large Intestines eliminate unwanted substances. The role of eliminator thus makes the skin part of the Metal energy field.

Let's look on a deeper level how skin as a soft tissue relates to Metal energy. Skin conditions and illnesses indicate our perception of our relationship to others: how we think other people see us and - how we see ourselves? We express our insecurities and problems through our skin. We blush with embarrassment, we redden with anger; we erupt with angry skin sores; we peel or flake in trying "to shed our old skin". We try to let go of old patterns. Skin is dry, because we withdraw inside, not letting enough fluid to the surface to keep the skin alive. One might well ask, is there nothing like simply having – dry skin? And the answer has to be "NO", if we believe in the interconnectedness of body, mind soul. All physical manifestation is related to the psychological or soul level; they are energy patterns with deeper truth!

In a metaphorical sense, the skin separating us from all else, is a symbol of our relationship with all else. Is our skin dry, hard, broken or tight it might refer to repelling, rejecting what is around us. Are we in fact, revolting against what life presents us with? A kind of deadening the sense of self, of protecting ourselves behind layers of dead skin just like hiding behind dead, outlived patterns, which shows especially in such skin disease as psoriasis, hives or rashes? On the other hand - is our relationship with our environment smooth, permeable and a well nourished ground for exchange, are we receptive and flexible in all interactions, then our skin is most likely also smooth, elastic and flexible. Thus, skin, it can be said, is about communication and as such, is a befitting contributor to the Metal energy.

The sense organ as well as the orifice connected with the Metal energy field, is the nose.

This is pretty obvious in terms of breathing, as well as in relation to the Lungs. Difficulties with the nose often have a direct link with the Lungs, as well as with the Large Intestines. In fact one of the most influential points of the Large Intestines meridian is directly in the groove at the flare of the nose. Recalling the last common cold you had and the elimination of mucus through the nose makes the link even clearer. The nose is like a gateway through which the air, the life-giving energy enters. Wide open nostrils speak of a generous gate, a free and easy exchange of intake and giving out of that energy which animates all life.

The Chinese attribute to the Lungs the quality of housing the soul. More accurately, they describe what we would call the soul or the spirit, in three concepts, each lodging in a different organ. *Shen* lodges in the heart; the ethereal soul or *hun* in the liver and *po*, the corporeal soul, in the lung.

Similarly in the Indian tradition, *atman*, the joyous self, lodges in the heart, *jivaatman* the individual, ethereal soul in the liver and *prana*, the animating spirit in the lungs. The latter is the physical counterpart of the ethereal soul. "It is closely linked to the body and could be described as the somatic expression of the soul, or the organisational principle of the body; the corporeal soul provides movement to the essence, i.e. it brings the essence into play in all physiological processes of the body, breathing can be seen as the pulsating of the corporeal soul; on a mental level the corporeal soul protects the individual from external psychic influences. Some people are easily affected by negative influences; this is due to weakness of the corporeal soul"[14], or as we would call it, the animistic soul. The nose is the gateway for this the most physically manifest form of life-energy, the entrance hall to our innermost being. This is well recognised in various forms of Yoga and in meditation, clear emphasis is placed on the form of breathing.

There is also another aspect of the nose. The nose releases mucus, unwanted germs and tissues that block the airway. In a metaphorical sense, at times when we feel disappointed, powerless or disillusioned; when we feel hopeless and frustrated, we might get a runny nose or even a cold to rid ourselves of whatever is bothering us, or even what is bothering our soul. Thorough cleansing of emotional as well as physical accumulated waste from the sinuses can happen through the nose. Thus people with permanently blocked noses, with polyps or chronic nasal congestion point towards an imbalance within the Metal energy.

The sense associated with Metal is smell, which is obvious after the above. Particular smells often trigger good or bad memories and associations. An inability to smell can thus be a particular way of blocking off experiences, which is a sign of congestion, of being stuck with a particular pattern and not being able or willing to let go of the associations with that

The Element Metal (Air)

smell. Conversely, people who open their minds to the soul or the heart often experience an improvement in their sense of smell, as though a new link, a new awareness has been established.

Life is full of smells. Just think of a flower that is not just beautiful in itself, but it gives us pleasure to smell it. It provides an extended awareness of beauty, of life itself. In this way, as we develop our awareness, our nasal passages can be opened in the widest sense to the 'smell of Life'. I remember well once when I was sitting in a room and suddenly the room smelled very strongly of burning human flesh, very acrid. No one else in the room smelled it; shortly afterwards I heard the news: all over central India burial pyres were burning thousands of earthquake victims. At the point in time when I smelled it, I had not heard anything about an earthquake!

The Fluid that relates to the Metal Element is mucus. Most of the body's eliminations are accompanied by the excretion of mucus. It is the transportation lubrication of the body and vital for elimination. A dry throat and nose, cough, a tickle in the throat, point just as much to a lubrication problem in the respiratory system as too much mucus with constantly oozing sinuses or dripping noses. The same is true for too dry faeces or certain forms of diarrhoea. On a mental or emotional level, lack of mucus can thus signify an inability or unwillingness to clear out old ideas and patterns.

External physical manifestations attributed to the Metal Element are the skin and body hair. The skin we have already considered. The body hair, whose follicles are embedded in the skin, has a close link to the skin and thus is useful as an indicator for the state of the skin. It is said that unusual amounts of body hair or the lack of it (within reason and considering racial and cultural background) indicate an imbalance of the Metal energy. The condition of the body hair shows whether the lungs are in splendid and flourishing condition. Ohashi explains this with the link the hair outside the body has with that inside the body, such as the cilia in the oesophagus and digestive tracts as well as in the lungs and intestines. Excessive cilia indicate mucus accumulation which in turn results in increased hair growth[15].

The colour linked to the Element of Metal is white. White light, and (taken from there) the colour white is really a combination of all colours. "The spectrum of colours which makes up white light ranges from the short violet and blue waves, through green, red and orange waves to red waves, which are the longest that the eye can detect"[16]. We speak of white noise, describing random sounds across the spectrum of all frequencies. Both perceptions (eyes and ears) register this quality of collecting, gathering things as white. This word "white" has from here found entrance into our every day language and is used to describe objects made of alloys (white metal) of a grey colour; it is a slang word for being honourable and square (white person); it describes a variety of fish (white fish) . This gathering mode is taken to extremes in cosmology, where we have "white dwarfs". White dwarfs are stars that "have a mass similar to that of the sun, but are only 1% of the sun's diameter, consist of degenerate matter... packed... together as tightly as is physically possible, so that a spoonful of it weighs several tonnes"[17]. The characteristic of collecting, gathering and condensing makes it obvious why this is linked to Metal.

Furthermore white is in some societies associated with purity. Purity stands for the state before; before the attachment to all clutter, all unnecessary things, or evil and thus some societies attached white to virgins, to virtue, to sacred spaces, the surplice of the clergy or choir, priest and priestess etc. It could be described as the pre-state, the state of emptiness, the state of before and after, and thus again is reminiscent of the cleansing activity of the Large Intestines or the pause between the in-breath and the out-breath. The notion letting go- makes white also into the colour for funerals in some societies.

In the Indian traditions, white is the colour of Shiva. White holds all colours, Shiva holds all: creation and destruction, as well as the interval. White ash, from the purifying and thanksgiving fire, the Yajna, is applied to the forehead; such white streaks of Bhasma are a sign of devotion and surrender to the divine consciousness, the *dharma* of Truth. In Buddhist tradition white is associated with the Dhyani Buddha Vairochana whose body-colour is white and Akshobhya whose radiance is pure white to symbolise mirror-like wisdom.

In Chinese medicine nuances in facial skin colouring (taking into account racial variations) are used for diagnosis. A white shading of the skin points the prudent observer in the direction of a Metal imbalance. It signifies that the physical, mental or spiritual aspects of the person, are suffering from an impaired function of the Lung or Large Intestines meridian, thus not fulfilling their role of purifying, condensing, absorbing and eliminating.

The smell relating to the Metal Element is rotten. As with the colour, the smell of skin (or person as a whole) is used for diagnosis. Large Intestines and the Lung energies, when inefficient, leave matter too long, thus lazy elimination allows matter to rot. Illnesses such as Tuberculosis and other infections have distinct rotten smells, as is often stated in the description of war - hospitals in fictional literature. The smell of rot is a smell of decomposition.

The taste associated with the Metal Element is that of pungency. Such strong flavours could relate to cheese, curry dishes, peppery dishes and in general, spicy food. People, who have a particular liking or dislike of such food, have most likely an imbalance in the Metal energy. These foods are said to open the pores and improve the circulation of saliva and mucus, - a desire of the body to help itself in the removal and elimination process that otherwise might be stuck. On the other hand, one should not eat too much pungent food "if too much pungent flavour is used in food, the muscles become knotted and the finger and toenails wither and decay"[18].

The grain indicative of the Metal Element is rice.

Chapter 4

The fruit chestnuts.

The meat that of the horse.

The vegetable is the onion.

These are foods that are said to have a specially balancing effect on the Lung and Large Intestines energy. If a special meridian is out of balance, these foods might help to redress the balance. Rice is a grain that easily absorbs moisture and also, when eaten with the husks (brown rice), carries a lot of fibre. Both characteristics help the Large Intestines in their function of absorption, condensing and eliminating. Chestnuts are a water carrying vegetable and as such lubricate, dilute and help constipation, as well as moisturising the Lungs, for as we will recall, air needs to be moisturised before the absorption process of the gasses can take place. Thus chestnuts are beneficial to both meridians. I have no idea why horse meat should be beneficial, unless its toughness helps the fibre and bulk that is needed in the Large Intestines.

Onions are rich in water and its sharp gasses penetrate the nostrils and bronchioles, stimulating their activity, as we have all experienced when peeling onions - with watering eyes and dripping noses. They clean the air passages. An old house remedy often used in rural areas is to make onion tea when children have bronchitis, or even to burn onion - skins in the room. This helps the bronchioles and the general respiratory tract.

The emotion linked to the Metal Element is grief. Grief is a stage of transition, it is a necessary step to say "goodbye" to appreciate what has been and then let it go and be free for the new. This applies to many situations. We have to grieve and indeed accept that we miss things or people before we can let go of them. For example, we need to accept that we miss our old home before we can really look forward to the new one; we grieve for a past job, and often we ritualise loss with a celebration. We grieve for losing a friend that has moved abroad. We also leave childhood and grieve for a while we do not quite know where we belong and feel awkward about it. In fact every such transition in life is accompanied by grief. Most 'primitive' cultures have initiation rituals for various stages of life and they usually have a set period of solitude first, to come to terms with whatever is taking place. Our own rituals, birthdays, weddings and funerals have always an element of grieving; why else do mothers cry at weddings, why else do we celebrate with our friends on the night before a wedding. We have farewell parties to let go off the previous year, our parents, children, our friends or - the dead.

In these celebrations we remember the shared times, we reconcile feuds, try to let go of problems and express our feelings for the person (places, situations), we tell them about our love for them and wish them well. We face our loneliness, we acknowledge the emptiness they leave in us, and then we let go of it, to be filled again with the new. Each step has to be taken, each is as important as the other. I remember when my father died (I was fifteen years old). I knew he was dying, he had been ill for a long time, but because of the circumstances I was not able to tell him that I loved him and to say "goodbye" to him. The pain of that unexpressed grief stayed with me for thirty years!

Obviously the most important grieving is connected to the loss of a close relation or next of kin, the loss of a child or parent are the most tragic, calling for the most extended period of grief and mourning. "If families can cry and talk together about the happy memories they share of the much missed person, then the real process of bereavement can be greatly enhanced"[19]. The emotional turmoil can be well digested and then let go, a process that is very familiar to the reader by now and linked to the Metal energy. People, who have unfinished business with a person who has died, (say in an accident, or of an illness that prevented the survivor saying "goodbye") might result in that person being unable to face "goodbyes" altogether. They might refuse to grieve, pretending that the other person did not die, and in not being able to truly let go.

This leads to severe emotional "constipation" and probably they will need outside help.

Even when a normal death occurs in a family, the etiquette might demand not to show emotions. One does not cry (not being allowed either by others or by exerting self-control) or some other such behaviour pattern suggesting "I have to be strong, I can survive, I'm all right Jack." These leads to suppressed anguish, sorrow and grief that clogs up the system of emotional flow, and so leads to withdrawal, introvertedness, depression, inability to communicate one's feelings in the future etc. Without letting go of these feelings there is no room for new energy, for new life to come in. There can be no growth, no change, without letting go of the old, without creating an empty space the new cannot be received. Such holding in can result in physical illness of the respiratory system or the bowels. On the other hand, people who grieve too much for an unreasonably long time (some widows or widowers) and never get beyond the stage of letting go, are also stuck. The Nei Ching says, "extreme grief is injurious to the lungs"[20]. Similarly the roots of extreme post-natal-depressions, diseases occurring after retirement (especially skin diseases), depression that causes pathological illness (i.e. after the children have left home) and aspects of the menopause (as well as the mid-life crisis) might well lie in the inability to grieve and then to let go. These might even be caused, by clinging to grief itself. Healthy grief is a transient state.

The expression associated with the Metal energy is weeping. The link to grief is obvious, as is the ability to weep and express ones feelings easily or conversely, the inability to weep (suppressing such emotions). But what is meant here is more a quality of the voice. It is a sound of the voice, a kind of whining, that "should be accompanied by tears". Some people always speak with a whine, it even accompanies joy and happiness. This sound in the everyday voice gives a clear indication of an imbalance in the Large Intestines and Lung meridians as it indicates how a person absorbs and eliminates. Some people have constantly watering eyes, or an expression in the eyes as though they are ready to cry at any time, these people obviously need some support for their Metal Element.

The sound linked to Metal is that of cracking. Metal is sensitive to heat and makes little cracking noises when it expands and contracts. Could this be what this refers to? Obviously Metal is also quite brittle (apart from special steels) and under pressure it breaks easily, the most obvious is cast iron. When it breaks it makes a sharp, pointed cracking sound. Furthermore it is a one off sound, unlike the sparkling, crackling of fire, or the slower cracking of dry wood. Metal breaks with a distinct, compact sound. This could refer to a person whose internal stress has built up so much, (or the suppressed emotions have reached such intensity) or the lungs have held the air for so long, that they literally burst with a big howl, bang or crack - to release the pressure. Explosions point to long-standing imbalances in the Metal Element.

The manner in times of excitement or change associated with Metal is that of coughing and nervous scratching. Both speak of irritants, one of the lung, one of the skin. Coughing gets rid of stagnant air, scratching the skin releases energy, a movement directed onto the self, a frustration of not being able to let go of ones feelings, energy turned inside, in the extreme, attacking the self. (Eczema etc.)

The Attitude associated with Metal is a deep breath, a sigh of relief or resignation.

The Movement of Energy described in the Metal Element is yawning. The last three expressions are to do with the lung and the way air is used, not only physiological, but also to express or hide feelings. "Our feelings are comprised of energy, and they function as a fluid, moving interface between body, mind, spirit and environment. When we experience loss of a loved one, or a cherished dream, we immediately generate energy to address the loss, and we feel sorrow. The sensation of sadness is the movement of energy needed to resolve our hurt". Indeed, all human feelings are forever balancing energy that rises in response to events of our daily life. Unfortunately we are not taught how to react to our feelings, contrarily we are often raised to resist the feeling of movement of energy, then the energy gets stuck, it remains in our body and contracts and becomes part of our continuing experience. "Unless we release and resolve such contraction, it will remain as a tangible wound, or scar or disruptive pattern in our emotional body, which in turn can lead to mental neurosis/or physical disease. We will have unconsciously transformed energy into specific and unhealthy mass"[21]. Unpleasant happenings of any kind can bring about such manifestations, be it a tragic loss, an accident, a way a teacher spoke to us or, - even the sound of the voice of a dominant father. The experiences are unavoidable, but how we deal with it, depends largely on ourselves, and/or our environment. To store it as old stuck energy creates foundations on which constantly more "injured feelings" get piled up and the energy contracts. The block gets bigger; we literally hold our breath. A deep breath is taken to force the energy further down, sometimes a slow controlled sigh allows a bit of the pent-up emotion to release; sometimes a cough attempts to let go more but all too often illness results. A yawn is an even slower way of controlled, hiding release. "I have to get rid of it, but I will disguise it!" On the other hand, if there is plenty of love and nurturing, understanding and physical comfort, enough positive energy is generated to quickly release the contracted energy then healing occurs.

Conversely deep breathing, sighing and yawning all can be signs of a need for (rather than of too much pent-up) energy. A lack of the vital energy of breath can create the spontaneous desire for a deep breath, followed by a sighing of relief. Similarly yawning can express the need to move stagnant air quickly. "Every feeling is a field of energy. A pleasant feeling is an energy, which can nourish. Irritation is a feeling, which can destroy. Under the light of awareness, the energy of irritation can be transformed into an energy which nourishes"[22]. A person that habitually shows either of these three expressions suffers from difficulties in the process of exchanging energies and thus shows an imbalance of the Metal Element.

The Quality connected to the Metal energy is: Vitality. The Oxford dictionary describes vitality as none other than the vital force, power or principle as possessed by living things; the principle of life. In fact the word itself means life: vitae; and in Sanskrit, the root of many of our languages, another word for Shiva, the highest principle of life is *Vitalle* (pronounced vital). What animates life, and who animates life are thus the same. Furthermore since it is intrinsic to living things, the creator and the creation are by definition the same. The breath is what animates us, thus we are the breath of God. Or as Swami Chetanananda writes "The breath you are usually aware of is nothing more than the gross manifestation of this pulsation that is what we are, nothing more than a form taken on briefly by the Breath of God. That is why we practise focusing on our breathing - to become aware of and to understand the flow of this breath inside our breath. You see, there is only one thing behind the appearance of many things, and that one thing is the energy of Life itself. The energy of Life - basic pulsation in all things - is really nothing but pure consciousness or pure awareness. This pure awareness is both infinite and vital. It must be vital because awareness without vitality would be inert. In the process of displaying its vitality, this infinite awareness pulsates. Its pulsation vibrate at different rates, giving rise to the appearance of different forms... it is all still one thing"[23].

Or in a more classical language:

> "The heart of Vedanta is *prana*, bringing the breath under complete control. Vedanta is the knowledge of the Indivisible... Vedanta has no form, it is indivisible, changeless. If the breath is not harmonious and rhythmical... the free flow of air and energy is obstructed: Water cannot flow through a blocked pipe. This imbalance leads to all disease"[24].

Vitality and breath are inseparably linked on all levels, body and mind and soul. Incorrect breathing, such as shallow breath, a-rhythmical breathing, wheezing and so on will thus affect the vitality of the person and lead to illness; the imbalance in the Metal energy will affect the whole of the body/mind/soul entity without further ado.

The activity of the Metal energy is that of analysing. In Buddhist art the Buddha of Wisdom, Manjushri, is depicted with a sharp, gleaming sword, with which he cuts away all, that is irrelevant. Moreover, Manjushri embodies "the transcendental knowledge that death is ultimately an illusion and that those who identify themselves with the ultimate reality, the plenum-void (*Sunyata*) of their inner centre, overcome death and are liberated from the chains of samsara"[25].

Manjushri is shown to cut down with his sword even death and is called "the Ender of Death". The sword, made of clear, refined metal stands for a sharp mind that not only takes apart or analyses (analysis is nothing else than cutting up into smaller and smaller bits to look at) - but sees even further than the bits to the pure essence. Such intellectual work is necessary and beneficial, as long as one does not lose sight of the whole. The sword (metal) seems to indicate that this ability has always been associated with Metal; yet how does it relate to the meridians? The Lung "takes apart" and analyses the air then splits it into oxygen, nitrogen and carbon dioxide etc. The Large Intestines analyse the chime and takes out the minerals etc. that the body needs. So both organ networks are involved in a dissecting and analysing. A person that is overly analytical and gets lost in the detail, could show an imbalance in the mental side of the Metal Element, just as much as somebody who finds it difficult to apply the mind to any sort of analytical work.

The condition associated with Metal is that of inhibition. In the wake of what has been said about blocking out emotions and experiences, it is obvious that such a person would appear inhibited. A person that has no intimate friendships, finds it difficult to relate to other people, other than in a business capacity, as acquaintances and mates, friendly, casual but not sharing, not intimate. Such inhibitions could affect all aspects of life; if they appear frequently and in a painful way, then it is time to investigate an imbalance in the Metal Element.

Qualities/steps in Sadhana that correspond to the Metal Element are that of the awakening intellect. One recognises the mind as a function of the body; the mind can be used to control the body and thus one can decide ones own life. The intellectual awareness enables one to let go of the firm identification with the body alone. "I am not only my body but a mind, conditioned by many influences".

As for the idea of spiritual advancement in the four levels of consciousness, the Element of Metal must surely belong to the dream state. The dream-state, the second stage of consciousness, is that where we identify with dreams, with concepts and ideas. Our ideas, our dreams are for us as real as the physical world. Our mind is caught in his shiniest colours. Can we see its limitations, it's conditioning- harbours the challenge to focus on the mind itself and use it to detach from physical being?

The relationship of Metal to the other Elements is like for all the Elements characterised by two sequences, the *Sheng* and *Ko* cycle. These act like good parents, one nourishes and gives birth, the other restricts and limits so that neither can get out of control. Metal is a mother to Water. The traditionally suggested is water springing forth from a rock. The implications are that Metal nourishes and replenishes Water. The connection goes beyond such a simple metaphor though. As mentioned earlier, Water and Metal have a close, intimate connection.

If we digress to the other traditional mode, that calls this Element Air, the link might be easier seen. Water is a combination of Hydrogen and Oxygen molecules; Air shares, chemically speaking much of the same molecules. Oxygen is particular vital, renewing water constantly. If we look at the function and meaning of the element we see that Metal/Air and Water have a close, intimate relationship. Even though it might be hard to imagine. Air without humility in the lungs is useless. The gas exchange within its cells could not take place without the air being enclosed in water vapour. The same is true within the work of the Large Intestines, water is absorbed but also used as a lubricant (since faeces is 70% water).

The Metal Element can be said to be connected to the Element Water in yet a different important way. The cerebrospinal fluid, a central part of the bodies system, is activated by the action of the Lungs. "The Breath of Life - this pulsation - moves through your spinal column twelve times a minute. The breath that you are aware of, is nothing more that the gross manifestation of this pulsation"[26]. Their relationship is characterised by help full co-operation.

Metal controls and limits Wood as the action of an axe or saw (sawing of a tree trunk) vividly illustrates this. If the Lung and the Large Intestines do not supply the blood with fresh oxygen and nutrients, the gallbladder and liver have nothing to process. Their relationship is characterised by control.

On the other hand Metal itself is controlled by Fire. Metal thrown into fire will melt and although it will not perish for a long time, it will lose its form and capacity to act. Even more so Air; it gets used up by the burning process and completely vanishes – as one can see when a candle in a jar is extinguished by simply putting a lid on it. Once the air is used up- a vacuum created inside. As far the working in the body: the heart, as the supreme organ, has to beat and work well otherwise even the life-spirit cannot operate in the being. Without the heart, the work of the lungs is unthinkable; yet an overactive heart can damage the capacity of the lungs. Lung and heart depend upon each other, the blood alone is useless to the rest of the body, unless the blood carries oxygen in sufficient quantities, the body is not healthy. They exist in mutual dependency.

Metal itself is the child of Mother Earth. It originates in earth, and in terms of the body, it can be said that "the lung extracts the Essence from Air, combining it with the essence from food sent by the spleen, distilling it into the pure, correct *Qi* of bodily life. The lung then guides this refined essence downward from the head into the chest and abdomen and outward towards the muscles and skin and extremities. Through exhalation, the lung eliminates the by-products of its alchemical work by expelling the turbid, used air"[27].

Having fulfilled its task, Metal then proceeds in the cycle and gives birth to Water.

CHAPTER FIVE

INVOCATION OF WATER

I am Varuna, the Vedic Lord of the waters who rules the mysterious seas
- whose eye of conscious awareness is in every drop of water
- whose intuition is natural guidance

I am divine consciousness within the waters of the Ganges of every country
I am Tialoc, the water snake of the Mayas,
I am Tiddalic and Gekko the water- beings of the Aboriginals,
I am Dagda of the Celts
I am the TAO, ground of being and non-being
I am the ten thousand things in the field of the TAO

I am the blood of the earth coming forth of metal and stone
I am in all living creatures;
- plants and trees gain their progression from me
- fruits and flowers obtain their measure from me
- bodies of bird and beast gain their potentialities through me
- their stripes, markings, hair and feathers are made through me

I am all those things, yet there is not one of the various things that is the result of any effort on my part, all is my natural property, my suchness; my Buddha nature, is emptiness. I am the ten thousand things, the question is not "What am I"? But, "How am I "?

I AM WATER
I am <u>moving, fluid</u> - <u>still</u> and <u>stagnant</u> taking up any form:
- changing effortlessly from the tiny vaporised particle to the most grand glacier
- moving gracefully as a ballerina and powerfully as a Sumo wrestler
- following a law unto myself, respecting no political borders
- adapting to water-pipes and sewers alike, unattached
- throwing back the image of the moon from brackish marshes
- carrying the lotus flower in the muddy Balinese temple lake

- suffocating all life in my sucking swamps in the Everglades
- breeding flies in a stinking puddle in the African village.

I am <u>refreshing</u>, <u>cooling</u> and <u>freezing</u>, <u>deadly</u>
- refreshing rainfall after a scorching summers day
- the icicles that delicately hug the holly leaf
- moisture gathered in the softest moss beside the river's bed
- the cool drink on the parched lips of the fevered child
- a pregnant cloud that bursts asunder
- the blizzard, the flood-wave crushing forests and villages
- the ice-cap of the frozen north, an endless reservoir of energy
- winter cold paralysing bones and joints with arthritic pain

I am <u>gentle</u> and <u>strong</u>
- the sacred water that washes the lingam
- the sweet nectar the hummingbird finds in the hibiscus flower
- the vibration creating the sound of Handel's music in your ear
- the slow drip from the ladle in the Zen garden
- the majestic wave that carries away the ballast of a lifetime
- the power in the churning electric turbines
- the current carrying Norwegian logs to build a Cornish roof
- seeping into the tiny crack of Ayers Rock, splitting it like dynamite

I am <u>nourishing</u> and <u>draining</u>
- morning dew that turns the seed into the date in the oasis
- summer rain that swells peas and leeks in an English garden
- bone marrow and "sea of marrow" so you can read this poem
- carrying the salt of the sea, the gold of tradesmen
- draining all life from the salt-pans of the world
- cutting the mountain, carrying him down his slopes
- bleeding out of the soldier, sapping his life's force
- washing the last bit of nutrient out of the table mountain in the Sierra

I am seemingly <u>permanent</u> - then <u>impermanent</u>
- the mist of a November day that hides life's continuity
- the dreams of journeys far away, sailing to distant shores
- the ebb and flow of the ocean for ever moving without goal

- the relentless drip of water in the torture chamber
- the dew on the cherry blossom, symbol of impermanence
- the primeval force of yesterdays whirlpools
- fear of the unknown, of losing oneself
- in the last out-breath of the dying

I am <u>creative</u> and <u>destructive</u>
- the medium for male and female cells to merge
- the cradle of the unborn child
- the paint depicting poppy flowers and the Medusa
- the nectar of the summer ripened peach
- the dampness of a rotting leaf, a decaying corpse
- the flood that drowns the Bangladeshi child
- the heavy water of nuclear fission

I am <u>controlled, guided and pent-up and explosive</u>
- gathered in an intricate system of reservoirs by the engineers of Ashoka
- arrested by dykes in the flat-lands by the North Sea
- measured in the smallest amounts in syringes in the hospital
- the sea of madness hurling the ship against the cliff
- boiling mud in the Yellowstone Park
- steam rising from the undersea volcano
- the geyser spurting forth through the earth's crust
- the force ejected from a blow hole in Australian

I am <u>crystal clear</u> - yet <u>hidden and deceptive</u>
- the mirror of Narcissus, the master's mind reflecting our ego
- the clear blue sky hidden behind the anthracite clouds
- crystal clear sharpness of an icicle, focusing perception
- the healing power, touching peoples eternal thirst
- the secret behind the unfathomable depths of mind
- the eyes focusing inwards to see the unseen mysteries
- the crushing power in a majestic waterfall
- the sulphur cloud hiding Mount Fuji in its stench

I am <u>wilful</u> and <u>surrender</u>
- will and determination forcing the floods through the canyon
- relentless unforgiving power carving giant's steps in Ireland

Chapter 5

- pushing and shoving, forcing my way into the Tokyo subway
- the willpower of the athlete running for a world record
- compassion and love pouring unlimited through your saints
- mutual surrender of two ancestral kidney energy's in orgasm
- giving one of my forms for another when I meet fire
- not questioning my own nature, but surrendering to the "watercourse way"

With so many forms my wisdom shows itself in balancing. My cycles know neither beginning nor end, but equipoise can be achieved:
- by respecting the Earth and accepting its helping limits
- by giving freely to Wood and other life forms
- by yielding and opening itself to the Fire of the sun
- by cleansing and replenishing itself from its source
- by moving, always moving in harmony with all others.

> As above so below;
> as inside so outside;
> as on the planet so in the body.
>
> As the Yellow River collects all sediments before he spills it into the South China Sea, so the
> bladder gathers the waste of the body ready to spill it.
> As the Wadi of the African Savannah has to adapt from floods to drought, so has the bladder.
> As the gravel beds and limestone layers of the earth filter the water, so the kidneys exchange
> fluids through freely swinging filtering membranes.
> As earth's waters are not filtered properly in the groves and swamps of Belize,
> plants, animals and people are poisoned. If the blood is not cleaned properly, the body becomes poisoned, the soul becomes depressed and disturbed.
> As all colours, all markings, all life is sustained by water there is no beauty, no paper, no paint, no sculpture, no pot, no photograph made without it.

As the body depends on the kidney and bladder, without their proper functioning there is no happiness, no beauty, no joy, no creativity in the person, indeed, ultimately there is only madness and death.
As above so below, as for the planet so in the body.

To keep these energies balanced is to keep the body and mind-

> Flexible but not without integrity
> still without getting stagnant
> refreshed without getting frozen
> gentle without getting insipid
> strong without getting overpowering
> nurturing without suffocating
> diluting without dispersing
> changing without getting lost
> creative without getting spent
> analysing without being destructive
> energised without exploding
> guided without being controlled
> mindful without being deceptive and secretive
> clear without cutting
> determined without being dictatorial
> surrendering without annihilation

To keep them balanced walk the middle path, attached neither to here nor to there. For ultimately the water's nature is to just flow.

> It is our mind that judges -
>   the slowly dripping water, as
>   the peace of a Zen garden
>   or the screaming pain in a torture chamber!

Character of Water

Let me summarise the characteristics of Water mentioned in the above invocation. Water is movement, is fluid, it is refreshing. It is cooling, gentle and nourishing. It is seemingly permanent, creative and adaptable, which implies it can be easily controlled and guided. Water is crystal clear, transparent even; it has purpose and is wilful. At the same time Water has inherent negative tendencies. It is freezing and stagnant and as such deadly; it is strong, it is draining, it is impermanent. It is destructive, explosive, pent-up force. It is hidden and it is deceptive. It surrenders.

Let's not fall into the trap that Hyemeyohsts Storm describes when he says " people do not know anymore what water is, for they think it comes out of a tap - that's all, - they forget that water is us, we are walking water, that water has spirit, is living." Let's widen our perception, to re-experience water.

Hildegard von Bingen describes Water as having 15 powers; "warmth, wetness, is wavelike, has speed, movement, giving sap to trees, taste to fruit, greenness to vegetation, lubrication to all things, holds birds, feeds the fish, enlivens the animals through its warmth, holds creepy crawleys encoated in mucus and encompasses all"[1]. This is a strange list. But it communicates the feeling, that nothing exist, that is not touched by water. She points out that water carries warmth (not just cold as we expect) and quite surprisingly, sees the movement of flowing not so much a quality of water, but of air. Both share this property which points to the mother-child connection of the *Chen Ko Cycle* for Metal/Air and Water; this means in terms of organs that there is a special connection between lungs and kidneys. She relates their dependency to the bottom of the sea for there we find the sand which contains the vital minerals the human body needs, salts. The minerals keep illness at bay, stimulating the kidneys, - the curative power of sea-salt is beyond doubt. Furthermore if lung-energy does not decent - kidney - energy cannot rise.

She does not rest there and takes the idea into the realm of consciousness - the ocean hides the deep; in the deep we not only find vital salts, but in the depth of ourselves we find consciousness . Her idea is closely linked to the Buddhist concept that beyond the deep is stillness the nothingness, the all containing "mirror of wisdom". In this way the aggregate of Water is "more powerful than fire, because it can extinguish fire"[2]. Even the fire of devotion and love has to be transcended to ultimate stillness.

Ayurvedic medicine too links Water and Air, both connect them because for them, Water carries *prana* (which essentially is Air/ oxygen/ life energy). The lung influences and provides direct energy to kidney and bladder, which in turn are linked to Vata and Kapha states characterised by fluidity and dryness[3].

Tibetan medicine ascribes to Water the qualities of: cohesion, assimilation, equilibrium, dissolution, liquification, being the elixir of life, lunar forces, fertility, the female principle, colourlessness, the receptive, the qualities of a mirror, the deep, the abysmal, the subconscious and unification[4].

Water's wider, more psychological connotation rise out of the link to movement and space, not from its form. Strictly speaking water has **no form,** it takes up what ever form is needed; from here it has becomes a symbol of "the dynamic principle per se" and in many cultures is used to describe "the flow of life". In terms of health and illness this means, "not to flow" is the root of all illness. It violates the principle of the universal consciousness (*alaya - vijnana*), which is movement, is change. It is often linked to the ocean on whose surface there are currents, waves and whirlpools, yet whose depth remains motionless, unperturbed, pure and clear.

In agreement with TCM most cultures agree, that the illnesses attributed to the Water Element are anxiety, panic, mania, stress, hysteria, hypertension, disorder of liver and gallbladder, blood and water related illnesses etc.[5]. On the other hand, in a positive state water energy is soft and patient and so let us try to match the attributes to a person that displays dominant characteristics of the Water Element (here after referred to as the Water Person).

The person will appear to be soft and gentle, with fluid movement and manner; he may be a family doctor; equally he may be in any helping profession; may be a teacher for small children, or for handicapped people. A Water Person has a unique ability to feel into other people, to sense their emotions and needs, and respond to them, without much ado they give support, healing or physical and emotional nourishment.

Water people can be refreshingly simple and have an open directness that might appear as coolness; but it is more because they are clear about their own feelings, their intentions and motives, it is more that they appear transparent and open for others to interpret, love or misuse.

They are steady people and build permanent honest relationships. They can control their emotions well, not so much by suppressing them (as Wood would) as by limiting their outbursts. They might express their emotions, but then not indulge in them, rather cultivate an acknowledgement and then they put their emotions out of their minds, allow them to flow away.

A balanced Water person is persistent. He/she does not easily give up ideals or plans, but work slowly and steadily at an obstacle wearing away the resistance -very different from say a Wood Person who also will not give up, yet in a driven, striving way, with the need to reach their aim.

The image that comes to mind is that of a country GP or midwife. He/she will in all weathers go for miles through snow and flood to get to a patient that needs them, and once there, they show no anger or frustration at their ordeal, just kindly, they get on with their job in an even, gentle manner. The clarity of purpose, together with persistence becomes their strength. This differs from the strength in a Wood Person, which is due to their vitality and drive. The water drips, wears stone away in time -Wood (e.g. the roots of a tree) just push the stone out of its way.

As a hobby, the Water person might paint or play music; they are very creative, expressing themselves in many different forms. Nothing is quite so important to a Water Person as deep personal relationships and human values, thus the will and persistence will be used to preserve these. Consequently we find Water people amongst many humanitarian giants, who might not listen to reason, but with their charm and insight, their sensitivity and strong sense of values, they can achieve great feats for humanity.

For more detail let us now turn to the meridian system itself.

Associations to the Water Meridians

The two meridians, or organ networks, that are connected to the Water Element are those named after the bladder (*Yang*) and kidney (*Yin*). Let us first look at the function of the traditional anatomical organs.

The Kidneys lie just below the diaphragm, on either side of the spine, the right kidney is slightly lower than the left and roughly between the twelfth thoracic vertebrae and the third lumbar vertebrae. Kidneys are bean shaped, about eleven centimetres long, six wide and three centimetres thick. There is a difference in the position though; the right kidney is close to the liver, the left to the spleen, stomach and pancreas.

The kidney's function is to synthesise urine; this happens in three stages, <u>simple filtration,</u> <u>selective re-absorption</u> and <u>secretion.</u> The kidney consists mainly of about a million units called nephrons, some tubules and blood vessels. The arterial blood enters the kidney passing into millions of tiny tubes, (nephrons); the nephrons enclose a knot-like bunch of blood vessels called glomerular. These have semi-permeable walls, which let water and small molecules pass through. Blood cells, plasma and other large molecules remain. These compositions that are filtered out, are altered in the tubules where the substances the body needs are re-absorbed, the rest is passed on to a collecting tubule where foreign matter is also gathered. The process of re-absorption is regulated by hormones (e.g. antidiuretic hormone, aldosterone etc). The secreted matter, urine, is a complex product that consists of 96% water, the rest being unwanted body chemicals, such as ammonia, potassium, chlorides etc., to name but a few.

The large amount of water taken into the body as food or drink is absorbed into the body by the metabolic process. The balance of fluid intake (and output)is also controlled by the kidneys, albeit in conjunction with cells in the hypothalamus; these sense the changes in osmotic pressure of the blood and send messages via the anti-diuretic hormone, released in the pituitary gland, to the kidneys. A feedback mechanism registers when the osmotic pressure is raised and instigates the decrease or increase of the fluid intake or output. Thus the filtering process of the kidney serves primarily to maintain the blood concentration of various substances within normal limits.

The kidneys also keep an electrolyte balance within the bodies water by regulating the sodium intake (sodium is the most common positively charged ion). Sodium is also in almost all foods, thus we take in much more than we need, so its secretion has to be assured and constantly monitored; this is the task of the hormone aldosterone which is secreted by the adrenal glands. They sit directly on top of the kidneys and also produce adrenaline and non-adrenaline. These hormones are responsible for the 'fight or flight' response in times of stress. This means they increase or decrease the metabolic rate, dilate or contract the bronchioles (allowing more or less air to be taken in) they instigate the constriction or dilation of blood vessels etc., in order to prepare for fight, or conversely for relaxing and withdrawing. The close involvement of kidneys and adrenals in this aspect leads to the association of the kidneys with fear.

It seems in various different forms, the main involvement of the kidney has to do with keeping balance. They clean and detoxify the body; yes, but mainly in order to keep a balance of nutrients. This seems different from the detoxification of the liver, the former is more subtle, a fine tuning, whereas the latter is directly involved in detoxification of ingested material. In a wider sense, it seems, the Wood energy gets rid of substances with conviction and strength, the Water Element gets rid of it with gentle coaxing (See the portrait of the Water Person).

The Bladder is a 'reservoir' for urine. It lies in the pelvic cavity and its size and position vary, depending on the amount of urine it contains. From it the urethra leads to the exterior world. Autonomic nerve fibres in the bladder wall trigger the micturation reflex in the brain. Micturation occurs when the wall of the bladder contracts and the internal and external sphincters are relaxed. The urine, once assembled, is propelled through the ureter (a 25 cm - 30 cm long tube) by peristaltic action of the bladder.

The main character trait of the bladder is its adaptability. It gathers and then releases. In a metaphorical sense we can relate that to emotions. Every new beginning is preceded by two phases; the cleaning out of the old and - letting it go! A vessel has to be empty to be filled. Old emotions, be they hurt pride, anger, fear or rejection, have to be collected and then let go. But not only emotions! Since all these organs symbolise a spiritual quality - in order to receive grace we have to be aware that we have to let go of our preconceptions and striving. As Meister Eckhardt suggests as his via negativa:

> The more you seek God, the less you will find God.
> If you do not seek God
> you will find God.
>
> God does not ask anything else of you
> except that you let yourself go
> and let God

be God in you
for;
God's exit is his entrance[6].

Considering that the body consists of 78% water and that the kidneys regulate the water intake and the bladder the disposal of excess water, then the importance of these meridians and their relationship to water as a whole is obvious. The basis of blood, lymph, endocrine fluids, urine, cerebral spinal fluid, sweat, saliva, tears, sexual secretions, breast milk - all are basically water. Furthermore an imbalance in any of these can obviously lead to disruption of the finely tuned energy system that is our body. It could result in creaking dry joints, even the inability to move. It could result in dryness and thirst, too frequent or too little micturation or a build up of chemicals. It could result in too much or too little sweating, a slow poisoning of the system etc.. In a metaphorical sense, if there is no fluidity in our thought processes and emotions, it can result in being swamped with emotions, fears and a general feeling of being overrun; or, conversely, we dry up and wither, become brittle and uncaring. Unexpressed emotions accumulate and cause irritation and frustration. Cystitis might result, as it is an irritation of the urinary system. So it can be said that the function of the Water Element or its meridians is to keep things flowing, to be fluid, to keep a balance.

Cormac, the Irish equivalent of Solomon, gave a list of things to follow for both king and warrior alike:

"Be not too wise, nor too foolish,
be not too conceited, nor too diffident,
be not too haughty, nor too humble,
be not too talkative, nor too silent,
be not too hard, nor too feeble
for:
If you be too wise, one will expect too much of you,
if you be foolish you will be deceived,
if you be too conceited, you will be thought vexatious,
if you be too humble, you will be without honour,

if you be too talkative, you will not be heeded,
if you be too silent, you will not be regarded,
if you be too hard, you will be broken,
if you be too feeble, you will be crushed"[7].

It seems written in perfect Water-spirit, from a point of balance.

There are two more aspects to consider about these two meridians before we go on.

The Bladder meridian is the longest meridian in the system, starting at the inner eye and running over the top of the head, down either side of the whole spine and back, down the back of the legs, along the outside of the foot to the little toe. Along the back there are special points which are directly connected to the function of the remaining organs. These points are called Yu - points and are related to the sympathetic nervous system and, (in terms of the sacrum) to the parasympathetic nervous system by nerve strands, which enter or leave the spinal cord through the openings in the vertebrae at certain points. These *Yu* points can be used very effectively to influence many different illnesses.

In terms of the Water Element, this feature can be linked to a river whose water reaches, through many tributaries, into the furthest corner and influences life in the most distant village. This is probably why in the Nei Ching, the Bladder meridian is called "a magistrate of a region or a district controlling the overflow and fluid secretions which have to regulate vaporisation"[8]. The Kidney meridian has an unusual importance as well. Although the meridian is bilateral and symmetrical, the function of the right and left kidney are associated with differing concepts. We have seen earlier that physically they are also in slightly different positions in the body and have different organs as their neighbours.

The right kidney is, in Chinese tradition, said to carry your ancestral energy, referring to the state of the kidney energy, which can be a very strong creative energy given to you by your ancestors, thus inherited. This also implies that it is not easy to replenish this energy, rather it is more a question of conserving it by an adequate lifestyle. For example a depleted kidney energy from a mother will be passed on as a low Kidney energy to a child. Since the Kidney energy is related to the endocrine system, which influences nearly all body systems; being born with such a weak energy will then effect the whole person. It is also called a constitutional energy. The left kidney is associated more with the obvious, the water system, the detoxification and the urine production. The detoxification will of course also effect all other organs in the body, so it comes as no surprise that the Nei Ching compares the kidneys to an officer who works effectively and is noted for his technical ability and expertise.

The Cycle

The movement of life flows from one to the other, is never still, is never the same as the moment before. This movement is responsible for the cyclic nature of energy even in our every day lives. The time for the Water Element is split into two sections. The peak functioning time for the Organ- network of the bladder is from three to five p.m., and for the Organ- network of the kidney it is from five to seven p.m. On the other hand the time of minimum functioning of the Bladder energy is from three to five a.m.; and respectively the time of minimum functioning for the Kidney energy if from five to seven a.m.

A person with the main characteristics of a Water-Person, might be aware of their peak energy time in the afternoon, and their lowest in the very early hours of the morning, where most people would sleep anyway, but getting up early in the morning could present a problem. Conversely if, let us say, a Water Person had weak Kidney energy, they would probably notice a lack of energy in the late afternoon. This cycle could easily accommodate many normal professional hours and probably would not even be noticed by most people.

Let us now consider the Water meridians in more detail by looking at the correspondence of the Element in the Chinese tradition.

The Season related to Water is winter. Winter is the time of gathering, of drawing inwards to reflect, of preparing for new growth. In terms of what we have said earlier it is easy to relate this to the bladder as a vessel for gathering and a vessel that has to be emptied at times, to make room for the new. If we think of water in its wintery aspect as ice, then the link is clear. Water condenses, crystallises, draws together and, as such, water gathers in the glaciers or even the rivers and stays, seemingly at rest, reflecting until the melting time in spring. If we picture icebergs or ice floes we realise the strength of such crystallisation; the power inherent in this quiet state of reflection. The stillness that is sung about in many poems about a winter's day can also be linked to the stillness we call death, and be regarded as a similar transitory state, preparing for the new growth of reincarnation.

But, moreover, the stillness of the icy, yet featureless landscape can also be suggestive of the stillness of meditation, the still endless void that is the necessary ground without which no initiation of creation, of action, of spring, can start. Yet there is also an inherent danger in this state. Ice can be so crisp - think of sheets of ice on a river - that it breaks and cracks. Slices of ice are cuttingly sharp, and used wrongly, can be weapons that kill - just like a knife. Where isolation of winter has created such sheets of dry ice, such "brittle-ness", there is danger of becoming maniac or insane. People who completely withdraw from activities of life, spending their life withdrawn into themselves, pondering life and fate in isolation and depression that can speak of Water – imbalance. On the other hand such people might have turned to the lifestyle of a contemplative and reach heights of spiritual achievement, only few can dream of.

If a person actively dislikes winter, being alone, being still, being quiet at appropriate times in the day and ones life, then this points to an imbalance, an inadequate use of the Water energy. Old people frequently have the tendency to escape from reflection of an unfulfilled, may be painful life, and resort to constant distraction. To prepare for and contemplate winter in the form of their own death is so frightening to some that they need endless rounds of meaningless socialising, e.g. bingo games etc. On the other hand, young, active people can have a similar problem; taking stock, thinking where they are in life, integrating experiences needs time and space, needs a "winter" to contemplate, but many bury this need in an endless round of parties, deafening music even drugs. The inability to enjoy "winter" in its literal and metaphoric sense point to an imbalance in the Water meridian.

The Direction associated with Water is north and spreading outward. It is easy to see why water is associated with – spreading outward. Spilt tea spreads everywhere.

In our latitude the north has similar associations as winter. The north is the area from where coldness comes, where freezing winds blow; northern countries are thought of as "cold"; we actually speak of "the frozen north". In a physical sense, we can say that people who suffer from the cold, who feel it more than to be expected, or people who are completely out of touch with their bodies and do not feel it at all, are showing an imbalance in the Water Element. For example: A landlord in a village pub (in England) wears, indoors and out short sleeved shirts. He wears no warm clothing, and looks like a person who is always too hot and never feels the cold - (even in cold winter) - would be worth investigating as to whether he has an imbalance in his Water- meridians.

The north is also known for its especially crisp, clear light. The air is pure and fractions the light, like a crystal. The aurora borealis is the most well known occurrence of these special lights. Standing at the furthest, northern point of Europe, at the North Cape, near Honigsveg in Norway, the majestic stillness, the feeling of infinite space, the awareness of limitless expansion and the shimmering light seemingly reflected in its own light, is unforgettable. And yet the North is also associated with darkness, long nights; dark feelings; long suffering; dark emotions and the fear of the unknown.

Somewhere in the stillness of the north, in the stillness of our very being, we experience the special light and darkness of existence, the two sides of life. This could be the reason why in the American Indian tradition the north is the location of wisdom, knowledge, sacred, ancient knowledge and wisdom represented by the Elders[9].

The Bladder meridian flows along either side of the spine. The sacred channel, in which the spiritual energy is rising, the *sushummna*, is said to be in the spine (as is the Governing Vessel). It may be due to this close association, the BL is associated with the experience of deepest phenomena. The spiritual energy itself is said to alter the cerebrospinal fluid when Kundalini is aroused[10]. Again here is a direct link between water's fluidity and spiritual energy.

Winter and the long nights of the north have another thing in common: there is nothing we can do about it. We might prefer sunshine, day-time, or... or ... but there is nothing we can do to change it. - To me this suggests patience, patience until the situation changes, patience and trust in the knowledge that one day spring will come, one day light will rise, one day - day will break, one day the suffering will be over. Water energy then points to our ability to wait, to accept, to trust, to be patient; not being able to do so suggests an imbalance, maybe just as much as hopeless resignation.

But this bids another thought. In all major spiritual traditions and many scriptures reference is made to the transition from the state of doing: doership to the state of being. Being is total integrity with who you are; is a state where one acts out of stillness, out of "no need". There is no need to achieve or take charge. It seems to me that this state of Being is the result of totally imbibing a balanced state of water, a state of acceptance. The ocean moves, - all the time, no need to stagnate, but also it needs to go nowhere.

The Climate related to Water is, not surprisingly, cold. As the winter and north suggest, the effects of cold are significant for Water. Many illnesses are created by cold or made worse by cold. Many arthritic problems are, for example, made a lot worse in cold weather, pains often increase and joints stiffen. But when we speak of a "cold person", we are not necessarily thinking of the body temperature, we think of people who are unable or unwilling to express human warmth. A mother who lacks the ability to hug, touch, stroke, warm and cuddle the child, could be said to have an imbalance in the Water Element. The heartless passer by, who sees somebody fall and yet just turns away so as not to be involved - could be said to be cold and uncaring. It could be said that many people in our society, especially those that live a stressful life, do not take time to care much about the suffering of others. Their own stress -their aggravated kidneys and adrenals, - stop them from caring, they have a Water imbalance.

The Tissues or parts of the body associated with Water are bones and bone marrow. At first glance this seems surprising, what can they have in common with Water? Bones, teeth, the skull, the vertebrae, all are nourished by the energy of the Bladder and Kidneys, e.g. they are supplied, by them, with clean blood, every cell is filled and washed with water in some way, especially in the bone marrow, where new cells are formed. Cells, even in bones, change and change and change. We are a slow river. But this is so everywhere in the body, even the brain is described as a "sea of marrow" and thus included as well.

In Ayurveda and Tibetan medicine bones belong to the Earth Element, it seems somehow more apt. It remains a bit of an enigma. Let's look again: Imagine a diamond, it is the hardest crystal which implies that it has the most dense form of matter; and according to the equation $E=mc^2$, it also has the densest energy. We can think of bones in the same way, they represent

The Element Water

the most crystalline energy in us. We are reminded of the icicle, which has a dense crystal structure, making ice strong enough to allow a plane to land on it; similarly bones are strong enough to hold us up, and to be able to sustain quite some pressure.

The second angle stems from embryology. The first manifestation of the energy that will become a human being, is the spine, around which the rest of the skeleton and the body develops. Thus bones, including the vertebrae (the spine) represents our deepest core, the crystalline energy that results from the initial urge to incarnate. The bone structure provides our form, it is the manifestation of our desire to live. Life has to have form; it can be said that bones represent our innermost being - even in a spiritual sense as our physical being cannot be without bones. As our Soul cannot follow a spiritual path without a physical body, so we can only do Sadhana and become enlightened in a physical body. Body and Spirit are intrinsically linked. Spirit has to condense to form in order to grow and fulfil its dharma, its suchness - just as the body has to solidify, has to have bones to exist.

Injury to our bones (broken bones) relates to our innermost core. This inner core of energy, that is the first manifestation in the spine of the embryo, represents our ancestral Kidney energy. The very energy we bring with us into this world, passed on to us by our parents, hold the potential from where all other structures (e.g. bones, appearance, character) develop. The Kidney, especially the right one, reflects the condition of the endocrine system as we saw earlier. The endocrine system includes the thyroids, whose function it is to secrete calcitonin which acts on the bones and the kidneys to regulate the blood calcium level; calcium is the main mineral in the composition of the bones. So physiologically the health and state of bones and kidney are related. Osteoporosis, for example, can be linked to an imbalance in the Kidney meridian.

Thus the most solid body part the bones, are connected to several aspects of the most fluid Element.

Chapter 5

The Sense organ connected to the Water Element is the ear, the sense is hearing. Again we have to go back and look at the embryo in its environment of water! Here it develops the first sense, that of hearing. Many stories exist of children being born with an awareness or skill that they must have heard while in utero. The importance of this organ and function for the entire development of the human being has only come recently to attention through the work of Professor A. Tomatis.[11] The ability to hear in, or rather, under water is never quite lost. Hearing itself is dependent on a liquid in the ear (perilymph in the bony labyrinth of the inner ear). Thus there is a strong connections to Water. Symptoms like nausea, dizziness, balance problems and inappropriate sound in the ears point to an imbalance in the Water Element.

The Orifice associated with Water energy is the Anus, coupled with the Genitals. Healthy procreation depends on the condition of the egg and the sperm, both are cells that consist largely of fluid and are surrounded by water, they also meet in liquid. Healthy cells can only be grown by healthy organs. The condition of the ovaries and the scrotum are also related to the Water Element. The sexual act itself is dependent on fluids, so difficulties connected to the sexual act, such as impotence, frigidity, infertility, illnesses of the uterus, low sperm count etc. are all linked to the Water Element. Our attitude and experiences to/with the sexual organs can then result in such irritations and weaknesses as Candida Albicans, Herpes etc; and these can be influenced by the Water meridians.

The anus is the orifice that releases faeces. If we realise that faeces, despite their solid appearance, consist of 60 to 70% water, then the link to the Water Element becomes understandable. Its activity of releasing can be linked to the character of the Bladder-organ- network.

The Fluid of the Water energy is urine, although all fluids are connected with water in its many forms; urine represents water in its cleaning function. The body needs an agent that removes the unwanted substances, constantly cleaning itself. The psyche too has to be cleaned constantly, unwanted emotions, stored feelings that have become useless, all need to be disposed of. Imbalances in the mechanism of disposal not only lead to poisoning of the physical and emotional body. Thus urine infections, imbalances in the composition of the urine etc. can point to an imbalance in the Water meridian. Similarly poisonous relationships, unexpressed accumulated emotions and irritation with life itself (which has presented us with unwanted problems and experiences) point to an imbalance in the Water energy. Here lies the root of the colloquial expression "I'm pissed off"! We have to understand what is happening to us is never bad, what causes suffering and pain is our reaction to what happens. Thus constantly check and clean out our points of reference, our accumulated judgmental patterns; they need cleaning out.

There seem many parallels here to the Metal Element, we need to recall that Metal is the mother of Water, therefore it will contain some close links. The difference here is that the letting go of old issues with Metal is a letting go of the useless, it does not include the actual cleaning process. The emphasis with Water is on the removal of the poisonous, the irritant, not just disposing of the useless; not just on <u>letting</u> it go, but actually <u>pushing it out</u> !

The External Physical Manifestation of Water is head hair. The condition of the hair, be it dry, broken, split, fine, silky, curled, strong, robust, receding, falling out or untimely greying hair gives an indication to the state of the Water Element (disregarding, of course, racial characteristics). What is the link to Water? The kidneys provide energy to the body, if the kidneys are weak, then those areas of the body that are not essential, are provided for last; if there is no more then they do not get anything at all. If the hair is healthy and full of bounce - so are the kidneys; if the hair is broken, lifeless, so are the kidneys; if the hair falls out, we have a warning sign that the kidneys are in trouble (terminal illness, chemotherapy, eating harmful foods).

Chapter 5

Heavy metals are difficult for the kidneys to clean from the body, in fact they poison it, thus they are injurious to hair. Similarly, prolonged emotional stress, affecting the adrenals and the kidney, could cause hair loss.

The Colour of Water is Blue. This is almost too obvious to mention, since we are so used to equating the sea with blue, (despite the fact that in Europe mostly the sea is varying shades of grey, even at times black). Yes, the sea and the still lake can be blue, but water itself ? In a glass the water is clear, taking up the colour of whatever is held close to it. Water reflects colour; it is blue because it reflects the sky. Water has no colour on its own; taken into a dark cave, it is dark, taken out into the light it is transparent. On a glorious evening at sunset, the sea will be golden or even red. So water and light are connected, e.g. it can be said that if the sea is blue, then it is reflecting the light of the sky. Water is not the sky; it is not the ultimate, although many use it as a metaphor, Water is only reflecting the sky. Water must remain aware of this; it must learn humility. It is very significant especially on its spiritual path[12]. Many times on the horizon the sea and the sky seem one, but it is an illusion. Water might be close to the ultimate truth, but it must stay humble, or it will fall prey to the illusion of grandeur. Such illusion can lead to just another form of insanity, for example to dictatorial visions.

In the Buddhist tradition the great Healer Aksobhya is connected to the Water Element. His qualities are, colourlessness, a mirror-like surface reflects the pure colourless light of alaya consciousness, the ocean "which reflects the void as well as things, which mirror the emptiness in the things, and the things in the emptiness"[13].

The Water-person must be aware that all others are just as much reflections of the divine. It must be aware that it is not blue, it only reflects the blue! Water is connected to everything by its nature it is part of all others, its blueness, its divine consciousness is shared. Blue has become the colour to depict sacred divinity. Indeed Shiva, Krishna and other gods are depicted with blue bodies or garments; the Virgin Mary is portrayed mainly in blue clothes, the halos of saints and God himself are painted as either gold or blue. Mystics testify that the divine energy they saw was transparently blue, the blue pearl of divine consciousness.

If a person has a strong like or dislike for the colour blue it points to an imbalance in the Water meridian, but it also may reveal something much deeper, either a severed link with the divine, an active denial - or a strong longing for - the divine.

The Smell associated with the Water Element is putrid. When water stands for a long time and matter decomposes in it, it has a special stink; swamps have this unmistakable foul odour. If we can detect this smell easily -not just a subtle hint- then we can safely assume that that person has a problem in the Water Element. It could be either, that the kidney cannot remove all the debris, or the urine stays too long in the bladder, in either case it leads to rotting. The flow of the Water energy needs to be increased, so that the body will get washed more easily.

The Taste related to Water is salty, the link to the sea is obvious. The tributaries have washed all the minerals, including salt, out of the earth and poured it into the sea. The sea is salted water. Too much salt in the water results in killing all life, as can be seen in some inland seas such as the Dead Sea and Lake Eyre in Australia. To maintain the right salt balance in the body is the task of the kidney - and also of the person. We can help the kidney by regulating our salt intake, a little salt stimulates the kidney, too much is harmful, especially when the kidney has to cope with other stress symptoms at the same time. Too little salt can deprive the body of needed minerals, yet there is, in a balanced diet, no danger of that, since most vegetables naturally contain salts. Excessive salt consumption can show up as darkness in the eye bags, the area underneath the eyes, which denotes the state of the kidneys.

Hildegard von Bingen describes many different levels of salty waters, their origin and relationship to harmful-ness or their curative powers. They "restore the health because they take the putrid smell (see above) and rottenness of the body juices away like a soothing balm" but if we go overboard and drink this cleaning fluid where there is nothing to clean, it results in ulcers.[14]

The Grain associated with the Water energy is beans and peas.

The Fruit is dates.

The Meat is pork.

The Vegetable is the leek.

As with the intake of salt, these can only be a guide and are supposed to be approached with care. It may be appropriate to eat more or less of these if the person's intake is unbalanced. As for the recommendation to eat pork? Many cultures refrain from eating pork because the pig is an animal that reputedly absorbs toxins faster than other animals, as revealed in recent years from hormone injected animals. So I would have thought that pork would create more work for the kidneys as an organ of detoxification, but on the other hand there are cultures where pork is the only meat addition to the diet, for example the Igorots of the Philippines. They are a strong, healthy tribe, but then their pigs are fed on water hyacinths and nettles, grown in pure mountain air! On a more serious note, the pig in many cultures, such as Greek, Latin, Egyptian etc., was related to the female, to motherhood and specifically to the uterus. It is often referred to as the symbol of Demeter's fertility - or "goddesses are all great white, round maternal sows" (Ishtar, Isis, Demeter etc) [15]. Even Tibetan Buddhism, referring to one aspect of the female energy of the daikini principle, talks of Vajra Varahi the "Diamond Sow", or the "Indestructible Sow".

What it relates to here, is the unleashed, riotous female passion - could it be that this is where we find the link? Could it be that the fire of female passion, that untamed female creative urge, is needed to warm the Water? In other words that the reference to eating pork implies that Water imbalances relate to the need to acknowledge or even incorporate the animalistic female side? In the Chinese horoscope, the Pig is described as innocent, gullible, trustful, honest, pure, sincere, devoted, easily taken advantage of by others e.g. sensitive and a victim. An astonishing correspondence of characteristics of the Water person; could here lie another link for the recommendation?

The Emotion related to Water is fear. The Nei Ching says that too much fear hurts the kidneys, and fear can be overcome by looking inward[16]. We have pondered this while looking at winter. It remains to add that all fears and phobias are related to Water, including fear of heights, fear of water, of new things, of people, of enclosed rooms, of sexuality, of darkness and death. Also such states as having bad premonitions, or a general, diffuse fear of life or the unknown, are related to these meridians giving us a clue to the origins of insanity and suicide. But why should fear be connected to Water. All fears are basically a holding on to what is known, and thus oppose the idea of life constantly changing, flowing like a river. Rather than letting go of what is outmoded or that which has fulfilled its usefulness, it is kept because it feels safe. This is an illusion, which poisons the system. Fear is like a paralysed sphincter that cannot let go of the urine and the vessel is not emptied. The illusion is that by holding the old nothing new can come in, but by necessity it does! The river of life flows on regardless, so gradually fear becomes panic and one suffocates into despair, deep depression, even paranoia.

The Expression associated with Water is groaning. We are looking at the subconscious undertone of a voice, a sound that is almost as if the speaker is under water, drowned, in emotions and fear. Obviously if this sound is very noticeable in the voice the person might suffer from an imbalance in Water.

The Sound is that of rushing; when a water person enters a room with too much of that energy, it feels like a pipe has just burst and energy flows bubbling here and there, rushing out in great gushes.

Chapter 5

The Manner in times of excitement or change is: trembling. Since fear is predominantly related to Water, it is obvious that trembling is too, when we experience fear, we contract to protect ourselves. Contraction builds tension, trembling is a natural release of tension. If a person trembles excessively, or habitually, the cause for it is probably an imbalance in the Water energy.

There is another not unrelated reason for excessive trembling in people. It can be caused by various nerve diseases, especially those of the motor nerves, for nerve impulses cause serial contraction of motor units in a muscle as each unit contracts. If there is any fault in the minute structures of the endings of the autonomic nervous system, trembling results. Since the bladder meridian is linked to the autonomic nervous system, we could still look at an imbalance in Water, especially because the original reason for the dis-functioning of the nerves could well be lying in trauma and be connected to fear.

The Attitude associated with Water is the need for stimulus.

The Movement of Energy is one of starting up to rush. Both these relate to a sudden burst of energy, the image of somebody suddenly getting out of a chair, and with a burst of energy proclaiming that they need to go to the cinema (party, book-fair, whatever) right now! The energy flow has been held by a dam and suddenly freed to roam. The constant need for stimulus is very different in character than that of Fire (as we will see later) for it is not an indiscriminate need for constant stimulus, but an aimed movement, like the river flowing vehemently down stream. The Water person needs the stimulus of the next project, the next fulfilling idea, the next job to expand his interest; they are for ever pushing themselves with new ideas. By contrast, a balanced Water person would have a steady energy flow, calmly considering and following the direction that needs to be explored. Bursts of activity are bound to be followed by dryness and exhaustion, so that the ideas or jobs might actually not be seen to the finish. Consider the differences between these two people: both have had many careers in their lives, many jobs. The first person has always started them with determination but after a few years something else was more appropriate. The second person also started the new career with much interest and determination, once the aim was reached, the degree awarded, the job tried out then another was chosen to build on the first job. The first person reacts from a Water energy, the second from a Wood energy; yet from the 'outside' both activities look very similar.

The Quality associated with Water is Will. The will is related to discipline; we need not only willpower to do things, but the discipline and clarity to carry it out. Only if we have both can we achieve our aim. Without discipline, and what is meant here primarily is self discipline, the will grows despotic and not only tyrannises others, but can harm the actual person. For example a child rules the whole family by its wants and wills. If they are denied, the result is shown in a bad temper that ruins the peace and puts a lot of strain on the family. In addition the relationship of the child to its expectations of what life 'should give it', become false. Action as well as reward come about to its will, rather than as timely and right choice.

Water might want to flow into a certain direction, but unless there are limitations and boundaries, that somehow harness its energy, all it achieves is "going all over the place". It floods the landscape; by implication, to reach their aim a Water-person needs limitations; self imposed boundaries, rituals, routines, in order to go where they want to go. In other words, they have either self- discipline - or they need discipline from the outside. This discipline, like the stimulus, is energy other than its own which is needed to trigger or contain. The danger of this is that the person might become dependent on such outside discipline, rely on the form rather than the contents, or even become subject to the will of others (Earth-Element makes good dams for Water, Metal provides sluices and gates etc.).

The ultimate challenge for the Water-person is to surrender its own will, deliberately and willingly to the divine will. This is a complex topic, but it might suffice to hint at it here. If the Divine created man in his image, or somehow man holds a spark of that divine likeness to God, then the Will of man and the Divine will can be said to be reflection of each other, in their purest form. And there lies the crux, its purest form means without the ego-pollution. If man can see beyond the reflection he can see the Divine original will in his own soul. Thus Christ could say : my will is the father's will. Divine will then becomes original purpose, original nature, the original state of being, the Buddhists call this suchness. The nature of Water is to flow. To fulfil its intrinsic will it needs to flow! It is the suchness of water to be fluid. The will of a person in this sense relates to the ability of the person to find out their own nature, their personal purpose in life. Then they can remove all unwanted debris, that is in the river of their Life, remove all obstacles to gain the clarity, that allows them to move, to flow into that direction.

The insight into the process of life, the increasing insight into the whole flow of the river, sets the being free from the illusion of individual ego-hood and reveals the concept of "Dependent Origination" which in turn reveals our interconnectedness, life as an ever-changing process. Being in tune with divine will then means being "in harmony with the forces of the universe...free from the will that opposes and finds opposition in reality" [17]. The Will then has the great task to guide the person to the fulfilment of their destiny. This includes the will needed, to get up and start again after a knock, trauma or some such devastating experience. It means having the guts to start a new creative way, making the best out of what there is or to choose to totally surrender with no self-designated purpose.

Water has the quality that is needed for the river of our life to reach the sea. People who have no determination and a weak will, be it to life's small everyday tasks, or to the realisation of life's purpose, or on the other hand are using their will for destruction, all have an imbalance in Water.

The Activity of Water is said to be scanning[18].

The Condition is one of withdrawal into one's own depth and isolation; either to recoup one's energy and replenish it, or in order to run away and hide. The danger for the Water person is obviously one of isolation. Scanning over the surface, gathering fleeting impressions. To me this speaks more of Wood energy, yet the mystery that unfolds inside a Water person continues through their hands and mind, outside themselves. Fleeting impressions gained by scanning on the surface can trigger profound ideas and concepts and thus a continuation is created between the inner and outer world which can find expression in music, artwork or flowing dance movement. The continuity of the Water person to the outside world is given by permeable fluid personal boundaries with which he/she has the capacity to feel into other people, scan their bodies and emotions and tune into them. Such people feel and share other's emotions, their joys and traumas, and can reach into them to heal and help.

Conversely, people who have a blocked Water energy have difficulties empathising with others, are so withdrawn and immersed in themselves that they become insensitive and unable to reach out to others. In a similar vein their potential to be expressive and in tune with their surroundings is undermined and their creativity blocked, for there is no continuity beyond themselves, they become like frozen ice crystals.

Qualities/steps in Sadhana The quality of Water effects Sadhana as a growing awareness of the dissolution of form. One becomes aware of the unlimited, infinite existence beyond time and space. Emotions are explored and transcended as temporary reactions, dissolved as temporary forms of life-energy.

As for the states of consciousness, I venture to say that Water shares the second stage of dream consciousness. The all-important emotions as well as the intuition which play such a vital part in the life of a Water-person must still be recognised as conditioning of our personality, our mind- make-up. It is the fibre our dreams and motivations are made off, and we get attached to those, holding them for real and important. C.G. Jung did much work on this, and even if we ban the dreams into the unconscious or archetypal, we still have to see that they are mind-made; may be not by ours but by the collective. For some their dreams might even be more important than physical or mental reality, such is the stuff artists are made off. Needs and wants arising out of dreams and even intuition are recognised as what they are, temporary forms, and as such they loose their value. Detachment from details grows and the bigger picture is increasingly addressed. Awareness of the shared spirit of all that exists is experienced. The wave gains awareness that it is ocean. A glimpse is caught of the divine in all.

The Relationship of Water to the other Elements has been mentioned now and again in the previous text. Here is a summary: Metal gives birth to Water; springs and rivers are seen to come out of rock, but also this could be a hint at the chemically bound water in minerals. The implications are that Metal provides constant nourishment for Water, like a mother. In real terms this means that the lung energy, *prana*, nourishes the kidney energy, thus there is a direct link between these two energies and if the energy of the lungs does not descend to the kidneys, these starve and illness results. The relationship is one of nurturing.

Water is controlled by Earth, she can stem its flow. Suffice to say that the Earth can be turned into a swamp or bog by Water, if the balance between the two is not respected. Here is an example. I remember two such occasions as a youngster: I lived near the mouth of the river Elbe in a marshland. Either side of the river about a mile inland were earth mounds, called dykes, to stem the river which flooded regularly, and protect the villages in the low lying marshland. This happened to some degree every spring and autumn. My family home was on the "dry side of the dyke". One Spring, the storms and spring moon excelled themselves, the river rose much more than usual. It kept rising into the night and then rose even more.

Sirens went off, men were called in, lorries with sand-bags were brought to fill any holes and to raise the level of the dyke. Soon several villages were in danger of being flooded; the water gurgled in the darkness with foreboding. The radio broadcast was that the waters were still rising and the villages might have to be evacuated. The water reached the top of the dyke, four metres high, the message came, "Evacuate now!" The water started to lap over the crown of the dyke, we were herded to shelter in the church on higher ground. The water was still rising. Sometime later the floodwaters won, a few hundred yards from our home the dyke burst- its gurgling powerful fingers ploughed up the land and rushed into the houses. The ground floor of many houses was flooded, that part of the village had turned into a sea; when the water subsided we found that many cows and other animals and some people had died in the treetops. The village (and many others in that area) had turned into a mud flat. Long months of cleaning had to follow and much of the damage was irreparable. This is a powerful example of how water loses its limitations when Earth is not strong enough to limit it and thus becomes a destructive force. Their relationship is one of respectful balance.

In the body this means that the Stomach and Spleen energy balance and limit the Water energy of kidney and bladder. Thus if the former is weak, depleted or overworked, it will be the kidneys that suffer, their energy gets dissipated - the energy of the bladder (emotions) go "all over the place". The power of this destruction is only equalled by Fire.

The Abbess from the 12th century pays great attention to the relationship of Water and Fire, and some of her observations are extremely inspired. Thus she not only writes that the Sun warms the fire, but from the viewpoint of the Water, "the sun draws the inherent warmth out of the Water" sort of bringing it to the surface. It is a bit like *yin* is inherent in *yang*); when combined with wind "the Water rises like Fire" (hurricanes, typhoons, etc). Out of this powerful union she sees salt is distilled and crystallised and that then can be used to pacify

Chapter 5

Water[19]. Water also is linked in its capacity of "mirror-like wisdom", to Fire; for inspiration, enthusiasm, devotion and qualities of Fire, are mirrored in water. Water is commonly seen as extinguishing Fire, yet it can also be seen as reflecting, thus enhancing the purest qualities of Fire - like a mirror reflects the sun; amplifying the effect and making a ray into a thousand suns! Who would have thought that water can multiply the effect of Fire! Their relationship is one of inspiration under careful control.

And finally Water gives birth to Wood; just one look into nature is sufficient to see that all that grows, all that lives is brought forth with the influence of Water that nourishes it, as a mother nourishes her child.

> For the source and what flows from it are one,
> as the drop and the ocean are one,
> as " I and the Father are one ",
> As Creator and Creation are one.

Chapter Six

Invocation of Wood (Space/Ether)

I am the Spirit of the mighty tree
standing aloof on the top of a hill,
gazing far over all lands.

Rising in me is the most powerful sap
- the sap of continuous creation, the greening power
I am nourished as much through my roots
- the roots, that reach deep into the bowels of the earth,
- the earth, that provides me with water and nutrients,
 as I am nourished through the crown of my many leaves
- leaves that reach into the limitless sky,
- sky that provides me with water and sunlight;
Thus I am a bridge between heaven and earth
A bridge between Man and God
A bridge whose feet rest either side of life's turbulent river.

The turbulent current of Life bends me this way and that
yet I stay steadfast in the most violent storm
rooted in my centre
my wisdom, acquired in rings-of-years;
from this centre I bring forth
blossoms and fruits in accordance with the seasons;
into this centre I withdraw to rest and gather strength.
I have the foresight of creation
according to a timeless blueprint, I create
each cell of new growth
to fit the vision of the species
one leaf, the same as another;
one oak the same as another

I am a host to many creatures;
the flighty birds rest in my crown,
the wise owl sleeps peacefully in my branches,
the robin builds its nest and the insects feed under my skin
the bees enjoy my blossoms, the squirrel feasts on my fruit,

the fox hides behind me, and deep hidden in the apex of my trunk,
lies the coiled serpent,
protecting me, protected by me,
to be awakened one auspicious day.
The shy violet looks for shelter, even the cultivated pea
enjoys the moisture dripping off my leaves,
the weary wanderer seeks my shade,
the children dance their nursery rhymes around me
it is not that I need them so much as they need me,
for I emit the oxygen they breathe.

I have been worshipped by most primitive man;
I have been worshipped by most venerable sages.
Just as God draws forth faith in me,
So I draw forth faith in you
For I am the mirror of your own divinity
forever reaching to heavens for divine light.
As is said: Faith can move mountains;
for the energy in me is boundless
how else could I nourish the tiny acorn to become the mighty tree?
how else could I help the tiny seed to grow into a giant palm?
how else could I nourish the heart's intention to become light?
how else could I bring lush, rich freshness to wilted shrivelled people?

I am the Spirit of the tree
- as I am greening-power in motion.
I am the Spirit of steadfastness,
- for without me, no direction would be safe
I am the Spirit of creation,
- for no creation can become manifest without me
I am the Spirit of truth,
- for it is my nature to be a tree, and nothing but a tree.
I am the Spirit of Man,
- for it is his nature to be blessed with divine energy.
I am the Spirit of Energy,
for I am the life.

Character of Wood (Space/Ether)

The Wood Element is more difficult to grasp because traditions name it differently. The Chinese tradition most prevalent and used in Acupuncture, Shiatsu and other complementary fields, calls this fourth stage Wood; others experience the energy as similar, but name it Ether, Faith or Space.

According to the Hutchinson Encyclopaedia, ether is either a colourless, volatile inflammable liquid used, for example, to sterilise and clean wounds, or a hypothetical concept introduced to explain some of the properties of light; the connection to Wood as a burnable substance giving birth to fire is certainly congruent. The idea of ether as a property of light can be linked in the more spiritual aspect to Wood, in so far as the tree reaches for light. The idea of ether as a cleansing agent can be linked to the task of the liver. Ether in Ayurveda is difficult to understand, as the actual word has such diverse meaning. "One of the meanings of the word originally is "sound", another 'root' and another radiation, that which does not provide resistance". It is linked to the qualities of cool and dry and to the personality type of Vata[1].

Pure Vedanta, the oldest and probably the original source of qualifying the energy in five elements, talks of this stage as "faith".

The reason for the discrepancies, in my opinion, is connected to a common phenomenon. We can not always express precisely what we feel and describe it with the full awareness; "some bits have to be left out, because they do not fit". This is especially so in Sanskrit, where associations are given for root-syllables. Different people try to say the same, but use different metaphors.

But let us look a bit deeper, because the words WOOD and SPACE just seem too different to pass light-heartedly as the same.

Chapter 6

It is beyond doubt, that before the established Religions, people deified the elemental forces in the phenomenal world. That this was also so in ancient China, as we know from documents like the Nei Ching (from 2-700 AD or its predecessors). Apparently the Yellow Emperor, legend or real, not only used the Five Elements but also referred to earlier times; (2000 BC or before). In its neighbouring culture; India, the Elements and accordingly deities were worshipped in Vedic and pre-vedic times, probably since 4-6000 BC. There always was fertilisation of thought between these neighbours.

In ancient Indian scriptures there is talk of the tree of life; it is a botanical tree (Pipal tree, Ficus Religiosa). According to Sankara, one of the most respected ancient Philosophers of India, this tree has been chosen to " represent the entire cosmos, because of its creative meaning", its called *Aswattha*. As previously mentioned, Sanskrit syllables carry great meaning: *Swa* means "tomorrow"; *Stha* means "that which remains"; *A - swattha* means "that which will not remain the same till tomorrow"; in other words the tree indicates the ephemeral, the ever-changing world, of phenomena. The word tree (*Vriksha*) furthermore denotes "that which can be cut down". Both meanings refer to the same - That which contains the phenomenal, ever changing world.

In the old texts, this tree is described as having its roots "up", up in space, up in the subtle; Space is the most subtle of the Five Elements. That which contains all phenomena, derives its sustenance from beyond. The human experience of change origins in the subtle, that is beyond, divine. Thus the world of plurality is allegorically pictured as a fig-tree, arising from and sustained by higher, subtler energies; Higher Consciousness.

In the Bhagavad Gita, (Chapter 15) the Aswattha tree is also mentioned at length. The roots reach into the eternal, its leaves and branches speak of spiritual growth and the necessary knowledge that lead to a noble life, enabling the knower to reach Self-realisation[2].

It seems to me, that such mystical representation should not be taken literally, but assuming one would, then the associations become superimposed and confused. Space, as the most subtle element, who's divine origin as "that which gives accommodation to things" (Sanskrit: *Akasa*) is source and womb of all phenomena. Just as this mystical tree is representative of all ever-changing phenomena. Space as the most subtle can not be conditioned by grosser factors and is thus all-pervasive. Similarly the poetic description of the fig-tree expresses the subtle philosophical truth conveying a deep religious message. In this sense we find the symbolic tree in many cultures in place of the fifth Element, thus it can be called Faith, Great Spirit - or Space.

What happens when this symbol is emptied of its meaning? May be through its travels into China it has become (as any fundamentalist approach), calcified and isolated and adapted to a different culture. We imported that adaptation, and are faced with looking for meaning in real trees, in real wood - luckily as everything is connected to everything else, we still can see beyond the "Wood", to the shared meanings.

Buddhism that travelled the same route, from India to China has a special interest in the element of Space. It connects it to the fundamental two properties of all existence, *prana* and a*kasa*. *Akasa* – as we have said, is that space that allows things to become manifest; - before that, there is <u>emptiness</u>. Nothing exists, that does not occupy space, that applies to three - dimensional space, space in infinite dimensions and spiritual ones. Referring to the former it is called mahakasa and in context of the latter it is called *cittacasa*, or ultimately *cidakasa*[3].

Space, the milieu where 'things happen' is devoid of anything; as such its quality is limitless and empty. The Avatamaka Sutra says:

"If you wish to enter the Karmic realm of the victorious Buddhas, you should train your mind to be pure like space.

Chapter 6

By abandoning thoughts, discrimination and clinging to cognition, you will enter the Buddha realm with a mind like space"[4].

Space has the capacity to hold phenomena. This is so in the visible, external world as well as within the body and mind, for these are nothing but a milieu with capacity to develop and manifest. Every atom consists mainly of vast quantities of many-dimensional space. Thus basically all atoms- and all phenomena are empty! In this empty-ness vibrating frequencies of energy are "motion in space". And that is all there is ; what we deem exists, because we perceive it with our senses, is on a microcosmic level space, that holds moving energy. So to talk about space in itself is rather odd, because there is nothing in it to qualify it, no adjective to describe it, this is why the sages to of Space itself, as pure. In this sense our body too is pure, "empty space" where energies constantly flow in and out. One can say, these energies pollute the original purity of the crystal-clear space which we are. The purity of the innocent space-body is what is described in the Guru Gita (Skanda Purana) Verse 64:

> I am everlasting, self-luminous, taintless
> and completely pure.
> I am the supreme Ether.
> I am immovable, blissful and imperishable.

This is our original nature, to become aware of it and sink into that pure space, is in Buddhist and Vedantic tradition seen as: the bliss of emptiness. This rings with the harmonies of the spheres and sparkles with luminosity. Such space has no limitations, no barriers, it spreads into all directions (just like the branches of a tree). To get into contact with our inner Space becomes a tool to un-block and free us from our "complicated, narrow, boring and limited reality"[5].

Returning to the Chinese description of this element as Wood, we recollect that the symbol for wood is a tree. One could say the tree is representative for plant-life, for living organisms in

The Element Wood (Space/Ether)

their multitude of forms. In this way "Tree"(like Space) is limitless.

Imagine a tree standing on a mountain top, exposed to all weathers, being pulled by winds this way and that. It spreads his branches in all direction, and it has a commanding view allowing vision far beyond. Similarly a balanced Wood person is a person that reaches this way and that and has far reaching connection and vision, enabling him/her to see beyond illusion. When, on the other hand, we are too limited in our movement, our vision and opinions are narrow and blocked we have imbalanced Wood Energy. The blocks prevent the sap of life from flowing; we are congested. A tree where the sap can't flow for what ever reasons of restrictions, withers and dies, so out of this congestion illness arises. To heal this, we need to clean the blockages, free ourselves from restrictions and relax back into pure space. Relaxing into Space is synonymous with surrendering to the all-embracing principle of higher unity where we become part of a many-dimensional living organism. Here inner and outer space become one; the point of meeting is traditionally called *bindu* (or *thigle*; Tibetan)[6].

To reach this point, we need the help of those, that have been able to do it before us, gurus, teachers or masters. In Tibetan Buddhism exist symbolic helpers, they too are called Buddhas. There are Five such symbolic Buddha, the "Supreme Healers for our five most serious problems, and three Healers for our three root poisons of attachment, hatred and ignorance"[7]. The supreme "Healer" who particularly helps in relationship to space, is Vairochana, whose colours are white and blue and whose sound is the OHM.

Without going further into details of the above, I choose the TCM symbol of Wood for further contemplation, even though due care will be taken to mention the other concepts where necessary. The reader will have no difficulty seeing the link between them and similar qualities.

Chapter 6

Let's contemplate Wood. It has the unique character of geotropism. On the one hand trees grow upwards for two reasons, they always grow towards the light and they grow opposite to the force of gravity. They sense and grow towards light. I remember a narrow valley in the Grampians of Australia where the trees grew horizontally, at a 45 degree angle to the slopes instead of straight up, in order to reach the little light that was let into the centre of the canyon. A Wood characteristic thus is to stretch towards light, a quality with many implications.

On the other hand, they also grow towards the force of gravity with their roots; trees have a special ability to tune into the earth magnetic field. They grow opposite to earth-magnetic forces too with the roots. One could say a tree stretches in two opposite directions, or into all directions (akin to the concept of multi-dimensional space).

Wood is an umbrella term for plant-life. Plants start as seeds. Their origins are the "parents-plants" thus the seed has ancestors, has history; it does not come into existence of its own volition. The seed contains a complete blueprint for what it is going to be. No cabbage seed has ever grown into a bushel of rice. The seed with its inherent plan - or its morphogenetic field - is put into the ground. There the earth protects it so that it can germinate. For this process to begin, the environment has to be just right for that individual seed in order to make the quantum leap from seed to seedling. For some plants it takes decades, for some days; for some it takes fire (to crack open seed-pods), for some it takes water; for some it takes sand, for others rich humus. Why and how these needs are shaped depends not only on the environment for which they are destined, but is also part of the mystery of life.

From the start, the tree has a very special relationship to its environment; the conditions for its development are crucial. This close relationship remains through out growing from seed to seedling. This first growth comes out of itself, it has the initial potential to grow roots, a certain measure of wholeness and independence. As our seedling grows, dependence grows on sunshine, rain, nutrients in the ground, shade, wind, adequate space etc. (it has to establish links between his inner needs and the outer world).

Once a young tree it needs to respond to its environment with flexibility. It needs to be subtle to bend in strong winds; winds that pull it to this side and that and could snap the trunk. It needs adequate water to dissolve the nutrients provided by the earth and to fill the cells with sap so it stays flexible. Thus trees especially are dependent on water. They cannot exist without it or will dry out and shrivel up only to be snapped off by the next encounter with wind, animal or man. If the tree should dry up all together it will easily fall prey to fire, whether it wants to or not. Although some trees, old and sturdy trees like the Redwoods, Mahogany, or other hardwoods can actually survive fires not only while green and living, but also when dried up, or cut. The reason lies in the density of their cell structure, which does not allow the oxygen the fire needs to penetrate. One could say these are so strong in their integrity, so true to themselves, their own nature, their "tree-ness" and conviction, that nothing can touch them. Indeed some of these trees are three thousand years old. Branches can be cut off, the trunk can be sawn off and still the sap is so strong that it makes new growth, new shoots and eventually a new tree (like the motion of *prana* is continually regenerated out of the emptiness of space).

It helps the young tree to withstand the hazards of nature to grow up in a group, for then the trees provide shelter for each other. But eventually they will outgrow this arrangement and need space. Trees fight for space and light. If they have not enough they wither. Let's assume our young tree survived and his companions made room for him; one could say that sacrifice is part of the nature of trees. The survivor can grow according to the seasons. He will make new cells, branches and leaves nourished by an ever rising sap. The branches will stretch in many directions, some bigger, stronger, longer, some smaller, shorter, weaker. Some of these branches will die. In

Chapter 6

the winter the sap will retreat to the centre of the trunk, or the roots, to avoid the frost. In order to prevent severe damage, the sap retreats avoiding a damaging confrontation, with icy winds or drying frost. This withdrawal from the harsh winter attacks might lead to branches dropping off, yet as long as the centre stays untouched "unimportant" shoots are sacrificed. The tree renounces items of lesser importance, but maintains faith and trust that spring will come again; or that after a dry period it will rain; or in endless rain that the sun will shine again. And when spring comes, he sees his faith rewarded. With confidence and vigour he produces new shoots, leaves, branches, flowers and fruit - only to withdraw again in the autumn into himself to integrate last summers experience. In this way he builds time and time more rings around himself, gathering strength ready to green again in another spring.

And so the tree grows according to its destiny, in harmony with the seasons, in constant battle with the natural forces. As it grows strong, the winds and weather do it less harm. The tree maintains enough flexibility to sway in the wind, yet stays firmly rooted in the ground.

In this way his roots grow too, reaching deep, like the anchor of a ship while his crown reaches high into the sky with a canopy of leaves that soaks up the sun and rain. He now has a beautiful vista over wide rolling hills, a view over life as it proceeds, unattached, contained and peaceful. His peace is not ego-centric and closed off - by no means; he gives generously and selflessly to others. Even though the earth and environment provide for his needs, in exchange he gives abundantly oxygen, life-sustaining energy, to all that live. Nothing could live without his emanation; all that breathes needs trees. Generosity is one of his characteristics, for not only does he give oxygen (vital prana) to others, but ultimately he gives his life to fire, and all along he gives small necessary gifts to those friends that join the tree. The tree although standing alone, provides a community for others. All sorts of animals and birds live in his branches, live in him or of him; he supports plenty of life unperturbed. The tree protects others throughout blizzards, draughts and floods because his roots are firmly planted and his energy is self- contained; he is not bothered by little inhabitants. They are living according to their nature, as he does to his. He loves them and is grateful for their droppings are of some benefit fertilising his earth. He might even share his version/vision of life with them.

One day the woodcutter comes and decides it is time to cut the tree. But even then it takes the tree trunk a long time to dry out or decay. Eventually when wood is ready to be used, the natural beauty of the tree is still recognised; its spirit still appreciated by those people who buy the wooden furniture, which might be enjoyed for hundreds of years. Yet some of the tree will be cut into logs and burned in the fireplace; but then the tree always was aware that it carried fire intrinsically in himself, for it is the wooden sticks, that rubbed together, create the fire. In its wisdom Wood knew and accepted that finally it would be transformed into pure energy, into pure spirit.

Now let us recollect the main characteristics: Wood is firmly rooted in it's past, firmly rooted in the ground; it contains a plan, a vision. It constantly metabolises creative energy; it lives in partnership with other trees, creatures, and its environment; it needs light, space and its own specialised ground; it bends to the wind, this way and that. It stretches to the sunshine; it thrives on water; it can endure real hardship and survive. It is bound to the seasonal cycle; it retreats into itself in order to recreate itself; it is vigorous and prolific in its constant creative expressions. It bears fruit; it gets tough and more resilient in the constant battle with nature; it reaches for the unreachable sky; it has trust and faith in nature; its creation might outlive it; its spirit might still be admired long after its death; it eventually surrenders.

Can you see these attributes applied to a human being? It might be a person with a strong sense of purpose, secure in his family relations or his world of ideas; yet he will outgrow his siblings and family to lead an independent life. He has lots of ideas and the energy to actually plan and then execute them; such a person might be a self-employed craftsperson, a managing director, or a great teacher and leader. He needs to be surrounded by people and nature to recharge but also to be challenged, yet he is not greatly emotionally involved with them. He lives an active private life, doing this and that, but always tries to stretch himself in doing so - to do it successfully. Eventually he might stand in a forest one amongst equals, or even alone on the top of his hill. He might live near the sea. He likes a life of high profile and has high ideals and standards in life. This has led to many conflicts in relationships, but integrating this, he grew stronger and in time more and more self-sufficient. Even physical hardships had only the result of teaching him how to deal with things better, how to grow a new way of doing things. Thus his trust in nature and life has made him strong and set him free to create much good work for which he has justly become renowned. He might be so dedicated to his children, job or ideas that he gives his life for it, - martyrs are made of this.

Before we consider the manifestation of Wood in the appropriate meridian systems, let us listen to a Celtic Legend telling us that

> Aengus Og goes to and fro in the world
> he is a deathless comrade of spring
> and we may well pray to him
> to let his green fire move in our veins
> whether he be, but eternal youth
> or even though he be likewise death himself[8]

Associations to the Wood meridians

The meridians linked to the Element of Wood are the gall bladder meridian (*yang*) and his sister, the liver meridian (*Yin*). First let us focus on the bodily function of the organs after which the above Organ network is named, for their functions reveal some worthwhile lessons.

The gall bladder is a pear shaped sac attached to the liver by connective tissue. It acts as a reservoir of bile. Bile is secreted by the liver and consists of water, mucus, bile pigment, salts and cholesterol. The gall bladder has a lining, which adds mucus to the bile, the lining also absorbs water, so that it concentrates the liver bile 10 to 15 times. By contraction of its muscular walls the bile is expelled and passed via the bile duct into the duodenum (part of the small intestines). Fat and hormones secreted by the duodenum, stimulate the gall bladder to contract. The workings of the gall bladder can be summed up as being a <u>reservoir; substances flows in and out (this way and that)</u>, it absorbs water, it <u>contracts and reacts</u> due to the will of some other. The latter might be responsible for the idea that the gall bladder is an "upright official who excels through his decisions and judgement"[9]. Such official acts to the plan of a general as a magistrate whose ideas he puts into practice. The gall bladder also controls the amount of bile (including some hormones) that is expelled. Since this effects the nutrients and their distribution around the whole of the body, <u>the gall bladder is linked to decision making.</u>

The Liver is the largest gland in the body, weighing between 1 and 2 kg. Its importance is hidden in its very name, which has the same root as life. It is situated in the upper right part of the abdominal cavity. It has four lobes, a right and left one, each in the front and back. Various structures enter the liver, the portal vein carrying blood from stomach, spleen, pancreas and intestines, an aorta from the abdomen, sympathetic and parasympathetic nerve fibres; the hepatic ducts carrying bile from the liver to the gall bladder; and lymph vessels. The close link to the related gall bladder is obvious, as is a link to stomach and spleen (earth element).

The functions of the gland are numerous; <u>it's an extremely active organ.</u> It deaminates amino acids (breaks down amino acids, into new proteins and waste; uric acid). It converts glucose to glycogen in the presence of insulin (important changes in the blood glucose level). It desaturates fat (converts it to useable forms). It produces heat due to its high metabolic

Chapter 6

rate. It secretes bile (the cells of the liver synthesise it). It stores vitamins (B_{12}, A, D, E, K and water soluble ones) and minerals (iron and copper). It synthesises vitamin A and nonessential amino acids, blood clotting agents, etc. It detoxifies drugs and noxious substances. It metabolises ethanol (in alcoholic drinks). It inactivates hormones (insulin, glucagon, cortisol, thyroid and sex hormones).

A varied and complex job, that can be summarised as: The liver processes nutrients, and stores them. It produces heat; it cleans and detoxifies, it destroys or converts unwanted substances. In the Chinese theory, the liver is linked to "a military leader who excels in his strategic planning"[10]. The liver has to decide what to store, what is needed, what to dispense and how much; what is poisonous and must be cleaned; when more hormones will be needed and how much. It does not only decide to store and then leaves it to others, but it actually stores materials itself, in order to have them on hand. It can be said, that the prime task of the liver is to plan and to store, keeping in mind the overall purpose.

In the Nei Ching, the liver is said to rule "flowing and spreading". Liver Energy is responsible for smooth effective movement of bodily substances and regular body activities. The liver is said to maintain evenness and harmony throughout the body.

How the liver relates to the gall bladder is mirrored in the relationship of the official who works together with his general in making necessary decisions at the front of the battle. The gall bladder does it in one area, where the general maintains the overall view of the body's needs. It is understandable why these two energy fields are linked to Wood. Wood metabolises nutrients, sunshine and water according to its inherent blueprint, with vitality and vigour. It stores some in its roots and some such as Chlorophyll, in its leaves. The energy field that is called the gall bladder meridian and its sister jointly relate to the ability to have wider vision and plan, organise and carry out the decisions in order to put that vision into practise.

Whether they use these skills appropriately will indicate the balance. Does the person use his resources and mental abilities appropriately, neither erratically nor exhaustively; is excess energy released after hard work? Does he display an even-ness and harmony in body movement, a harmony of mind and emotions? Or does he suffer from erratic mood changes, shortness of temper and lack of emotional equilibrium?

Imbalances in the activity of the gall bladder and liver meridians might result in various forms of migraines. Most likely the liver energy gets out of hand and rises much too fast into the head and cannot assure appropriate supplies to the eye, ears, or brain. Arthritis results, if the element fails to neutralise acids and other poisonous substances. Menstruation problems can arise if the liver cannot discharge the necessary blood evenly to the uterus at the start of menstruation, it will cramp and periods pains will be experienced or there may be a disturbed sugar metabolism. Inappropriate bile release will affect the peristalsis of the stomach and intestines, thus can produce interference in the assimilation and elimination of food, constipation can be the result; in a metaphorical sense it may affect clarity of vision, thought decision making and the ability to make appropriate judgement.

GB imparts the power to make decisions, LV the power of planning and carrying them out. Dissonance between these two functions may result in action without discernment, without appropriate consideration - or an in ability to actualise decisions leaving the person in a state of feeling "there is no way out".

The Cycle

The circulation of Life's energy creates the meridians Life-Cycle. The time of peak functioning for GB is 11pm to 1 am, and for LV the maximum working time is 1 am to 3 am. Conversely, the time of minimum function is 11 am to 1pm for GB and 1pm to 3pm for LV. Symptoms of imbalances will be especially noticed at these times.

A person with the main characteristics of Wood Element might find that his peak functioning time is in the middle of the night: during the day time, morning to afternoon, he feels low and tired. Since most people sleep at night, this is a potential "problem". These people might adjust their life to being a night person, or they might use the sleep time for decision making. This sounds intriguing? I am sure, if we learn how to work with our sub-conscious and use our dreams, a lot of work can be accomplished, especially creative work, while asleep. The result ? One wakes up with a host of ideas, ready to put them into action. Work does itself, literally "over night". This can be useful with emotional adjustments or problems: after a good night's sleep such people literally feel different. On the other hand, even a person balanced in Wood Energy, might find the slight fatigue over lunch-time disturbing. This fatigue could be made a lot worse by having a large lunch, since the Liver and Gall Bladder organ network will not be of much assistance to the digestive process. A rhythm like this would suit artists, craftsmen, to some extent business people who are able to "take a siesta".

As a potter I used to wake up seeing the shapes of pots I wanted to make that day in front of me; but never used sketch-books to work on shapes while awake! My Wood Energy prepared the work while I was asleep. Creative dreaming used in some traditions and therapies has its place here. As we have seen before, each Element has, in the Chinese tradition, a host of correspondences.

The season associated with Wood is spring, the time of new growth. In Greek mythology, spring is associated with Persephone; married to Hades, the God of the Underworld, she is allowed to come to the surface of the earth, to be reunited with her mother Demeter, who is summer and brings forth fruit and grain for humanity to nourish. (She goes into the underworld , i.e. sub-consciousness or sleep, dream- and awakens in the morning with fresh ideas.)

Spring is power coming alive, spring is the greening power Hildegard of Bingen calls *Viriditas*. It is the germinating force, it is the blessing of nature that enables to bear fruit. The energy of spring is intimately connected to creativity. If a person loses the ability to grow or to bring new concepts into their life; if a person does not allow himself to take new roots, make new shoots in the extreme one loses interest in life itself. It is an imbalance in the Wood Element.

If a person has symptoms that get periodically better or worse in the spring, they might be considered to have a Wood-imbalance. A person's elasticity or stiffness in muscle tone or muscle tension might indicate such an imbalance. There might be dullness or rigidity of mind too, as some people dry and shrivelled up inside. They lose their sense of purpose, their spirit, "the soul is the freshness of the flesh, for the body grows and thrives through it, just as the Earth becomes fruitful through moisture" [11]. Spring as we know it, is abundance breaking out in the presence of moisture. That is also what the Chinese must have had in mind, yet having lived in the tropics, and the Southern Hemisphere, I am aware of the limitations of this metaphor and frequently use the term "greening power", which has a wider application.

The significance of moisture for growth points to two important aspects. Firstly it shows the close link to Water which reinforces that Wood, is the child of Water. The child cannot exist without the mother. Secondly it might explains why in some Element theories for example the Greek tradition and that C. G. Jung omitted Wood altogether. The link to Water is so close it might seem unnecessary to have a separate category.

The Directions associated with Wood are east and upwards. The sunrises in the east, the day begins from the east, dawn hints at a new beginning. All these relate beginning and creation, to new growth. It is obvious how this relates to a person: if, for example, a person finds it difficult to tune into new phases in their life, accept new ideas or processes it is possible that their Wood Element is out of balance.

The second concept of moving upwards relates to the movement of sap and the growth of the tree in general. The latter is easily to observe in the posture of a Wood-Person; they are easily flushed, with too much heat rising to the head, and have raised shoulders and hold their neck and head stiff when imbalances are present. The person carries himself upright seemingly filled with too much rising energy. On the other hand a slumped person that seems to lack energy, and seems withered and sunk also points to imbalance.

I feel there is another concept hiding behind the "upwards" movement. People of the Wood Element for ever seem to strive higher and higher they need a challenge to do their best; they are always searching, always reaching out. Imbalances show when this ambition gets out of hand and the connection to the earth is lost by moving upwards to the stars, by reaching for the impossible; or people with no ambition, no interest in reaching up at all show imbalance.

Reaching upwards is also relate to spiritual growth it expresses itself in the interest in philosophy; the expansion of faith and the ever- present drive to explain the mysteries of Life. That upwards movement denotes the longing of the soul to achieve the union with the divine consciousness. This spiritual longing is linked to the Kundalini energy, about which is said, that she lies like a coiled serpent at the bottom of the spine. Many people asked whether this energy really exists. There is no doubt in my experience, yet ultimately it depends on the myth we build around it. All our energy is spiritual energy. The bottom of our spine is activated through our breath and pumps the spino-sacral fluid up to the brain, - as it feeds the brain it surely is exceptional, it is volatile and it leads to "better or different use of our brain". So hopefully on day these reserves or this mechanism will be free to move up and fulfil its destiny.

The American Indians see in the East the Door "that leads to all other levels of awareness and understanding; one example is the artists creativity, by using any talent or creativity you have you will know illumination... The second path to illumination is healing and transmuting poison... The third is in knowing how to properly use and exchange energy; (it) will bring understanding of all material and non-physical forms of energy, true exchange is sharing"[12].

The climate associated with Wood, is wind. In oriental medicine wind is considered a powerful force, which can injure a person's energy. "Wind is the cause of a hundred diseases"[13].

If a person suffers badly from the effects of wind, or finds it extremely exhilarating, it may suggest an imbalance. Especially the East wind might make people with a strong Wood tendency very bad tempered or even ill.

Wind, in the days of old in many legends and stories, is linked to the 'Spirit of Life', the moving force of life. In the Atharva Veda (XI 4) breath, the supreme spirit and wind are all linked together.

> The mighty Wind they call him,
> or Breeze
> The future and the past
> exists in him
> On Breath of Life all things are based[14].

In the Buddhist tradition of Tibet, the wind plays a major role in medicine. The moving force or current of life is called wind. Wind is defined as dynamic energy that influences, connects or interacts with all Elements. In order to support all elements we need to keep the winds clean, pure, and health - in the inner world of our own body, as well as the outer world, the environment, the cosmos and planets. Lama Gangchen, Tulku Rinpoche, one of Tibet's most venerated Lamas, Abbot of Gangchen Monastery and Tibet's foremost expert on Medicine and Healing writes:

We need to transform our impure space energy into pure space energy, our impure wind energy into pure wind energy... We need to learn about and deeply understand the interdependence of our bodies and minds, the five elements and the environment we live in. According to the idea of wind as a current of the movement of life, each Element also has its own current ...wind and furthermore minor winds are attached to the five senses"[15].

These energy currents are something we usually are not aware of, we have lost the sensitivity to tune into such pure energy; may be we can relearn this by focusing awareness on the upwards direction.

An Aboriginal fable from Australia suggests, there are six winds, three male and three female. The "South East Wind" has three wives, he makes love to them and they begin to grow and put forth "flowers and fruit as a sign that Yarrageh, the spirit of spring, has arrived". Twice a year the East Wind Gunyahmoo and his colleagues come together in a corroboree and the love of the male winds "causes trees to put on their leaves, and to flower and fruit, and the earth to blossom in its green mantle"[16]. Why is wind part of the Wood Element? As with the direction 'upwards' could be linked to the tradition of ether, yet maybe, like the Aboriginal story suggests, the lies way back in the Dreamtime.

The Tissues or Parts of the body associated with Wood are the tendons, ligaments and muscles. These are parts of the body that make movement possible and hold various bits together. They govern the suppleness and flexibility of the body; they remind me of the supple young tree that bends under the winds, this way and that.

It is understandable that rigidity, stiffness, tension, cramps, spasm and certain types of paralysis may all be caused by an imbalance in the Wood Element. There may be spinal problems, or conversely, over-flexibility, looseness of joints, in fact a kind of floppiness in the general body stance.

The joints themselves deserve special mention, since it is ligaments and tendons, which hold them together and make 'them' work, their condition and consequently all mishaps with joints, including arthritis are governed by Wood. Wood-people tend to have a lot of physical energy (like the tree) - or indeed a marked lack of it, thus physical exercise is especially beneficial for Wood people, it frees the energy trapped in joints, muscles etc.

The sense organ connected to Wood is the eye and **the Sense** is sight. The quality of vision, clarity of purpose, planning and decision making is connected to sight, literally and metaphysically. Blurred eyesight, short of long- sighted-ness, blindness, astigmatism, distorted vision, cataracts, eye strain and pain, how eyes adapt to light and any other eye symptoms relate to Wood Energy. The ability to see clearly through a problem to gather and sift information with one glance, the ability to really see - grasping the essence of something, is governed by Wood. Obviously any blocks in such matters are due to Wood imbalances.

The Orifice associated with the Wood Energy is the eye. The eye is actually an interesting organ, the process of seeing a fascinating problem. We see only in the presents of light. Without light we do not see, yet who's light helps to "see" dreams or visions? We see clearly pictures in our mind, yet without participation of the organ of seeing, and with self-generated "light". R. Sheldrake suggests we share an electro-magnetic field, inside and out.

Seeing needs light, yet the interior of the eye is dark. It reflects the light that hits the outside objects. It is thus more of a mirror, than an autonomous organ. But seeing and light are intrinsically linked. All light comes from the sun. So the sun is the one that "sees everything" - since time immemorial eye and sun are linked. In Malay the sun is called "Mata Hari", meaning the eye of the day.

As we are dealing here with the orifice, we must stay with the actual organ of seeing, they then according to the above become a door, an open link, for light to walk in and out. But not alone, it brings with it what is seen, our whole visual experience of the world, including a connection to the sun – our creator? The eyes have, not without reason, been termed the door to the soul. From here even our dream pictures make sense, they then are created by the light of the soul.

On a more basic level, we have to acknowledge that all eye "dis-eases" are linked to Wood Energy, all light sensitivity, and even the ability to have visions and dreams. May be even the ability to relate, to walk through the door to our soul- is connected to Wood energy and thus imbalances in that energy will show here.

The function of seeing concepts with clarity is an integral part of making decisions. Having visions and foresight and any visual interaction between the external and internal world. Belong here. If the Element is in balance, then the passage will be neither blocked nor over open and thus provide an adequate and efficient exchange. An imbalance in Wood is indicated when the eyes show tension which prevents them from taking information in, they might be experienced as vacantly staring, seeing without seeing; or the opposite they might be too open and receptive, taking in without selection and be overwhelmed or over-stimulated.

The Fluid connected to the Wood Element is - tears. This does not mean just because somebody cries they have an imbalance, although excessive tears may be. Tears in this context refer to smarting or conversely unusually watering eyes. We must not forget that weeping or crying is one way of cleansing stagnant energy or rather getting rid of excess energy. On the other hand dryness of the eyes is often encountered when the person is very tired and stressed thus it is an indication when that "the general" is overworked .

The External Physical Manifestations of the Wood Element are nails, hands and feet. Thus the condition of the finger and toe nails show when the Liver is in splendid condition. Cracking, discoloration, splitting, peeling or ridging of nails all is indicative of a Wood imbalance. The condition of the hands and feet of a person may give further clues, do they look thin and brittle, do they look overly swollen, fleshy, too wide, flat and as though there is too much weight on them? Do they look strong, adequate in size and well maintained?

We use the feet to step forward in life. So feet that are well equipped for their task point to a person with a strong sense of purpose and determination, actively going where they want to go. On the other hand people with lifeless, weak feet may tend to lack a firm footing in life, they may even "drag their feet". Sometimes one sees feet that seem to have a lot of tension in them, in such a way that the toes seem to grasp the ground. This usually denotes an imbalance in Wood, since LV and GB run along the 1st and the fourth toe respectively, on top of the foot. The big toe is indispensable for balance. When the toes curl inward then the owner might have a very rigid outlook of life and resists changes, or is desperately trying to maintain a link to the earth, its roots, its something we find amongst people who have been uprooted.

How about the hands? Now here is another complex feature to observe. Although few people see each other's feet, we all see each other's hands. From the hands as well as from the feet, one can read much about a person, and gain an overview of the body. Why? Hands and feet are said to have nerve reflex points and zones that are connected to the whole body. For example there is the fleshy part underneath where the fingers (or toes) root, which is, in part representative of the lungs and chest. There is the inside of the tip of the thumb (or big toe) which is representative of the pituitary or master gland of the body, and so on. The condition, sensitivity etc., of such areas can give clues to the state of well being of the related organs.

Chapter 6

The hands as such, have also strong connections to the heart and circulation because of the central position of HC that runs straight through the palm of the hand and to the top of the middle finger. And furthermore HT and Si (the meridians of heart and small intestines) both run on the outside ridge of the hand along the little finger. This can be understood as a special connection between the supreme ruler (see Fire Element) and his general (Wood).

Most meridians have endpoints on the hand and feet thus they represent the whole body energy. Rough patches, gnarly joints, rough nail-beds, flexibility or stiffness of fingers, thick, worn skin; all are indications of the state of the Wood Element and the relevant areas of the body . For example: a woman might have a thickened stiff joint on the index finger, it points to arthritis but the arthritis manifested itself on the finger that is connected to the energy field of the large intestines. Further investigation of her large intestines are asked; the question of her mental ability to let go might also need investigating. It shows, that hands and feet can not only reveal intrinsic imbalances in the Wood Element, but "reaches further" into the body as a whole. This "reaching out" itself is characteristic of the Wood Element.

The Colour associated with the Wood Element is green. It is interesting to note that this corresponds to the colour of the heart chakra, as mentioned earlier. The heart as we will see later, has been in many cultures revered as the seat of the soul or spirit. Spirit that is life-giving energy, "greening-power". Green, love, the heart are connected. Energy that manifests as sap in the tree, providing lush vigorous growth, is green in nature. The colour has been used in mythology and legends to depict splendour and virility of heroes and gods, their jewels are often a mixture of red and green. The Indian Goddess of abundance, Lakshmi, wears a green blouse, the colour of healthy vegetation, of chlorophyll. Green is also the colour the Indian bridegroom often wears, a sign of the abundance of seeds, of greening-power. A person who wears or surrounds himself/herself always with green may be feeding an imbalance in the Wood Element, or may be consciously or not, trying to right it.

The personification of male fertile energy in the Celtic tradition is simply called the Green Man. The Healing Buddha Amoghasiddhi, who represents all – accomplishing wisdom (successful action), – is green.

The colours of the other Elements are blue, red, yellow, thus primary colours; the Wood Element has a combination of colours: Yellow (earth) and Blue (sky). White - the other complex colour is attached to Air (Metal); thus again we are led back to recognise the special place of Space and Motion, the two original energies

The smell associated with the Wood Element is a rancid and offensive, 'goatish' smell; the dictionary describes rancid as "smelling like rank stale fat". This points to the idea of food gone off. At the root might be a defect in the working of the liver to help digestion.

The Taste associated with Wood is sour. The origin here might be found in decomposing plant matter, which goes sour or even starts to ferment. Fresh fermented leaves or grass are strongly acid, thus wood soil is often acid and acid-loving plants such as rhododendrons, azaleas etc. thrive on it. Someone who either loves or detests sour, or vinegary foods, or conversely has great cravings for sour food may have an imbalance in the Wood Element. Very careful and considered advice must be given here, for there is easily the danger of overdoing it and making the imbalance worse, in either direction, by avoidance, or over indulgence.

The Grain associated with Wood is wheat. What might be interesting to note here is the ever increasing wheat-allergies in the West. It will definitely effect the liver. The question arises- are we becoming a society that has overindulged in breads /cakes so that the "Good Life", our indulgent way of life is poisoning us? Or, is our wheat being poisoned by pesticides, fertilisers and genetically modification? A point worth investigating.

The Fruit is Peaches. The peach in Chinese culture is a symbol, for long-vitae. So if the gallbladder and liver are kept happy it bides well.

The Meat is Chicken.

The Vegetable is Mallow (mallow is a plant of the Malvaceae family, like the holly hock, which is not commonly associated with food in the West). As with the sour taste, these must be approached carefully. It may be appropriate to eat more or less depending on ones practice to reach a balanced intake.

What needs also to be carefully watched is the intake of stimulants and relaxants. Tea, Coffee, sugar or alcohol are in excess, not good for anyone, but the person with a strong Wood Element will feel its adverse effect sooner. Wood Persons tend to over-indulge especially in alcohol, which has a negative effect on the Liver and easily throws the Wood Energy off balance, resulting in nervous energy and uncoordinated movement, destroying the harmony of Life. We will now look at some correspondences with less tangible concepts.

The Emotion related to Wood is anger. Wood provides abundant energy, it rises so strongly; the sap of new life lets seeds shoot up, reaching up rapidly but what if this flow is barred or if it is not channelled at all? The rising energy gets frustrated. Anger is such frustration. It comes from spoiled plans, from obstruction to the blue print. It is the body's cry for help, an indication that the Movement-of-Life is frustrated, needs to be channelled or the accumulated blocked excess energy needs to be worked off. Anger thus can be seen as a positive abundance of "rising sap" that can be channelled into positive growth, used to assert oneself and provide the courage to act – only something doesn't allow it to reach it's goal.

A person with a lot of anger will be helped, by doing a lot of sport. The energy needs to be released. Left alone, the excess energy will harm the Organ Networks and be displayed as irritability or frustration, being constantly on edge, wanting to pick a fight and even violence. On the other hand if a person does not get angry or has difficulty expressing anger even when appropriate; or has the feeling of being stuck, or being paralysed by the anger; he is also showing an imbalance in Wood. Such anger is often stored in muscles and again we see that exercise, regular, vigorous exercise is good for Wood people, because it stops their muscles from holding them in such patterns. The jaw of people or the pelvis and hips are a prime sight where people hold anger.

The Expression associated with Wood is shouting. Shouting is a release mechanism for Anger People that shout a lot, or conversely feel it difficult to use their voice loudly might have an imbalance. Yet shouting relates not only to such extremes, but also to a quality of the voice, a tone of voice that always sounds like 'a general' on the parade ground, no matter what they say, or how it is meant when they say it.

The Sound associated with Wood is that of crashing, which is self-explanatory. We just have to think of a falling tree. It also suggests the bursting force of spring, of plenty - or too much energy. People like that might walk into a room and it is almost audible.

The Manner in times of excitement or change associated with Wood is that of control. The obvious connection is the function of GB and LV as the instigators of actions, through planning judging and deciding and their correspondence with muscle, tendons and ligaments that enable physical and mental control. Someone who shows rigid control in times of stress, or loses all control and physical co-ordination and panics, shows an imbalance in Wood. In a less extreme situation people might need to take over, become bossy, or conversely they feel insecure, bump into desks and tables, drop objects and their vision becomes poor – they have no control.

To exert control can become manipulation. This can be observed in children if they feel powerless they resort to manipulation of emotions, events and people.

Control is also an issue linked to spiritual development. Breath control is an intrinsic part of any Yoga, meditation practice, singing and chanting. The ultimate aim is to calm the constantly chattering monkey mind. Although control here does not simply mean dominance, but the mind can be guided like horses in front of a chariot to focus on one point. Such one pointed concentration is seen as the gateway to the Self. "That is why for every effort for control of breath, the mind should be made one pointed with a particular thought"[17].

> "In the Bhagavad Gita, Arjuna says to the Lord:
> impetuous, stubborn, violent
> and fickle is the human mind,
> I believe that to restrain it
> is as hard as to confine the wind.
>
> The Lord answered:
> It is true the mind is fickle
> and hardly anyway controlled
> yet by untiring exercise
> and practice it is yet controlled"[18].

The Attitude associated with the Wood Element is Irresolution and **the Movement** of *Ki* is Vacillation. Both have a parallel in nature,- what bends the tree this way and that. Destiny deals us blows that make us swing in different directions, opportunities present themselves for this path and that. Planning and decision making incorporates the act of choosing a path or a direction into which to proceed. A Wood person who cannot decide which way to go, constantly changing his mind, as well as the person who blunders ahead in one direction without considering the options, are both showing imbalances in Wood.

When I grew up there was a joke going around: What do you do after school? Well there are two possibilities, I can go home, or I can stay at school. So? - If I go home there are two possibilities, I can do my homework, or I could play. So? - If I do my homework, then there are two possibilities, I can start with Maths or English. So? - If I start with Maths, then there are two possibilities, ad infinitum... A Wood person might explore the opposite directions in Life in all sorts of ways, like having many professions, travelling many countries, getting involved in many causes etc. He is a person who basically explores life in all directions.

As long as the person does not get lost in any of the directions and always comes back to centre, can be called balanced. What can be done to come back to centre will vary. But a person who cannot decide what food to order in a restaurant, what job to take, what cause to support etc., could be said to be imbalanced. Just as much as somebody who walks rigidly in a straight line, follows one interest all his life, sticks to one holiday resort all his life and lives in one place, eating the same food etc.

The Quality associated with the Wood Element is Spiritual. As we have seen the Chinese did not see the body and the soul as separate entities, but rather as two equal sides of the human. The tree is rooted in the earth and reaches to the sky. The tree then can be described as being a bridge between man and God. The Chinese acknowledge a soul, Hun, that is housed in the liver and gives direction to our lives by showing a striving for a greater sense of purpose beyond the everyday material existence. It expresses itself in the need to find sense and meaning in this existence; it might, of course, also reveal itself in the complete absents, and loss of interest in such matters.

The Faculty associated with Wood is active awareness. This not only relates to the ability to look in all directions, but also the ability to have an overview, to see what is needed, and to keep in mind a vision: all these need active awareness, even self-awareness. One needs not only being aware of what is going on in life outside, but inside oneself, be it physical, emotional or spiritual. This is the role of the onlooker, the

Chapter 6

ability to detach and observe oneself and the outside world with suspended judgement. Meditation is due to such faculty.

People who display either no awareness or awareness to the point of hypersensitivity, then show an imbalance in Wood energy.

The Activity following awareness is: implementing. It is linked to GB and LV providing energy for action. It talks of the energy that not only makes plans, but also carries them out. A person that cannot carry out their plans, or on the other hand, has too many plans; or implements inappropriate actions without planning may also express a Wood imbalance.

The Condition associated with Wood is one of Arousal. Similar to the ability of expressing anger, arousal relates to rising energy and its opposite - withdrawing. Wood is able to handle both, one in spring, the other in winter, each to its appropriate occasion. Wood persons obviously can deal with highly charged situations potent, intense times occur at certain intervals for a purpose; in spring for growth, in winter for rest. An addiction to either would point in the direction of imbalance. A Wood person then has to be aware of addiction to highly charged situations, his susceptibility to these as well as drugs in general, is great.

Conversely the very quiet, withdrawn person whose enthusiasm cannot be aroused by anything is just as much out of balance as the business tycoon who lives off constant excitement, exhausting his energy, keeping abreast of fatigue by using "pep-pills", coffee, or even cocaine.

Qualities/steps in Sadhana
The perception of the world has changed; with a Water perspective one had started to see the common source, now the focus is on equal vision, where individual differences disappear. The poles of opposites are both seen and can be held as one. Awareness of now and focus on future have become one vision (the path and the purpose are the same); similarly

categories disappear, there are no more male and female, only divine beings. The physical manifestations have become irrelevant and with it the ordinary process of life, the world as others see it holds little meaning. The 'upward' nature of Wood energy, means there is still push in the person, pushing for the frontiers of spiritual awareness through spiritual practises, meditation and contemplation but that drive becomes futile, with the realisation that surrender holds the only promise of grace. "Thy will be done". Grace is shared through mere existence, self-effort looses its power; the tree accepts its role, of just being, sharing its insights with others, for the benefit of all yet knowing that ultimately burning alone will free the embodied pure energy.

As for the level of consciousness, the Wood or Space energy relates to the state of Deep Sleep consciousness. As the contours that divide become wiped away, the universal, that which is shared becomes more and more relevant. In fact in deep sleep consciousness there are no definitions. There is no discriminating awareness of the physical, there are no more ideas, dreams or emotions. Yet something of us is aware that we are, but not as individuals – rather as parts of a unified whole. Deep sleep conscious is universal consciousness, is no more, no less, than the awareness of "I am the universe"; Aham brahmasi; mere existence; purity of being within one divine organism.

The Relationship of Wood to the other Elements has been mentioned throughout the text where appropriate, but let us summarise.

Water gives birth to Wood, like a mother it provides constant nourishment and fulfils important intrinsic needs.

Earth is controlled by Wood. We have seen a practical link to this in the function of the liver. To use a metaphor, we can think of a jungle where growth is so dense that there is no room for earth. Farming techniques today constantly demand more crops and exhaust the ground. The relationship is one of negotiating, giving and dominating.

Metal is the arch-opponent of Wood. The axe or chain-saw cuts its life, and, apart from exceptions, there is no cure, it is the end of the tree. Yet Wood survives its death, and changes form: the tree becomes furniture. That leads far of the topic here. Switching to Air we know that polluted Air kills trees invariably and storms uproot trees, - yet woods used as windbreaks stop Air. And most important of all they co-operate in the production of oxygen. They co-operate when it concerns the lively-hood of others. In Ayurvedic medicine Ether can destroy Air; "by overheating it, causing dryness (as in a desert) and aggravate...the nervous system" [19].

Finally it remains to acknowledge that Fire is the child of Wood. Wood as the mother of Fire, totally surrenders itself to that task.

So we move on to the Fire Element.

Chapter Seven

Invocation of Fire

I will meet you
I will touch you
I will burn you
I will destroy you
out of your ashes I will rebuild you

I will meet you
A flame has no face, it expands in all directions
Agni the Vedic God of fire is never the same in two moments,
Amaterasu-omi-kami, shining deity of Japan, a reflecting mirror,
La Maue, of the Igorots lives high in the tree to observe all,
Ra's eye ruled all corners of the world with its insight,
Odin hides his golden chariot across the firmament,
the cosmic Christ illuminates the corners of the world,

So rest assured,
I will find you,
even when I hide in the sparkle of a bonfire,
even when I tame the amber's of your hearth,
even when I illumine your way at night,
even when I wax and wane as pale moonlight,
even when at dawn I shower you with grace,
From the chariot I ride across the sky -
I peer in each niche and crevice -
and when I find you, there will be joy and happiness,
there will be lampions, candles and fire-work,
there will be flickering lights and warming fires,
there will be dancing and merry making,
there will be passions kindled,
for since time began, there was no ceremony without me.

I will meet you
I will touch you
you feel my touch in the delicate kiss of the rays of spring,
you see my touch in the abundance of life,

Chapter 7

you taste my touch in the sweetness of the berry
you smell my touch in the fragrance of the morning glory,
you hear my touch in the crackle of the log fire,

you sense my touch in the light of meditation,
you are awareness of my existence in the light of your Self,

you hear me in the explosions of warfare,
you smell me near the ovens of Auschwitz and Treblinka
you taste me in the bitterness of raging hate
you see me laying waste the Amazon forests,
you feel my touch in your feverish body,
for I reside not only in the centre of the earth,
but also deep inside your being.

Yes, I will meet you,
I will touch you,
I will burn you,

although born from rubbing sticks, I burn wood,
although melting her core the earth arrests my furious flames,
although liquidising steel, my gait is stopped by metal doors,
although vaporising water, rain stops even my tiniest spark,
although I burn you body, I cannot touch your soul,
for your soul is pure, is light and as light is my-Self,

Oh yes, I will meet you,
I will touch you,
I will burn you,
I will destroy you,

as wood is destroyed to give warmth,
as chaos is destroyed to create order,
as illness is destroyed to reveal health,
as weeds have to be destroyed to make space for crops,
as ore has to be destroyed to yield gold,
as water has to be destroyed to fill the clouds,
so injustice, bad habits, desires, attachment have to be renounced to grow love

The Element Fire

so your body has to be cleansed and purified,
in order to work in harmony with itself and all else;

Fear not, I will meet you,
I will touch you,
I will burn you,
I will destroy you,
out of your ashes I will rebuild you.

Truly is it not the same gold, whether ring or ore?
Truly is it not the same wheat whether grain or bread?
Truly is it not the same tree, whether acorn or oak?

As seeds need the sun's light and heat to grow, so you need the internal fire, heat and light, for it is "Shakti", the movement of life that inspires, sustains and purifies in order to guide you on the path of righteousness and wisdom.

Yes, I will transform you, so that the seed of your life's happiness can grow;

> so that the Phoenix that is you will radiate
> > with love and compassion and
> > > eternal light.

Chapter 7

Characteristics of Fire

There is hardly a culture that has not a myth about the sun and fire. For mankind fire has always had two strong connotations, it was a great helper and a destroyer. Its power might have been the reason why Zeus kept fire out of reach of man, yet Prometheus, with the intention of giving mankind protection from the elements, stole the fire from the Gods and gave it to the humans. For this Zeus punished him severely, and in addition sent a flood to earth to quench the uncontrollable fire.

Many of the main characteristics of the fire can already be seen in this story, e.g. it can protect man, it serves and warms man, it rules over most other elements, it gets easily out of control, and its arch opponent is water. But let us look closer at fire in nature, as well as in the more esoteric sense where fire is linked to joy, inspiration and intuition, to love, devotion and finally enlightenment.

Fire comes into existence by friction between two different components, (e.g. sticks, stones, a cigarette lighter, matches etc.) Once a spark exists, which is actually energy released by friction, the spark exists in its own right and has to be fed and nourished to grow. The growth is rapid and has to be monitored carefully for further sparks easily fly off and create new fires as in forest fires! Fire is creative, it takes many shapes and forms, yet unlike water it seemingly creates the shapes out of its own - and here is the root for its association with 'inspiration' and 'intuition' - rather than being poured into a shape or a vessel like water. Have you ever watched the dancing flames? - None is ever like its predecessor. I remember many years ago at a festive gathering of Gypsies in the Carmargue (South of France); we stared for hours in the flames, seeing our future, our lovers, our lives in the dancing flames; it did inspire many stories and legendary tales.

When fire is burning, it is strong, energetic and full of vitality; it has many colours, it looks friendly, joyous even; it moves incessantly, it can not be still; even the glowing coals in its

The Element Fire

centre constantly change its nuances of colours. Fire is driven to consume all, if we let it. Fire in its hunger, eats everything in its wake. The destruction of whole landscapes devastated by it, give ample evidence; no house, no tree, neither animal nor human life is safe. Ultimately there is little one can do to stop it.

In its centre fire is capable of vast temperatures, so much so that it melts all existing matter we know off, even the core of the earth is molten. But much higher temperatures are reached in the stars and sun - to eventual dissolution. The inherent potential for destruction creates the need of control.

Fire can be controlled (as long as it is reasonably small) by earth. In large bush-fires, earth walls are built to contain the fire within a specific area. Water too controls it, yet there is between them a delicate balance, too little water evaporates - too much extinguishes rather than controls. Water also draws the energy (warmth) out of Fire, (heating the water).

Fire feeds on oxygen in the Air that is freely available, since water has chemically bound oxygen water cuts fire off from its vital supply. This points to another source of control, the withdrawal of oxygen (air). This is why, throwing a blanket especially a wet blanket over the fire, extinguishes it. Moreover, when fire meets another fire, they compete for oxygen, and in the process consume each other. When they meet on a small scale they are playful, happy; flame dancing around flame. But soon their hunger takes over and they explode into each other, burning all available fuel. This too is used to control fire. A forest fire might only be stopped, by burning forest strips (by an artificially started fire) so that the raging fire cannot 'feed'. Oil-fires are stopped by explosions.

In places like Hiroshima, Dresden and Berlin that have seen the most raging manmade firestorms ever, one found that some buildings in the centre or close to it, were relatively untouched by the fire. The fire coming from all sides, swirling like a hurricane simply ran out of oxygen, it simply annihilated itself by its own force.

Let us look closer at what happens in the actual process of burning. One kind of matter changes, in the presence of energy, into another kind of matter. Wood turns to ashes. In the process more energy is generated and given off. Warmth is created - so fire really is a process of transformation, the by-product of this activity is warmth and light. Light though is not so much a by-product in the strict sense, but more the visual impact of the process. Light is different in character. Think of a burning candle, if you go close to it, you feel the warmth; if you touch it, it burns; its light is safe. Light from a fireplace, or campfire signals safety, rest security.

The biggest light, the sun, - is light for us because we can't see the activity of the fire itself; in the distance the fire is really a fierce boiling cauldron. If Fire is active energy, light is its radiance. Thinking back to the energy of life we remember, that for scientists matter and light are the same; both are different forms of energy. So fire is the process of transforming one kind of matter into another kind of matter; light too is the result from a process of transformation albeit in another "dimension"; jumping across the abyss in a quantum leap.

Light is the effect of transformation, fire the process. Fire exists also in us, for our bodies are constantly transforming one thing into another. Air is transformed into vital oxygen; food and drink is transformed into life. Orange Juice, potatoes, bread and chicken for example are transformed into carbohydrates, proteins, fats and minerals; these are transformed into amino acids, lactic acids etc. They then on a cellular level, with the help of oxygen are changed into energy. Energy is then used in activities, or to form new muscle cells (e.g. from amino acids, carbon dioxide and water). In fact our whole body is constantly metabolising or burning, - in other words transforming one matter into another. The wise of old spoke of the 'gastric fire' referring to the fire in our belly, that transforms base matter like food items into energy.

The Element Fire

If we think back to the beginning of this work, we might remember that there are many different frequencies of energy in our body. We grouped those of similar frequencies together as auric bodies, or energy fields. Changing energy in chakras from one level into the next, one energy-field to the next then is also a kind of fire. The Fire inside us also refers to constant other changes not only to the basic physical level (minerals into bones, for example), but to emotions, the energy changes of hate into love, the frequency of a dark mood into joy and happiness. This constant transformation, gave rise to the idea that life-energy itself is Fire. We ourselves are children of fire, or rather children of the sun. The sun (Fire) is on the physical level the source of our existence. Without whom nobody would live, as we, our planet belongs to the cosmic solar-system and without whom nobody and nothing can live;

> as above, so below
> as outside, so inside.

In many tradition and esoteric literature the sun thus is worshipped, its light and graces greeted and honoured, in awareness of our total dependency.

> Dawn comes shining like
> a lady of the light,
> stirring to life all creatures.
> Now it is time
> to kindle the Fire.
> The light of Dawn scatters the shadows.
>
> (Hiranyavarna)[1]

The sun itself gets worshipped, (that is the physical level) furthermore on the subtler levels it is her light, that becomes *the light* and is heralded as the essence of life, truth and the divine. It is a well used metaphor in Christian traditions

> "I am the light of the world"
>
> (St. John 8,12)

Chapter 7

> "I am the way, I am the truth and I am life"
>
> (St. John 14,16)

> "While you have the light, trust the light,
> "The Lord is my light and my salvation"
>
> (Ps. 27,1)

Furthermore probably the oldest prayer we remember, is the Gayatry.

Om Bhúr Bhuvah Svah;	Oh effulgent light,
Tat Savitur verenyam	that has given birth to all spheres of consciousness
Bhargo devasya dhimahi;	Oh God who appears through the shining sun
Dhiyo yo nah pracodayāt.	Illumine our intellect [2]

On an inter-religious conference I met a Indian-Shaman from the Amazone forests. He stated categorically that: there can be no life without Padre de LUZ, he is life. (Father of light)

It might be interesting to note that ancient India would have agreed with the Shaman, for the sun, or fire was not experienced as destructive, as it is in other parts of the globe. Natural disaster in India came from Water. (floods, landslides etc. Fire thus was from early on associated with the life-creating energy, and timely dissolution (rather than violent distraction) Thus it was celebrated as Surya, and as Shiva and Fire ceremonies were important part of worship. Until today such Yajnas are held.

This benevolent character of fire plays a great part in Ayurvedic medicine, where Fire meridians are frequently used to generate or distribute heat. On the other hand Chinese medicine is much more respectful and careful towards the "Supreme ruler of life" (HT) and some schools advocate not to use the main Fire meridian at all.

The Element Fire

Now let us recollect the main characteristics: Fire is pleasant warmth, healing heat, illuminating, giving safety, joy and happiness. Fir is creative, inspiring; enthusiastic, prolific, quick, active, spreading easily, explosive, in constant need of nourishment, full of vitality, driven, passionate, volatile, consuming, transforming, powerful over most others, irresponsible, indiscriminate, potentially unstoppable, destructive, purifying, devotional and enlightening.

It is not difficult to see how the attributes of Fire can apply to a human being. If the Fire-Energy is balanced, the person will be full of vitality and of a happy, joyful disposition. The creative force in him/her will be boundless and display a colourful array of talents; she might even have amusing skills and inspire her peers and the community. We could find her involved in some kind of performing arts. Yet she could also have a special warmth in human contact, that would provide a happy focus at home, like the warming home-fires of old; she could be giving caring, compassionate and even healing support to another; we could even find her in the nursing professions. She would be a person with seemingly limitless energy that leads an active life, her intimate relationship would be characterised by warmth and passion.

But what happens to a person where the fire is not balanced? It is time we look at the manifestation of the Fire Energy in the Meridians.

Associations to the Fire Meridians

In Aryuveda, it is pointed out that the source of Fire is Wood (rubbing sticks together), Ether or Air (lightning). In medical terms this would point to the liver. The heat that is found in the environment is akin to the heat found firstly in the small intestines and liver, and thought to spread from there through the body. If not adequately cooled, it can result in fever, high blood heat, inflamed tissue, heart conditions etc. Hildegard von Bingen agrees with Fire's origination in the liver; she describes it as going from there to other internal organs, and if not adequately cooled it breaks out on the skin[3].

Four meridians associated with the Fire Element. There are two classical ones: Heart (HT) related to the energy field and organ network of the heart, and Small Intestines (SI) related to the energy field of the physical organ of the small intestines. The remaining two meridians, referred to as the "supplementary fire", are connected less specifically to the organs, but relate more to their function; they are called in oriental medicine the Triple Heater (TH) and the Heart Constrictor (HC). Let us first look at the function of the heart and the function of the small intestines and see what the ancient sages might have observed that made them link these to the Element Fire.

The Heart is the centre of the human organism, it governs the circulatory system which means it is responsible for carrying warmth and oxygen and nutrients throughout the body into its most distant cell and brings back waste products to be dealt with by the respective organs.

It is itself a muscular sac; it pumps the blood through its four chambers and into the blood vessels which transport the blood to the lungs, where oxygen is absorbed and carbon dioxide excreted; and brings it eventually to the cells. Thus the heart is constantly active; it cannot take a rest. If it stops the organism is dead within minutes. Just like a king or a "supreme ruler" as it is called in oriental medicine, it is always in charge. As Fire, it always needs to be active, constantly nourishing itself, if it stops the flames soon die down and the fire extinguishes.

The heart activity is characterised by waves of expansion and contraction, created by an intrinsic system that has no need for a nerve supply from the brain; however the intrinsic system can be stimulated or depressed by nerve impulses initiated in the brain or by some hormones. There are some nerves that originate in the cardiac centre in the medulla oblongata which reach it through the autonomic nervous system. They reduce the rate at which the impulses are produced, or decrease the rate and force of the heart beat. Adrenaline and nonadrenaline, hormones of the Adrenal Glands, have the same task.

This means the activity of the heart though not under control of the will, can receive messages from the brain that are triggered by sensory input and translated into more - or less - activity. Fire is like a master over all other elements, and yet (like in a democratic setting)it can be controlled by adequate use of the other elements.

Apart from this central physiological task, the heart is seen in many cultures as the seat of Love and other emotions. The reason is probably found in the impact that emotions have on it by releasing adrenaline or non-adrenaline, as for example in the fittingly named 'flight or fight' response.

Chinese medicine distinguishes three different 'Souls'. There is the corporeal soul or spirit, which we have encountered in connection with the lungs, which dies with the lungs and becomes part of the earth again. There is the ethereal soul or HUN which houses in the liver and gives direction to life, it is yang in character, and on death, leaves the body to become part of the subtle non-material energies. Lastly there is the Soul, or Shen which is Yin in character and said to correspond to the mind. It is responsible for complex mental, emotional and spiritual feelings and affecting areas like consciousness, mental activities, memory, thinking and sleep. It receives its input from the senses, thus the events outside the body are directly related to a change in heart rate. This corresponds with the nature of fire, which is quick and volatile and direct in its response to what ever it finds in its wake.

The second major organ network in the fire element is **the Small Intestine** (Si). The organ itself is in a way a continuation of the stomach, a little over five metres long and lies in the abdominal cavity. Its function is the chemical digestion of food. It has the vital task of separating out the food the body can digest and moving the waste on. It secretes

Chapter 7

digestive hormones, enzymes, and protects against microbic infection of the organism.

Most of the digestible food here is either absorbed as carbohydrates, proteins or fats etc., and/or prepared for further use. The energy of the Si also, in a manner of speaking, assists the heart by keeping energy and blood occupied low in the body (*hara*) in situations of anger, shock, trauma etc. Otherwise the heart would be 'flooded' by a rush of blood and soon exhausted by its effort to cope with it. In severe cases, keeping the blood in the lower belly can lead to stagnation of blood in the area, which relates to the fact that emotional outbursts are felt mostly in the lower belly. Stagnation, as a result of trauma, is felt as 'tummy ache' (especially with children) or experienced as back pain, as well as chilling of the legs; as a result, the reproductive system can be affected, especially in women.

We can find these characteristics also in fire, fire purifies, it separates that which it can melt, at certain temperatures, from that which it cannot. As for instance in the process of winning gold. The ore the miner digs out of the ground looks like any clump of earth, yet in the furnace, the gold, with a lower melting point than the rest, melts and seeps out. The rock itself stays untouched, and eventually floats on a river of molten precious metal, to be siphoned off and discarded. Likewise Si, separates out what the body can deal with and use, and what not.

The first energy field of the supplementary Fire is the **Heart Constrictor** (HC) which supports the heart. Physiologically it relates to the pericardium, which is a set of fibrous sacs filled with fluid, which provide a space around the heart in order to protect it. It is also responsible for the nutrition of the heart; and because of this dual task, it is also sometimes called the Heart Protector.

If we refer back to fire as such, we find a parallel in the way it naturally gives protection against wild animals, cold or even as warmth against illness. This protecting and nourishing relationship between Heart and Heart Constrictor can also be recognised in the way that fire feeds fire e.g. how flames unite to create a more effective fire. HC in particular is said to influence the area of the centre of the thorax. In an emotional context, it means that HC is the source of joy and happiness, much like our romantic associations with the heart. We can look at this "joy" in a different way, HC's service of taking a buffer position to protect the heart is an act of love! HC "loving the Heart" reminds us of loving ourselves, having a sense of self-value. A lack of such, or an inflated sense of self-worth both point to an imbalance.

The second major energy field of the supplementary Fire, is called the '**Triple Heater**' (TH), although not an organ in the Western sense, it is considered to be a supplementary function to the small intestine. The TH controls the energy circulation in the body and with it warmth and heat, it regulates the metabolic activity, including the fluids. It is envisaged as distributing *Ki* in three parts: to the chest (the Upper Heater directs *Ki* to the Lung [heart and HC]), to the area of the solar plexus and navel (the Middle Heater directs *Ki* to all the Organs [Stomach, Spleen, Gall Bladder]), and thirdly below the navel down to the extremities (the Lower Heater directs Body Fluids to the Bladder [but also acts on Liver, Kidney and Li, Si]).

"The Triple Heater controls peripheral circulation and lymphatic flow. This means that the Triple Heater is also closely related to the skin, mucus membranes and serous membranes which are supplied by peripheral capillary and lymphatic networks"[4]. Their work is akin to a bridge between the outer world and the inner body.

Since energy and/or heat comes from burning nutrition and burning gives off heat as a by-product, which is in turn needed for metabolising nutrients, it makes sense that "Heating" has its own meridian, it is thus also called The Triple Burner.

Both HC and TH can be understood as having the function of circulation (of heat and nutrients) and protection, protection means interaction with the other, even if potentially harmfully. Often these meridians are the ones that 'fight off' illness, or disturbing influences. They can suffer for this, thus are most easily put out of balance.

We can observe the working of these two meridians in our bodies when flu viruses are 'in the air', or we fight off a cold; then, the outside of the upper arms hurt (along TH) or the outside of our calves are sensitive. The same applies when we have an acute emotional problem like a piece of bad news or an argument with a loved one. We can feel, in these cases, also a pain on the inside of the arm or even the palm of the hand. Even more obvious is the quick response of our bodies to an outside influence, or the inability to rebalance in cases of car, sea or airsickness. Industry has produced wrist- bands that press on the HC meridian to bring about a quick re-balancing.

Our language uses descriptive metaphors that describe HC as a "punch bag" for pain, trauma and shock. "A stand-in" so that the sovereign itself does not get hurt. The effects of "taking the blow" are that the person finds it difficult to relax, is always *en-garde*.

The Heart meridian, the Heart Constrictor and Triple Heater represent then a person's vitality in a physical and psychological sense. They are responsible for bringing us back to balance. They integrate external stimuli and transform foreign energy into useable, own energy, transform stimuli that is received from the environment through the senses into appropriate internal responses, into appropriate personal energies. For example: if somebody sees a new- born child happy in his mothers arms, smiling - and his own heart leaps with joy-, the response could be said to be appropriate. On the other hand, if a child is five minutes late coming home from school. The mother fears and frets that something terrible has happened, she rushes to the phone and rings the police or hospital; only to find, as soon as they answer, the doorbell rings and the child is home safe and sound, just having had an interesting chat with the teacher. Over reaction, if it is frequent, over-exhausts the heart and people like the above tend to have blood rushing to their head easily, suffer from sweaty palms, palpitations and blood related symptoms that show imbalances in the circulatory system, which can develop into heart problems. On the other hand 'under reaction' goes more easily unnoticed. Such signs as disinterest, a feeling of giving up, perpetual fatigue which soon can lead to depression are signs of imbalances in HT. For example this is the case, if a person never laughs, has lost all zest for life and finds it difficult to express joy in any way, even when presented with a lovely bunch of flowers, or the most desirable news. When the same person finds it difficult to have fun and is like a colloquially called 'party-pooper' -then this inappropriate response to good things in life could also relate to an imbalance in the HT. Other imbalances are: nervous tension, over-sensitivity, poor appetite, restlessness, anxiousness, lack of memory, no will power, a stiffness in the solar plexus, thirst and speech impediments, like stuttering.

Imbalances in HC also lead to palpitation, even to *angina pectoris* but also to milder forms of disturbances like cold extremities, heartburn, insomnia, frequent dreaming and a nervousness in social situations, for the person is unsure of the input she might receive and whether she can deal appropriately with it. Nervousness or shyness result.

Imbalances in TH are linked to distribution. Malfunctioning will lead to headaches and dizziness, hypertension, constantly clenched fists, tight arms, signs of insecurity, sensitivity to changes in the environment, tendencies to allergies, colds and skin irritations, itching from eczema. A fight is going on between the world inside the body and the outside environment.

In general what is said about the other Fire meridians is true also for the 4th meridian of this Element. The Small Intestine meridian (Si) though is more responsible for the separation of "usable and unusable" food particles, and for moving the unusable substances on (separation is an intricate part of transformation). Malfunctioning in the area of nutritional assimilation can cause all sorts of deficiency illnesses. It can lead to pollution or starvation, to such 'simple' matters as irregular bowel movements. Looking at it in a wider sense, one can link the area of 'thinking' to that of food intake. Thinking is a kind of mental digestive process; thus people with an imbalanced Si energy often have difficulties in separating what ideas for them are useable, what not; or who is best for them, who not, it leads to confusion. Think of a student who wants to be a biologist, but finds it hard to decide whether to take a course in mathematics, statistics or anatomy.

A woman might be unable to decide between her two lovers, whom does she want? Who is good for her? She can be obsessed with her thoughts of them, unable to concentrate on anything else. She gets over-anxious and agonises over the decision, yet she cannot decide between the pure and impure. Rather different from the inability to decide in the case of someone with a strong Wood tendency, who is pulled into opposite directions by equal attraction to either, the indecision of Fire is more a question of not knowing what is better for me.

Another facet of Si, on a mental level, is concerned about "moving" things on; or its opposite "holding things inside". Imbalances in this area express themselves in holding in anger or deep sadness, controlling emotions too much. Such holding on can result in determination or stubbornness. A person with an imbalance here might be a very determined person who is driven to accomplishing things. Such a person might always want to see a situation to an end, even when it is unwise; so much so, that he/she totally overworks, suffers from headaches and eventually "burns out". This can be relevant in personal relationships. When a relationship does not work, or there are strong signs of incompatibility, the person with an imbalance here might hang on to the partner, even though he/she mistreats her/him, even though there might be abuse etc. The person will not let go, and even take pride in his/her determination on "for life or death".

The activity of ingesting - transforming and integrating the outside world, are governed by energy fields of the Fire meridians. The world from outside be it as experiences, foods or ideas are transformed by the fire meridians into useful personal energy including moving on unwanted energy fields, by-products, unsuitable experiences, unwanted emotions, un-digestible food, unsuitable ideas. In contrast to the Metal Element, which has similar functions, there the relationship between outside and inside world is governed by creating boundaries, here the main concern is that of transforming the input.

The Cycle

As previously explained, meridians have a cycle. The time of maximum or peak functioning for HT is around lunch time from 11 am to 1pm, for Si it is from 1 to 3pm, for HC from 7 to 9pm, and for TH from 9 to 11pm. Conversely the time of minimum function is 11pm to 1 am for HT; for Si from 1 to 3 am; for HC from 7 to 9 am and for TH from 9 to 11 am. Symptoms of imbalances will be especially noticeable at these times. For example: a person might feel full of vitality and be very active around lunch time or might feel extremely fatigued during these periods. Even in a person balanced in their Fire Energy, there may be signs of change between maximum and minimum function. For instance a person with the main Element Fire might feel that working at lunch time and at evening (HC/TH) suits them best, but they are no good in the early morning; then they feel tired and exhausted. A rhythm like this would suit people in the performing arts (Matinees and Evening performances), or any shift-workers who can decide not to work in the morning.

The Season associated with Fire is summer, for the obvious reason it is the time of great vitality, of generous growth and abundance of life. Similar in human terms, the years of family life and career are associated with it; we talk of the summer of life, with its warmth of family life, its abundance and achievement orientation, with the ripening of ideas and direction in life.

Imbalances then are shown in lack of a drive to achieve, in uncaring behaviour especially towards the family and disinterest in life in general, or conversely in being driven to success, in over-achievement which leads to later burn out. This is indicative of the high rate of relatively young businessmen with heart conditions.

The Direction associated with Fire is south and the further outer circumference (we look at that later). The sun is the highest in the south, it is warmest in the south (at least for the Northern Hemisphere, which is probably all the Chinese considered). In the south fire is most potent. Here is where we find enjoyment and merry making, the Indian tradition associates love and celebrations with the south, much like the North American Indian tradition. There the South is related to childlike innocence, to laughter and joy. We can just see the dancing flames playing like children, singing and dancing to nursery rhymes, even rolling about, laughing in the grass. The South is about enjoying life, the capacity to have fun! It's about humour. Obviously people who can not laugh, or are too serious and have lost the ability to " be like a child", have an imbalance. The South is home to the Coyote, the trickster and its laughter, the clowning animal of great physical fitness that leads us into illusions and teaches us that "when you can destroy the illusion of who you are to others and be yourself, you will have restored your innocence"[5]. To destroy the illusion of who we are is an aspect of the childlike. The person we think we are is a construct of our own mind and an assimilation of the opinions of others. We are told that we are beautiful, ugly, stupid, clever, strong or clumsy and we live up to those opinions. On deeper reflection, we will find that what we are is mainly the result of such conditioning through others, – right down to genes and ancestral influences. Who than is the "I", the pure "I"? The real me? The me purified and innocent? That original "Me" is cleansed and purified by self-inquiry, spiritual practices and transformation of pure energy. Once we have found our pure self, that what we really originally are, we found "the gold of the alchemist", we become "innocent" again, like a child. Fire and the South speak of this process of purification to "innocence".

The Climate associated with Fire is heat. A person balanced in the Fire Element should feel good in a warm, or even hot climates, contrary to that, an imbalance is present if a person dislikes hot weather strongly or desires it passionately, in fact "can't live anywhere else". It would be interesting to check the relevant meridians of the thousands of people who leave such countries as England to "live in the sun". They seek heat, but what are they really missing? Do we use sunny climates to substitute emotional warmth? Inner fire? Love?

The Tissue or parts of the body associated with Fire are the blood vessels. The condition of the blood vessels then, can give clues to the state of the meridians, e.g. burst surface vessels in the face, especially around the nose and cheeks, or varicose veins indicate imbalances. Blood itself is, in its various qualities, linked to all elements. Its colour links it to Fire, yet its liquidity links it to water. Hildegard von Bingen writes; "without warmth it would not be liquid, without being liquid it would fall off like small scales"[6].

The Sense Organ is the tongue, its association with Fire might surprise us, yet in Oriental diagnosis the tongue is seen as a miniature picture of the whole organism. We find the link when we realise that the heart is the ruler of the whole organism. The colour, texture and general appearance of the tongue is correlated directly to the condition of the heart. Here is the origin of the practice of tongue scraping in the Orient, where the plaque is scraped off the tongue, just as we scrape it off the teeth, in order to keep the heart healthy.

The Sense related to Fire is Speech. Effects and modes of unclear speech, too fast or too slow speech, a lack of willingness - or the constant need to express oneself verbally indicate imbalances.

A 74 year old lady told me that she needs to study (at colleges and university etc.) at her age, so that she always has a topic to discuss with people of a similar intellectual standard. Why - I asked - does she need the constant talk? Her answer gives a surprising insight into the link between Speech and Fire. She said: "Talking to people, always having something to exchange with people, attracts people to me; that is a very important source of human contact, in fact it is my only source of warmth, yes, talking, exchanging ideas for me creates human warmth. No, even more, talking creates warmth inside me".

Here is a case of somebody who attempts to balance an obvious problem in the Fire Element by exercising the Fire energy in the mode of speech to generate warmth; that for some unknown reason can not be generated else where. But speech has always been known as a special sense in many traditions. It is seen as the transforming power that brings thought or ideas into manifest form. The creation myth in the Judeo-Christian tradition starts with: God said "let there be light ... and there was light"; God said " Let there be water ... and so it was" (Gen. 1,3 & 4) etc. The Word of God created the world, or "In the beginning was the Word, and the Word was with God, and the Word was God" (St John 1).

A Japanese story tells about the priest, Kuya, who speaks a *mantras* (spiritual verse) and each one forms manifestations, in this way creation literally emerges from his mouth.

The Australian Aboriginals, have a very special relationship to speech but no written records. They say in the Djanggawal, the creation story of the Dreamtime, each Ancestor gave an original cry of "I am", followed by "I am Snake, Cockatoo... Crocodile... Honeysuckle... Spinifex...". Each of the ancient ones put his left foot down and calling "I am ...(name). Their naming created the water-holes, gum-trees, rivers and salt-pans; called all things into being. This first act of naming goes

The Element Fire

on and on all over the world until the present time and is revered as the most sacred part of the Ancestors song, that created the world. So in all corners of the world Speech has been associated with creation, with that step of creating, where out of spirit the form manifests, or where out of subtle energy of fire, - form appears: earth - (ashes!)

The Orifice associated with Fire is the outer ear, because like the tongue, the ear represents the whole body. Imagine a human embryo upside down with the earlobe being the head. Acupuncture points for the whole body are found here, thus the ear represents the realm, of the supreme ruler, the heart. On the other hand Hildegard von Bingen attributes the sense of seeing - to fire [7]. Could it be because looking at people, one has the impression light emanates from their eyes? (see the eyes as orifice; Wood)

The Fluid connected to Fire is sweat. The Yin and Yang symbol each hold the opposite in their centre as a tiny seed. I see sweat in this way, as fire producing its opposite pole.

The External Manifestation linked to Fire is the complexion. It is not the skin organ itself, but its tone, radiance and appearance. The outer circumference, the furthest extension of a person, it glows like an invisible circle around him/her; just as the rings around a candle light. A person might glow with this inner light.

The Colour associated with Fire is red, obviously from what we have just said. Fire itself has many colours, yet the dominant one seems to be red. Red is used as a colour to display passion. In Europe it is also associated with blood and war (e.g. the red poppy in memory of soldiers dying). In Japan and India red has a different significance. Red there denotes happiness, the bride wears red, and special gifts are wrapped in red, re is the joy to give; the joy to receive.

In other parts of Asia, red symbolises independence and courage, the courage to be active, to do better in adversity. All

Chapter 7

over Asia red is also used to indicate spirituality. Temple gates in Japan (*Tori*) are painted red, temples have often a red roof, columns, flowers or sculptures. In India whole temples are painted red. The reason I think lies, like so many of the cultural and spiritual traditions, in the old Indian Vedic tradition where the life-energy itself is called *Shakti* and revered as a goddess. The *Devi* has many forms; as that original energy she is dressed in flowing red robes. Red flowers are offered to her; she is said to be the fire that purifies the spirit, she is also known in one of her forms as *Kundalini*. *Maha-Kundalini* is the spiritual energy that raises us to the supreme awareness of consciousness, a symbol for active grace, abundance and wealth. Red has become a way to honour the creative energy.

In Central and East Africa the colour worn by the Masai and Samburu is bright red. They wear this colour, because it typifies fire and thus the wild animals fear it; so Red has become the colour of safety for the owner, warning off others. How well this works can only be appreciated if one has seen the vast expanses of grey, green savannah, seemingly endless and then many, many miles away there is one bright red dot, - a lone Masai with his herd of goats.

In Ghana red has become the colour of sorrow. At funerals the family as well as the deceased is clad in red cotton clothes called *Kobene*; for the 'destructive force' has been victorious; transforming the physical Life to the other realms.

In the American Indian tradition red is the colour of the south.

A person who has either a passion for the colour or an acute dislike has an imbalance.

The Smell associated with Fire is a definite, un-mistakable smell of scorched matter; a very individual smell. The taste associated with Fire is bitter, to me the root for this lies in the need of the Fire for stimulus, coffee, tea, chocolate, all grilled or burned foods have such a bitter flavour as does alcohol

(Beer, Gin etc.) has a bitter flavour. Extreme dislike for this taste, points to an imbalance just as much, as an extreme like.

The Grain that is associated with Fire and best serves it is glutinous millet, **the fruit** are plums, **the meat** is lamb, **the vegetable** cabbage.

These must be considered carefully. It may be appropriate to eat more or less of these foods if they are neglected, or have been indulged in.

The Emotion related to the Fire Energy is Joy and to some extent its counterpart, of being able to feel sadness and pain adequately. It makes sense that the volatile fire should give us both great joy and with it the ability to experience and accept sadness. It's sadness of departing, of "moving on".

The experience of Joy has always been associated with the heart by poets of almost all cultures. HC is responsible for the balance of joy, so that its measure does not over excite the heart. Too much joy is as hurtful as is too much rage, or too little joy. Those who live a life in constant search of excitement in order to find constant happiness are prone to too high blood pressure, or to heart attacks, for these are the ways of the body telling us to take it easy. This constant search for joy is a state of imbalance. It can be observed in relationships where one sexual partner is exchanged for the next, out of sexual frustration of not finding the fulfilling constant joy. Boredom creeps in fast and commitment is out of the question, because the next person, the next situation might provide more joy. The result is an unending stream of unfulfilled relationships that leave the person empty, their energy is drained; they feel desperate and humanly exhausted as in an emotional desert.

The Expression associated with Fire is laughter, which can be a subtle undertone of everyday speech, humour, or a constant giggle. A balance of appropriateness is here, like always, the key. An endless joker is the other extreme to the humourless, always serious, closed person.

Chapter 7

The Sound of laughter is like crackles of the fire, and sometimes like fireworks.

The Manner in times of excitement or change associated with the Fire Element, is sadness and melancholy. The reason for this is linked to the emotion of parting. The Si moves things on, yes, but before that, it has to say good-bye to that part of life. To acknowledge no emotion on such parting, points to imbalances just as much as exaggerated lamentations, such as one would see on the stage in a burlesque show. Such outbursts we call, very discreetly, "theatrical". Loss of a glove by a flamboyant film-diva, might well cause a display of colourful sadness and maddening grief, which in turn might results in firing a servant, or calling the fire brigade.

The Attitude associated with the Fire Energy is one of Receiving. Receiving is used in the sense of taking in, and holding in the centre. So far we have associated the HT with receiving input from the senses, and Si with receiving food - ready for transformation. But to receive, or to be receptive, i.e. open to receive, has much wider implications. The Chinese saw the life-energy divided into two complementary Energies those of *Yin* and *Yang*. The cardinal description of *Yin* is as "the receptive", thus it is not surprising that HT is a so called a *Yin*-Meridian, yet it is also the supreme ruler who holds all things together in the centre. This relates to the tasks of the small intestine meridian, which holds blood in cases of trauma, in the belly.

Fire is constantly feeding itself on what is presented to it, what it can receive. Fire cannot, in by itself "go out and get it" for in the meantime it would starve, die down. It is thus in a constant state of receiving, constantly in the present. There is no planning, there is no preserving the past. For the Fire the past is wasteland, the future is not yet consumable. This is of great benefit if one wants to understand a Fire person; she/he needs constant confirmation, needs to receive constant attention, trinkets, applause, food etc. It is no good to say: make a plan, ..get your own... the person can't and won't, unless balanced by the other elements. Here is the origin of the idea, that people who are dominated by their Fire Element, are irresponsible and indiscriminate. It is difficult to keep a balance in life without planning at least for the morrow and near impossible to totally forget the past; but people who live these to extreme are obviously out of balance. On the other hand, the much loved philosophical concept of : ;living in the now, living in the moment is very accessible for this element- yet it has to be made a conscious step, not just become a default explanation to justify behaviour.

The supreme ruler, the HT has to exert some measure of control from the centre. He has to control his servants and receive their service. He has to control the desires, the senses, the mind – the Fire person might be extremely good at manipulation! On the other to be able to receive, means also to surrender all control of wanting to "get it", or of "I can do it myself", or "I cannot trust anybody to give it to me", or "doing it anyway". Receiving requires an openness and a trust in the universe itself that it will provide. And here we come close to another association, that of **the Movement of *Ki***, which for the Fire Element is that of meditation and deep thinking. In order to allow us to be receptive we have to be able to become still ourselves. Our very persona, our *Ego* has to stop shouting: Me, me, me; our brain, our mind that we are so proud of, has to give up its grip, and decide on a path of non-doing, only then can we be empty enough to receive. Obviously meditation is the tool for such a task.

The Fire Element holds a deeply spiritual energy, and because it does, it is not surprising that the Quality associated with it is that of Inspiration; or even spirit or soul. "The heart takes the spirit and the divine Grace and gives it a home"[7]. Hildegard van Bingen writes that man gets his feelings of sensitivity, his longings, his devotion, from Fire.

This is not only meant in a spiritual sense, but the human being is seen with an inherent longing and striving towards a healthy life-energy. Life-energy is constantly changing, moving towards a healthy balanced state. Input happens and it will be integrated, transformed and adjusted to health. This is the constant throbbing of the Movement-of-Life. In a physical sense, in a psychological sense, and even in a spiritual sense, constantly trying to realign, to fulfil the longing for a higher energy, with the ultimate aim of re-merging with the divine Self.

If this longing in any of the three levels is destroyed or lacking then the result is disorientation, desperation, illness, a state of joyless-ness, then as we say: the heart has gone out of a person. The result of it is that the life-energy gives up, *Ki* collapses. From the above said it is understandable, that religious frenzy, despotism and simple over-indulgence is just as much due to an imbalance in the Fire as rejection of anything spiritual, as is total denial to fulfil that longing for health and balance.

For instance there are people who thrive on being sick, hypochondriacs, they use their illness to feed their e*go* in order to manipulate others, or simply because it allows them not to bother. This is like the child who screams and suffers greatly, because something really, really hurts, e.g., the finger got stuck in the hole of a soft blanket. By the screaming not only will all the adults rush to her/him and give attention but behind it is a sense that life itself has let him/her down. There is a need to confirm that 'somebody still cares', a deep longing for love, to know that somewhere there is a heart ready to embrace her/him.

Imbalances could also show themselves in an every day way, by lack of inspiration, a drying up of ideas, a loss of sparkle.

Qualities/Steps in Sadhana , Fire has too sides, it burns. This burning power is called the fire of love. Being filled with such love and devotion and living accordingly is in India called Bhakti Yoga, some say it is the highest Yoga. It purifies, bringing about a state of light, delight and ecstasy; the Indians call it bliss or Ananda. But such divine love is found in all major religious traditions. It was for example the essence of

The Element Fire

Jesus Christ's teachings, - just as it's cousin, compassion – is the centre of the Buddhist tradition.

Intellectual understanding is left behind; a knowing replaces it that has no words. Absorption might be a word to describe it. This absorption in creation, its beauty and magnificence can be seen and enjoyed totally unattached to "real" appearance, for what is seen is seen through the eyes of love. Not a love that has an object, judgement or criteria but love, that sees only the divine creative energy in all its splendour behind the apparent form. From here the "furthest extension", the highest goal is reached, human potential fully realised, man becomes of pure spirit and the world can be enjoyed for what it is - a play of energies; the goal is joy, pure and eternal bliss – Nitya-ananda.

As for the level of consciousness, it speaks for itself, Fire is the power of transformation with which one enters the last stage, Turya, the state of bliss and the Beyond; – that final stage is only reached through grace. The agent for that transformation is divine grace.

The relationship of Fire to the other Elements has been mentioned here and there but let us now summarise. Fire gives birth to Earth. The ashes the fire leaves behind, the minerals and molten waste, make up the earth. A volcano's slowly cooling lava, weathering over thousands of years of weathering, will become fertile soil. I have witnessed that in such places as Kagoshima in Japan, where the still warm dust of relatively young volcanoes was already used for growing oranges, in the region of Satsuma.

Fire controls Metal, it melts it into its purest form. If we care to remember, Metal is associated with the intellect; it means that fire melts the intellect. We do not have to look far to find an example for it. If we fall in love, we forget all rhyme and reason. But there is also another aspect to think about. We live through our mind - we perceive the world through our mind and decide how to act.(On varying depth of course) Fire is the agent, that makes it possible to use the mind to transcend itself.

Chapter 7

This plays a major role in Buddhist practise and the wisdom of lojong; but also in the universal practise of meditation. It reminds me of the Gayatri – in this 6ooo year old prayer humanity prays for "illumination of the intellect", for transcendence of our ordinary mental perception, so that we can go beyond our limitations to freedom, to a pure "golden mind".

Fire consumes Air, in its extreme it means total annihilation, the Ozone-layer problem is a loud witness. Or from the spiritual realm: Intellectual knowledge has to be totally surrendered, it does not "go" any further; a quantum leap is necessary.

Water and Fire have a two way relationship, in one way water controls fire, yet without water fire cannot live either, for the limitations water gives, sets fire free from the urge of self-destruction. Water is to Fire, like the North Pole to the South Pole; neither can exist without the other. Hildegard von Bingen is quite strong in her conviction that Water itself holds the seed of Fire. It sounds strange, but she reasons that without any warmth Water would be ice; on the other hand without coldness inherent in it, Fire would implode [8].

When I was a younger woman, I drove through the Nevada desert in an old car. The fan-belt broke and the car overheated. To press on, to reach the next village I poured the drinking water into the car. In these conditions it lasted but a few miles, and the next village was 60 miles away. Now I had no water and no transport. Thinking I might hitch a lift I walked and soon collapsed with de-hydration; vultures circling above me was my last conscious awareness. Apart from learning about my own foolish actions, I had a powerful lesson in the relationship of Water and Fire; outside and inside my body; without the limiting influence of water, Fire is deadly - luckily I was found by a ranger-patrol.

Wood finally is the mother of Fire. It gives birth to it and nourishes it and there the cycle ends, or rather begins again.

With Fire, it's spark, it's inspiration the circle begins. It begins in the world of ideas, but so far the thing in question is "still amorphous, plasmic, and yet possessed of great energy to inspire action". The original inspiration results in the birth divine creative energy, Shakti. "The sages looked for an analogy in nature and found fire, which though highly amorphous, is nevertheless possessed of great energy that inspires change. From Fire, the cycle moves on to a more solid, grounded state, in which the idea begins to take shape as a perceivable reality. This stage is known as Earth. From Earth, the process continues to its most dense and material form, signified as Metal. The thing in question is born. It is real. From the Metal phase the process continues to Water, its most flexible and enduring stage, from Water the evolutionary process moves on to the Wood phase, in which we see the fruits of the dream. Here the original inspiration has gone through its necessary development to bring forth rewards... Wood signifies the culmination of the cycle... and begins the process of regeneration all over again" [9].

Within each of these five elements interacting with each other are - the five elements. Let's say the Fire element contains in itself the Earth, Metal, Water, Wood and Fire and so on *ad infinitum*. Such is the complexity of the ever changing Movement of Life, the incomprehensible mystery, - the unfathomable Mystery of Life.

Conclusion

Truly comprehending that we are the Elements,
not just linking parts of ourselves to them,

One realises:

I am Earth
I am Metal
I am Water
I am Space
I am Fire

There is nothing outside that is not me

Rejoice

I need no boundaries
I need no defences
I need no separation
There is nothing but me
There is only the Self

There is only One

Energy expresses itself in five different forms. The forms are constantly interacting, they effect each other, they are in constant movement; they are the Movement-of-Life.

We have seen the Movement-of-Life unfolding from the physical organ, to emotions, mental attitudes and even affects the spiritual aspects of the person. Vice versa: the spiritual state of a person affects the person's mental and emotional make up and manifests itself in the physical body, thus the energy moves through all aspects of life. It constantly creates and recreates itself through different, interacting fields with its different vibrations, or even bodies and *chakras* .

Intervention in any of these processes gives us a wonderful chance to recreate or heal ourselves. In order to do that, we need to be aware of these processes. It is necessary to observe closely, to recognise these manifestations, interpret them correctly and relate them to their source. From there we can redress imbalances.

Chapter 7

PART III

RESTORING THE BALANCE IN THE ELEMENTS

PROLOGUE

The Movement of Life manifests itself in various energy fields. Due to their different character, different distortions occur and depending on the severity of the distortion, we speak of health or illness. A totally healthy person has the ability to regain equilibrium in body, mind and soul quickly. A permanent state of equilibrium is impossible to imagine, not only because of its complexity but also because such a person would be dead! Why? If life-energy is *Movement*, as we have seen earlier, the distortions occur with every wave of incoming energy, all experiences from taking a breath to being struck by a falling brick. Distortions happen constantly; health can only be defined as an ability to bring about balance; to come back to centre after impact; or simply "health denotes how quickly someone heals". It can however never be a static state.

The emphasis on "health" as the relative ability to bring back balance can be illustrated by the role, a doctor played in China. He was paid, as long as he was capable of maintaining a person's health. If the person under his care became ill, he would not be paid. If the person that became ill was a high official or even the emperor, the doctor might well be killed, for he had failed in his job. This explains why people in the Orient keep adjusting and balancing the body - preventative medicine. In Japan people might go to have Shiatsu, Amma or Acupuncture at the beginning of each season, to adjust their bodies to the new season's energy and to clean up any distortions in themselves, "sweeping clean the inside world".

In the West, under the influence of a science, which sees the body as a machine, the emphasis on health care is on fixing the part that <u>appears</u> to be ill, the symptom of illness. An interesting thought has to be considered here. If all is energy, even thought forms are energy that become manifest, (e.g. create matter) then such focus on illness could be said to actually create illness, for it distorts, by the power of its nature, the balance of the Movement-of-Life. Indeed it can be observed that highly civilised countries with technically very advanced medical systems, have actually more sick people than other nations. For example America, with its advanced system of medicine, recognises that the health of its people has deteriorated, more people get ill. The Americans are unhealthier than their fathers and mothers, and "were actually dying younger... we have more doctors, more dentists, more and better equipped hospitals, better drugs and a greater supply of food than any other nation we still are, by far, the sickest nation in the world" [1.]

> We are what we think
> having become what we thought,
> Like the wheel that follows the cart-pulling ox,
> Sorrow follows evil thought.
>
> And joy follows a pure thought,
> like a shadow faithfully tailing a man.
> We are what we think,
> having become what we thought.
>
> (the Dhammapada)[2]

Not only are we becoming what we thought, but also how we act and react effects us. For example if we experience fear, we breathe in and hold our breath in a shocked reaction and we don't breathe out fully, too scared of what might happen next. Now if we repeatedly experience such fear we condition ourselves to withhold our breath, learn not to breathe out fully. A habit of holding the breath is formed, - and here we have the symptoms of an asthmatic person. Indeed we can easily observe, that a person suffering from asthma holds the breath so much, it feels like suffocating. The question to be asked of such a person is what are you afraid of? What were you afraid of in the past? What is this underlying fear? Fear is an emotion that anticipates loss of life, respect, self, etc.

Why do we anticipate this loss? We can only lose something we have got. We seriously need to ask ourselves: what have we got, what is ours, what is mine? Is the house "mine"? In what way? Fire, flood, war, divorce, can take it away - so it is not mine for ever - it is just given, borrowed for a certain amount of time for me to use. If nothing else, certainly after my death it belongs no more to me. Is my family "mine"? What if they die, go away? I have borrowed the time with them, haven't I? What is marriage? What if the relationship brakes apart? How long are I allowed to enjoy my children? Are all of these there only for a time, to enjoy, to learn from? How long are they there for, certainly for a limited time, a month, a year, a life? What about our body? How long can we enjoy its beauty, my belly/my face? Is this my face now, for how long? What if I get old, die? Is my body mine? Mine? Who is the owner? What does the owner have? What have I got to call my own, what is it that I truly have? Or even more pronounced, what is so separate from me, that I can own it? Ownership needs two, one who owns and one that is owned. Only then can we fear the loss. We fear loss of life, so who is this "I" that owns my life, from whom it can be lost? Do you think you are separate from life? Can you even think you and That are separate? It is totally illogical and irrational, yet this is our most common fear underlying all others. We fear to be separated from the house, the family, the other person, the body because we feel separate from life itself!

If our worth fear happens, what dies, what is annihilated? Dying is a word describing transformation of one state of manifestation into another. Flowers become compost. When I die what dies, what undergoes this change of transformation from one physical state to another, my body, my mind? Was that me? Am I identified with this physical matter? But the matter that is my body would not function, is a corpse without the life in it. Only physical things can die- thus what dies cannot be the life that is housed in that body. If I am not limited to that physical form which changes into compost, than "I" that is life, - cannot die. Wow, "I" am immortal; "I am THAT". There is nothing to fear, because death does not happen to "me", yet this existential fear is the deepest imaginable root of all other fear. We believe we are separate, alone, left to the powers to be – and forget that we ourselves, are that life, are those powers! How can we be separated from the very thing we are? .

We are blinded by the different forms life has taken. As long as we cling to this view of duality, of seeing us and everything else as separate, we fear. But, as we have seen we are the same energy as everything else; there is no duality only unity. No death – no fear, there is only energy, mere existence.

Grief is intimately connected to loss. Fear and grief are intrinsically connected emotions leading to patterns of holding breath, holding energy. Eventually this forms a habit that manifests as observable illness we call asthma (Metal that supports Water = grief and fear). To restore health one has to unlearn these patterns and to rebalance the movement of energy in such a way that new patterns of breathing can be established. The widely used inhalers do no such thing; they give a chemical shock to the system so it breathes differently. As they do not re-educate the system, the situation appears again a few minutes later and possibly they themselves become a habit or addiction that reinforces a disturbed lung energy pattern.

OK. I hear you say but new born, or nearly new-born babies have asthma, how can they have a reinforced habit that is asthma? Here we need yet to address a different question of health and illness. You rightly ask, how can a child, we see as innocent, as not old enough, have a habitual pattern that causes breathing difficulties? We can extend this thought: why do good people who seem to live an ordinary, healthy, considerate life, come down with terribly destructive inexplicable diseases such as Multiple Sclerosis, Cancer etc.? Or how about illness caused by traumatic accidents due to other people's intervention (e.g. being killed)? How come even young children have bone cancer, or are born with other afflictions and illness?

If the thesis is right, that illness is based on a distortion of a pattern, or a "bad habitual behaviour", then I see only one solution: to examine the theory of "dependent – arising" and looking in the related aspect of reincarnation.

The concept of "dependent rising" relates in Buddhism to the view that everything is interconnected. Look at one instant: I take some bread into my mouth. - This is one clip of a whole film! At that time I do not see all that moment depends upon. The bread is bought at a supermarket, that has staff who put it on the shelf, lorries, builders, their families etc. without their help the bread could not have been bought by me, I could not put it in my mouth. For the bread to exist, a baker has to make it, he somehow has to mix flour, water, yeast - the whole of the electricity network and waterworks are connected with that job. The flour has to be grown by the farmer, fertiliser, tractors, harvesters, the whole of industry is behind that. For the grain to grow, sun and rain, earth and minerals are needed. It can only rain, shine this year in this constellation due to previous constellations of sun, moon, and the whole cosmos. My bread thus is linked to all of creation, in all times, to the past as well as to the future. To the future - because the bread becomes my energy and thus affects all my actions I do today, which in turn will affect all of tomorrow *ad infinitum*. I am thus embedded intrinsically to all events that have and will happen. I am part of an enormous complicated *Web of Life*, in which all is interdependent

This has far reaching implications. Let's just take the first simple idea. I am connected to everything - so where does "mine" begin? Is there any such thing as mine, or can there only be "ours"? (Remember the bread? Is it my piece or the bakers, the farmers, the...) "If it is not 'mine' - I cannot loose it. Thus we realise that no thing and no being can exist in itself or for itself, but that each form of life has the whole universe as its basis and that therefore the meaning of individual form can only be found in its relationship to the whole"[3].

That is easily grasped, but what about life itself, our body? Once we realise that we, as individuals, are embedded in the universe then we become aware that our body, "our life", is sustained by the rest of the universe. The life we experience in this body is in all its fullness an expression of all those factors "working" together in the universe, in past, present and future;

we cannot isolate any bits of us; just like a drop of water cannot be isolated within the ocean. Or as the Tibetan Yogi Milarepa sings:

"Accustomed, as I've been, to meditating on this life and the future life as one, I have forgot the dread of birth and death"[4].

Life is linked to past, present and future and all else, thus it is of universal nature. How it is linked is speculated upon in the theory of *karma*.

The energy-field, I call "my present existence" is as we have seen not limited nor is it finite. Just as genes get passed on from one generation to the next, so energy-patterns are fluid, they are movement, reaching over past, present and future. If we follow the path of our genes, we find we are probably related to half of the world, and if we go on probably to all that existed since time began. The same is true of course beyond genes and biological energy-fields, to all other energy-fields that crystallise into a space and time frame called "Me". It is said that this periodically manifests its lower frequencies as a physical body, which undergoes changes of form that we call physical death. Bodies live, die many times, thus hundreds, thousands of lives are lived. The "Me-ing" consciousness, energy of high frequencies plays, learns, remembers and eventually merges back into the Absolute. This process is called reincarnation, divine energy reincarnates in a physical body, again and again only it forgets where it came from or veils this, so it can fully live and explore the physical manifestation it has becomes now. Reincarnation theory is part of many religions. Contrary to common believe - even Christianity held this concept for most of its history (Origen, Memosias, Justin Martyr etc.)

This is relevant here, because it means that we may look for the cause of disease in an earlier life! This is not meant in the sense of punishment, a common misunderstanding, but in the sense of a spiritual law, the law of *Karma*. We incarnate with subconscious memories and patterns from previous lives in order to learn whatever lesson is necessary for the soul's growth, including patterns that might have evolved due to some memory of a traumatic experience.

What remains simply is an underlying idea that in some cases of severe inexplicable causes for an illness, there might be only one answer that makes sense; the energy flow and its inherent pattern has been influenced long before the person was born. *Karma* refers to that past and *Destiny* is the future we are growing into. *Karma* is where we come from, what propels us to go to our destiny. Karma is much more complicated than the common idea, that "I have done something bad - so I get punished". It is too simplistic to think that because I have pneumonia now, I must have hurt somebody's lungs in a past life. The general concept of cause and effect is well explained by Lama Gangchen Rinpoche. In order to help understand it, he suggests that we imagine a computer disc with billions of Megabytes. This disc hangs around our heart and all positive and self-destructive actions we perform are recorded there over the continuum of our present and previous lives up to now: this record is like a telephone bill. We enjoy using the phone, but we never notice that somewhere a record is being made of what we did. Then one day the bill arrives and we get a big shock, we have to pay! The 'disc' in its totality is the only luggage that we are able to take with us, as our mind migrates, on the soul's journey from life to life. "The inner Space disc is like a small mirror". We can even see the reflections of a huge city like Madrid, Kathmandu or Milan or even the entire planet in a small mirror, because the mirror is successfully using the quality of space... What kind of new reality we project for ourselves depends upon what kind of actions we have programmed into our inner disc[5].

Some illnesses then, are due to patterns of interference in this life, yesterday or 'yester-year'; and some are due to habitual patterns of interference before birth; or even in a previous Life. Consequently to unlearn such habits and restore the balance in the energy fields, varies in the effort required as well as in the possibilities and the nature of success. Obviously a habit fallen into a few months or years ago is easier to unlearn and replace with new behaviour, new thinking or new attitudes than to unlearn or heal distortions that are years old or even a lifetime or several lifetimes old. A smoker that has smoked a few cigarettes can give up relatively easily. Somebody who has smoked for twenty or thirty years will find it much more difficult to unlearn that habit. It is nearly impossible to unlearn or heal patterns that are older than this life. However deeply we look at the sources of our habits, afflictions or distortions in this life; however much we try to heal ourselves, we have to accept that there are limits to what we can achieve by ourselves. These limits are subject to our *Karma* and *Destiny*; they are shrouded in previous lives (previous effects on our energy patterns).

A. Young[6] suggests three possibilities of healing such past life patterns:

1. to become conscious of them and their teaching for this life, but disconnect the fact that the root is in the past; this is a new life and one is free to let the old go;

2. to heal it by seeing the connection and healing it, behaving as though it did happen in this life (e.g. forgive a person that has wronged you); and

3. to believe that because there is no time continuum really, that it is possible to change the past (e.g. visualise the event and change its end). But really it is far beyond this work to go deeper into these concepts, there are however, therapies that can be suggested, such as past-life therapy, metamorphic and re-birthing therapies etc. What is important here though, is to realise that there are apparent limits to healing or unlearning such energy patterns, especially those shrouded in previous *Karma*.

These limits can however be effected by something I call "Grace", or the love of God. Grace is the one limitless power that alludes our efforts or attempts. Grace comes from an altogether different source; it is divine energy itself. It is the compassion of the divine, the hand of God that reaches out to us with pure love (pure benevolent creative energy), for no rhyme or reason. It is said, that if we are fortunate enough (which is grace already) to meet a fully realised person, a Guru, Saint or Avadhuta that their energy, due to its purity can effect our *Karma* and erase our old energy patterns. Such is the grace of God, Guru or Avadhuta. Grace is the compassion of God, the compassion of the Guru. Like the compassion of man who forgives and helps without regarding whether the person deserves it or not, so divine compassion just washes *Karma* away, like we wash clothes. It restores life, makes new, for no reason at all other. Grace is the source of the abundance of Earth, it just is.

Without this grace our attempts to heal ourselves are limited, and limited not just by the depth and veils of *Karma*, but also by the complicated pattern of the many levels of life's interaction. But we cannot but try; we must put forth the effort to heal ourselves, self-effort draws grace. If we think back to the movement of life through the Elements, we recall the sequence of *Sheng* and *Ko*. Along the circular sequence (*Sheng*) each Element brings forth and nourishes the next, in the *Ko* sequence, representing the dynamic concept, each restrains or controls and limits another. The Elements are thus in constant interaction of "creation and destruction", of encouraging and controlling. For example, Water nourishes and creates Wood (as we have mentioned before) and it restrains, controls and even destroys Fire, but by doing so it take its own nourishment from Metal (Air) as well as being limited by the boundaries that Earth imposes. Thus the action of one will effect the whole.

One intrusion of any new stimulus or habit triggers a different pattern in the whole system. If the Liver energy (Wood) gets assaulted by overuse of alcohol, for example, the Spleen (Earth) and Lung energies (Metal) grow unduly strong and the Heart energy (Fire) becomes exhausted and tired because the Wood energy is too weak to nourish it. A collapse of one

Element not being able to do its job sufficiently, thus results in a pattern of disharmony and finally disease and illness.

To heal our Movement-of-Life then is mainly a re-education of energy patterns in body, mind and soul into balanced interacting fields of energy. How long does this take; how far is it to relative wholeness, how can we recognise the distortions?

The answers are shrouded for each one of us in the veil of destiny, but we must embark on the path - just as the Hoopoe bird describes in the "Conference of the Birds":

> "Before we reach our goal' the Hoopoe said,
> 'the journey's seven valleys lie ahead;
> How far this is the world has never learned,
> For no one who has gone there has returned-
> Impatient bird, who would retrace this trail?
> There is no messenger to tell the tale
> And they are lost to our concerns below-
> How can men tell you what they do not know?
> (yet...)
> Till you are drawn- the impulse is not yours-
> A drop absorbed in seas that have no shores"[7].

Part III

CHAPTER EIGHT

BALANCING THE EARTH ELEMENT

Long standing patterns and distortions of the Energy field we call Earth, can be observed in the posture and the habits of a person. Let us recall the location of the Earth meridians: ST and SP. The ST meridian starts at the centre of the lower orbital bone (eye socket) and runs down the middle of each side of the body, further down along the outside crest of the leg to the second toe. A branch runs along the back of the shoulders down the arm to the ring finger. SP runs from the temples down the outside of the neck, along the outside edge of the chest, continuing along the inside crest of the leg; a branch goes through the inside arm to the inside top of the index finger (Masunaga).

Imagine a puppet where these lines are strings and they are contracted, pulled too tight, the puppet would not stand up straight, but would bend over to the front, shoulders rounded; head pulled down towards the chest much like a caricature of a perching vulture. Now imagine the puppet with these strings too loose, flabby, lifeless, empty and the puppet would sag head down to chest, shoulders rounded but sagging and legs floppy, slouching, it might have slightly inwards turned, dragging feet. Indeed their feet might be the most prominent pointer. They will be heavy and appear either immovably stuck to the earth, or people might appear as though on their tip-toes, cut off from the earth.

Yet a person who has a strong, balanced Earth looks as though gliding parallel to the earth, in constant even contact with it. There focus and balance seems to come from the centre, their belly. They stand well rooted in the earth, poised strong and stable. They have presence, a stance; as we have mentioned earlier in context of the *Hara*.

Persons with marked imbalances develop habits to adjust themselves, either to stimulate or calm these energies.

Remember the Spleen meridian ends on the inside of the index finger; people might habitually rub their fingertips constantly, nervously over the surface of the tablecloth or against their clothes or even against another finger. In order to stimulate or sedate the ST energy they might stroke or rub their cheeks, maybe even with the index finger, thus working ST and SP in a pensive kind of way; some people might have the habit of stroking the side of their throat, along the ST meridian. I have seen people rubbing the lower rim of their eye sockets habitually. All these really are variations of the same theme.

People who have "loose, empty strings" might have difficulty in sitting upright for long; they will slouch into a chair, head down, sliding further and further.

Because of the position of the related meridians in the legs, the person might walk with a slight inward shuffle, such as can be observed in old people. This is described as "an apraxia of gait, which is characterised as a slow, halting, short-stepped, shuffling or sliding gait"[1]. These are some of the outer manifestations of distorted Earth energy patterns, about others, physical and emotional patterns, we have previously talked about in detail.

Now the question arises what can we do about it, can we rebalance energy fields, energy patterns? In ancient Chinese times, the sages were said to heal people by the grace of God (as is happening, on occasion, even today); the sages restored the disturbed Energy-patterns by merely transmitting "the Essence and the transformation of the life giving principle. One could invoke the gods and this was the way to treat... But the present world is a different one. Grief, calamity and evil cause inner bitterness, while the body receives wounds from the outside, moreover there is neglect against the laws of the four seasons, there is disobedience and rebellion; hence the minor illnesses are bound to become grave and the serious diseases are bound to result in death. Therefore the invocation of the gods is no longer the way to cure"[2]. So explained Ch'i Po to the Emperor of China thousands of years ago. It sounds like it could have been said yesterday. He suggests that the laws of God are manifest and easier to understand in the seasons, by observing those as well as the Elements we can find the way to heal. Even though the supreme law and wisdom must be maintained "the law of unity".

The law of unity refers to correspondences between the cosmos out there, and the microcosms in us. It means that by considering the Earth energy we heal the earth and our whole body or vice versa. To heal ourselves, is to heal the world. The Buddhist teachings, and various healing practices are in total agreement with the Chinese stance, so Lama Gangchen Rinpoche explains that "we have caused overwhelming outer and inner pollution, the decline and misuse of natural resources, massive environmental destruction and the destruction of many species. Also both, social and political, we can see our inner negative energy exploding... resulting in ever increasing wars, famine, plagues, natural disasters... violent crime, drug abuse and ever increasing body and mind sickness and suffering... Modern society needs to recognise that individually we all possess a precious human body; if we use it negatively, we can contribute to our personal and planetary suicide. We can choose to go from darkness to darkness, from light to darkness, or from darkness to light or from light to light. The choice is ours. Once we understand, we automatically stop and develop an interest in how to take care of it. We need to take care of our body with natural food and medicines"[3]. More concrete, we need to heal the Earth-Element in us, which will affect each other Element in the body and in turn earth itself.

Let us recall what the role of the Earth-Energy is. Taking Chi Po's advice, we can observe earth in nature. We are aware that earth is the central source, the womb of all life. It has many different states; from fertile fields, to swamps and desert, they all exist, they all have their function; so the first thing to relearn is to step back from and leave our tendency to classify and judge behind. The swamp is a vital and splendid environment for some creatures (and some learning) as the desert is, for its purpose. Each creature has its own adequate Earth - so your Earth is different from mine; your needs are different from mine and they are both equally good; for we are ONE in many forms. No valuation, no pain, no judgement, no discriminating against.

The first step then is to find the state of your Earth - find out who you are, what your needs are, what Earth is right for your growth. Once you have found it then you must find what you can do to ensure that Earth can fulfil its promise, fulfils its potential? In nature, it needs to be ploughed over, dug up, opened up - to let the air in; it needs to be watered to provide moisture for growth; it needs seeds that fulfil the need to create many abundant forms; it needs the sun to warm the earth. In other words Earth needs to work in conjunction with the other Elements, for it is central to all else. It receives and assimilates all other important energies and transforms them, bringing forth new forms of energy. It is obvious why it has been called the centre, or the central churning stick. The Earth-Mother, the goddess has many faces, from life giving mother to giver of learning and wisdom, to upholder of the laws and their defender as warrior and destroyer. Hardly any tradition and culture exists without some Earth-myths, about her as the beginning and the end, the source and the goal.

From earliest times, this has lead to attributing healing qualities to earth itself; starting with modern facial mud-packs to ancient healing groves where Hippocrates practised in the tradition of Asclepius. Our medical culture is based on these and Serapius in Egypt. It was said "not a human, but a divine physician" who worked through priests or "therapeuts" and were "attendants of the cult and who served the god by carrying out prescribed rituals"[4], healed people.

The rituals were held in sacred enclosures, marked off with stones. Epidarus was one such healing sanctuary, but there were thousands all across the ancient world. Later, temples were built there, with either sacred incubation chambers or even holes in the ground where people descended into the earth itself to be cured (*catachthonioi*). The cure was envisaged to happen through energies of the place, or through the appearance of the goddess, associated with such a place (Asclepius, Diana, Gaia) in a dream[5].

These sanctuaries were always near springs and groves, (as can still be seen in Celtic healing traditions in Wales, Cornwall and other places in Britain). The actual treatment consisted of ritual purification and of people sleeping, and or being put in a trance state on the floor in the innermost sanctuary (or on a couch, called clinic!). Many traditions, in East and West and through all ages attribute the earth itself with healing qualities.

Getting back to the analogy of Earth outside and in the body, the above would then mean, that the ST/SP network can heal the other Elements. Indeed one could say that through the stomach we take medicine and the spleen distributes it. Yet in a wider sense it means that the Earth energy in the body is central to healing. When the Earth Element itself is ill, then not only all else will be affected but serious disruptions of the energy flow is at stake. And in order to heal the Earth we have to recall its ability to transform. It transforms manure into roses, and roses into manure. It transforms oranges and potatoes into vital nutritious life essence that sustains the whole organism - including itself.

To heal Earth we have to get back to Earth - Earth only can heal Earth. To understand this apparent non-sense, we have to go back and remember the many levels of our energy system. The ST/SP network does not only relate to the physical but also to the emotional and spiritual. The physical Earth in us (ST/SP), in order to heal itself then has to call on higher levels of energy (e.g. the emotional or spiritual). Since Earth is the centre, it has to go to a higher energy centre. The power to heal then comes from the emotional level or the spiritual centre, which is the Higher Self. How can we do that? How can we call on it?

Chapter 8

The North American Indian tradition shows us a way that combines both the physical earth outside and the Earth at the core of our being, our higher centre. To connect with that centre, to know one's purpose, to find one's identity or healing, they suggest we go on a 'vision quest'. The person is sent under the guidance of a Medicine Person, to a remote location to fast and pray for three or four days. The place where he will do this is very personal; some people walk a long time - they walk literally (or metaphorically) a lifetime to find such a place.

Jesus is said to have gone to the desert or to the sea; Buddha went to the Bodhi Tree; Indian Sadhus go into caves; Merlin went into the crystal cave in Wales (UK), Abraham went into the wilderness. To find our inner centre we seek a place that has power for us, it speaks to us. Once we have found it, "the attention of Mother Earth is directed to that spot, and energy begins to flow to that area, the Earth Mother is there to nurture and give solace to that person" or a vision, direction or healing. "In learning how to find an individual Power Place it is important to walk the land until we feel a drawing within us to an exact spot. The keynote is trusting one's feelings and then being quiet, when our Earth connection is strong, we come to at-one-ment with the Clan Chiefs of Air, Earth, Water and Fire"[6].

The reader might ask why bring all this stuff into the picture that is totally impractical: just imagine one million Londoners go walking into the countryside to find their power place, to heal their stomach ulcer by lying on the ground dreaming! - Ridiculous!

Yes, well said, but strip away the many forms and go to the essence, what does it mean, what was the wisdom behind those traditions? To spend time, out of the routine of ordinary life, quietly, alone, not distracted by anything else, in order to get in touch with our inner core energy. In that totally quiet space the energy of the spirit, the higher Self, our essence can speak. The Self can only speak in that stillness - or rather we can only hear it in that stillness. There it can tell us what is wrong with our lives, where we need to adjust our lifestyle, relearn behaviour and it can feed us healing energy.

This, in essence is meditation! We do not have to go all around the countryside, but the countryside can be in us! We can all stay at home - calming our minds - and merely looking inside, seeking the centre of our being. From here the energy comes to renew ourselves. Here we can realise that the energy of the Earth is the energy of our self; so worship the Self, worship the Earth- they are the same! The tallest task is to heal ourselves; to connect to our centre, become the creative earth we can be, to become our SELF.

Well, I hear you say - fine how do I do that? What about my stomach energy, my ulcers, my wasting muscles, the lumps in my breasts, my low immune system, my infertility, my lack of energy etc.? In the final analysis, there can be only one answer, embark on the path that leads to the inner core, from where all comes in abundance. Sooner or later you will get in touch with some original creative energy. Increasing and tapping into that energy in time and with much devotion and practise will filter down. It will manifest in forms of energy filtered through the various energy bodies and *chakras*, so that our physical and emotional deficiencies will change. Our bodies will have the necessary healing energy to heal themselves and create a healthy new energy flow.

The power of healing is within each of us, and since the path and the purpose are the same, to embark on the way towards the divine healing power - some call it LOVE or God - is to change things on the way. This might even get rid of your ulcer very soon.

We do not have to look far. Even conventional medicine uses meditation these days to heal people. "Research has shown, for example, that even the most elementary meditation practice, repeating a *mantra* or focusing on one's breath, tends to have a beneficial effect on the immune system, and it improves such conditions as hypertension, angina and arrhythmia, high cholesterol, anxieties, stress, chronic pain, phobias and addictions"[7].

Meanwhile other practical help might be sought. Obviously treatments like Shiatsu, Acupuncture and Zero Balancing as well as other methods that focus on energy, like Spiritual Healing and Reiki might help.

In fact the Nei Ching recommends: "these diseases are most fittingly treated with breathing exercises, massage of skin and flesh, and exercises of hand and feet"[8]. Breathing exercises can be learned in various ways. Anybody who likes to sing could try voice lessons, singing helps to learn to breathe. Exercises such as Yoga, Makkaho exercises, Tai Chi, Aikido and even dance therapy can be helpful. Even simple deep breathing exercises or a change of focus and awareness towards breathing can help, especially while doing everyday activities like walking, cooking, cleaning, desk- work etc.

Massage can easily and professionally be obtained, from specific sports massage to rolfing (a deep tissue massage, which seeks to liberate the physical structure of the body, so that they are capable of realigning themselves, without lifelong distortions). The re-balancing will often release the emotional pain and memories of traumatic episodes that led to the distortions.

Exercises of hands and feet again can be varied, from walking bare foot on the ground (all surfaces and in all weathers) to using such available practices as Foot-Reflexology or wearing shoes that massage the soles of the feet while walking. As for the hands, massage such as Hand- Reflexology could be suggested. Some jobs are automatically massage and thus one heals oneself practising these. (Masseur, Reflexologist, Shiatsu practitioner) The same is true for mundane jobs such as a craftsman of clay, e.g. a potter, practising crafts like papier-mâché or weaving and spinning, the hands are used therapeutically in gardening and cooking - not surprisingly we connect images such as women kneading bread with the Earth

Element. All the above can be used to balance the Earth energy successfully.

Hands and feet of course hold the end-points of meridians, which helps all of them. Looking back to the Sheng Ko cycle, we see Earth's special connection with Wood and Water. As we have seen Wood controls Earth, imbalance results from overpowering Wood. By lowering the Wood dominance, we might help the Earth to become stronger. (e.g. minimise responsibilities, avoid stress, give plenty of rest, avoid insecurity, toning down the overly vigorous striving for such things as. travel, adventure, anger etc.)

All too often I have heard on suggestions how to help: this means I have to totally change my life-style, - I can't do that!

Or: what you are asking is not to change some bit, but the whole way I live; I rather take a doctor's pill! Or a patient just treated for chest pains- leaves the house- to grab for a cigarette! - Nothing happens without the will to change; old patterns get just more ingrained. But even that is an earth problem. People have lost the energy to take charge, to act from their own power, they rather had over to others; they are dis-empowered. They have lost their Centre. There is so much going on in their life- they suffers from stress: a wood dominance, they have to change in order to minimise 'striving towards' in favour of stable nurturing activities.

On the other hand if the reason for the imbalance is that Earth energy is too strong, the controlling function of the Wood Element should be increased and revitalised in order to hold the Earth in check. Activities should be suggested that kindle the spirit of movement, of adventure of doing .

As for Water? As we recall, Earth controls Water. A weak Earth Element cannot do its job adequately and Water flows out everywhere, as a result it washes the earth away. In order to allow Earth to regenerate, Water needs to be somewhat drained in order not to make such demands on Earth. How can that be?

Chapter 8

Always, if there is a problem, we can refer to nature to find the solution in the cosmic laws. How does nature deal with such a problem? Wind dries up Water, and so does sun. Thus by exposing Earth to dry heat, the relationship between the two could be bettered.

Conversely, if the Earth is too powerful, then in order to rebalance it the Water has to rise, to break the narrow confines of the dykes and dams and to moisten the Earth. We have to nurture Water. The river gets bigger through its contributors, thus working the meridian to make sure all water is gathered and flows well. Another way is to look for water's mother, Air. To do breathing exercises, to strengthen the lungs will in time produce more Water energy.

If the problem is a constitutional, one might have to look at the climate in which the person lives. In one case one has to ensure that one lives in a dry climate and in the other case one has to live in a moist climate. To drink more, or less, liquid; wearing clothes of the right colour (more or less yellows, browns and blues); choosing ones holidays consciously (mountains versus sea) and other balancing acts of styles will help to regenerate the Earth Energy. Once we get used to thinking in these terms, a lot of our patterns of daily life might have to be re-thought, re-educated and adjusted to what our bodies need in order to heal our Earth Element.

One of the major aspects of course is diet, beside the air we breathe, food is the most obvious source of taking in energy to nourish ourselves. Food as a healing agent, was chosen in Oriental medicine under very specific guidelines. Food has to represent, "a mixture of essences of heaven and earth in proper proportions" (referring to *Yin* and *Yang* foods); secondly it was important to cut or eat the foods "during the season having the closest affinity to the affected organ"[9]. In practise, if for example, a person's root of the Earth imbalance was a weak Spleen Energy, then we are talking about a weak *Yin* organ. The time associated with it is the late summer; thus we should be looking at food that strengthens the *Yin*; (nourishes the *Qi*) and is based on food harvested in summer.

Medicinal Food is also chosen for the effect and qualities it has, that are similar to the energy field 'Earth'. "A cooked yam is yellow, moist, soft, slightly sticky and sweet. Yams are considered excellent food for supplementing *Qi* and strengthening the Spleen and Stomach. Because they are so nourishing and digestible they are a good food for relieving weakness, fatigue and building tissues"[10]. In the same sense other vegetables like pumpkins, potatoes, carrots, turnips, millet and rice are recommended.

In the same way late summer fruit should be chosen, especially those that fit in texture, colour or shape (round, yellow, soft) such as apricots, pears etc. they are ideal for balancing the Earth (shape, colour and taste, are linked to Earth). Minerals are very important for the Earth, (they constitute a large part of it) we too need them in our diet. Since all vegetables contain minerals "all vegetables enhance the stomach and spleen and pancreas function. Particularly helpful are collard greens, which are rich in minerals and calcium" [11]. How important these are, I experienced one year in India. I stayed for a prolonged time in an ashram (monastic environment). As advised I drank a lot of water, as the heat of the day made me sweat a lot, especially during work periods. I got weaker and weaker- the water, although in itself important, washed out important minerals. Eventually an Ayurvedic doctor suggested to add ionised minerals to the water, I drank loads of such water- in 24 hours I was fine!

As a herb, dioscorea root, which is soft and starchy, could be recommended, as it replenishes *Qi*, as well as other herbs such as astragalus and poria; and if the Earth meridians need warming, fresh ginger, cardamom and even rice wine should be used in cooking.

In general, it can be said that extremes of either a very *Yang* food such as salt, eggs, red meat should be avoided, as well as extreme *Yin* food. Yin foods are chemical additives, sugar, spices, stimulants (carob, coffee, strong tea etc.) alcoholic beverages, tropical fruit, tropical vegetables, cream, yoghurt and milk. The balance should be around a diet of fish, cheese, much and more grains, beans, seeds, vegetables, nuts and fruit (the latter three of the climate where the person lives)[12].

To heal our Earth is to heal our Being. We need to change focus to reconnect with, and/or rebalance ourselves with the ground from which we originate and which, at the same time, we are. We need to heal our Core into *sat-chid-ananda*, to Being-consciousness-bliss. "Man draws life from the Earth, but his fate depends upon Heaven. Heaven and Earth unite to bestow life-giving vigour as well as destiny upon man, (to be) effective one must first cure the spirit"[13].

To sum up, the way to heal the Earth is to renew it from its own core, which is its source. A person that has Earth as their main characteristic might find this means that the purpose of their Life is to find that Source, that centre of being. By implication the greatest fear or danger for such a person, then, is that of getting lost.

> And yet, we and that centre are one:
> "We are the mirror as well as the face in it.
> we are tasting the taste this minute of eternity.
> We are pain and what cures pain
> We are the sweet, cold water,
> and the jar that pours".
>
> J. Rumi[14]

CHAPTER NINE

BALANCING THE METAL ELEMENT

As the Earth Element has as its special focus, (character or theme) the notion of "being the Centre", so does Metal Energy have a special "theme", it is that of contraction, moving from the outside inward to the core. The image linked to Metal Energy is, to start at the furthest extension, gather together and then take it all in and consolidate. The classical authority, the Nei Ching talks frequently about this point where outside turns to inside, for example the air from outside gets gathered, sucked into the lungs, then taken as oxygen into the tiniest, deepest vessels in our body and gives us life, it animates us. In fact the Nei Ching calls this vital function the animating spirit, or *PO*[1].

Recalling how God breathed life into the clay figure to change it into the first man, (Adam) in the Judeo-Christian tradition, one could indeed say, we are the "Breath of God".

Another important insight into the nature of Metal Energy can be derived from contemplating our skin. The skin is the outer periphery of the body. Its condition reveals how we literally "hold ourselves together"; how we deal with the "onslaught" of the outside world. How do we take in what life confronts us with; how do we turn what is on the periphery inwards. How do we choose, what to take in what to repel? We reject some things that we shouldn't have taken in and erupt in sores and spots, or even eczema! We tighten and tense the skin in an attempt to keep things in and literally "crack up". Do we feel stretched and exhausted from trying to contain what we have, letting no new experiences in, forever trying to stay the same, to stay young? Is our skin slack and tired and wrinkled from all the action and reaction, the demands that the outside world has made? Do we look clear and adequate for our age and coping well because we react appropriately? These are just a few examples of how we can observe the state of the Metal Energy field just by observing our outer periphery, our appearance, ourselves.

Like always our posture and our habits also give insights. To recall the exact meridians of the Metal Energy, Lung (LU) and Large Intestines (LI) and their position, see Part two. Here only a brief recap: Starting either side of the nostrils LI runs along the crest of the shoulder-bone to the hollow in front of the arm. In the hollow in front of the arm-socket LU starts. Then they run along the outside of the front of the upper body and along the outside back edge of the legs (with a branch along the upper ridge of each arm to the thumb and index finger).

If these lines were strings and they are either too tight or too loose, the puppeteer would not be pleased. In the first instance the puppet would have drawn-up shoulders, arching forward with the head pulled down (similar to the person with characteristic Earth Energy). The arms would look tensed up along the outside, they may also be bent forward; a posture of drawing inward, closing oneself off, like armour to protect ones emotions and to keep others out. The legs would also be tensed at the outside edge of the back, which gives a slight forward bend in the knees, towards the outside (seemingly opening the knees). The feet too point outwards, pulled away from the mid-line; -an altogether hard, stiff, inflexible looking puppet, walking heavy but upright; with a top-heavy chest and a "disconnected lower body".

In the second case, with the meridian too slack, the posture of the puppet would have a more collapsed feel at the shoulders, arms and legs, collapsing towards the inside of the body.

When observing a person with strong Metal characteristics, we might find that they are constantly involved in the thumb and index finger; from a simple habitual stroking of various parts of their face, to constant fidgeting, or very pointed movements. For instance a person might frequently sit with their elbow supported on the table, their head resting on the thumb that is tucked under the chin, and the index finger either resting at the side of the nostrils, or rubbing the side of the nostrils. Another person could be sitting pinching the side of the jawbone half way between chin and ear, pulling the skin. These examples show how the two ends of the meridian are used to activate various localities on the lines of the meridians in the face.

A gesture one can often observe in smokers is the rubbing or circling of the index finger and thumb against each other, or a picking or clicking of the nails of the two fingers, while the hand forms a circle. It looks just like a nervous distraction, but is subconscious stimulation or calming of the Metal meridians.

Another example that comes to mind is the thumb sucking baby (and child). Could it be that it is not just for comfort, or in remembrance of 'food' as is most commonly believed, but could it be a stimulation mechanism of the lung-meridian, to strengthen the breathing? Some people twiddle their hair and pull it habitually with, and around, the thumb and index finger, thus stimulating LU/LI organ network. And there are many more of these outer manifestations of "involuntary" stimulation of Metal Energy, such as scratching and itching which is obviously linked to the skin.

Once we recognise that these habits, gestures and even postures are due to an imbalance in the Metal Element, what can we do about it? And what can we do when the body shows serious tendencies that have manifested themselves in physical illness or emotional patterns as we have seen in part two? What can we do to redress them? Obviously many practises of complementary medicine like Shiatsu, Acupuncture, Kinesiology and other methods of healing the body's energy system can be drawn upon. Can we help ourselves and others to a more whole and balanced state?

Balanced, appropriate and effective working Metal Energy is one of contraction, one that takes in what it needs, to the centre and <u>leaves behind</u>, or gives off what it does not need. It concentrates on the essential. That is the function of the lung, the large intestines and their organ network, including connected emotions and spiritual aspirations. If this function is disturbed or fails we need to find ways of restoring it.

The solution is almost too obvious to mention and yet most of us forget it. I am talking about <u>breathing</u>. Most of us breathe shallowly and use only a small part of our full breathing potential. In fact we habitually deny ourselves the taking in of life-energy or *Prana*. Why do we do it? Some would say, we are simply lazy! Others say, it is because we do not really want to be here - here on this earth, - here in this incarnation, - here in this family. I find that hard to believe, since we, or rather our Soul chooses to be here (who else?) Some say, it is because of the experience of birth: it is such a traumatic experience that we don't want to be here, we are afraid of life, we fear our lives are threatened. Be that as it may, we are conscious energy; the way we are born, the way we choose to be born, the where and why, all are the choice of our consciousness; our conscious self. So why do we not breathe in life fully? The fact is, we don't! We can change it! We can learn how to breathe properly. Not to breathe properly, means to slow down or even hinder the movement of life itself, which seriously impairs and is the source of many troubles and illness.

The first step in learning how to breathe fully is to become aware of the breath, from moment to moment. Be aware of it when you walk to work, when you watch television, when you brush your teeth or sit on the toilet. Follow with your attention, the flow of the air as it touches your nostrils, feel the temperature change in your nose. Become aware how it fills your throat, how it fills your lungs, how your chest expands, (even sideways) how your diaphragm lift and relaxes. Now, do it now, while you read. - Watch your breath, feel your body relaxing with it; focus on the out- breath, a long, long conscious out-breath. Let it go. Don't hold on to it, it has done its job, let it go. All of it! When it is all gone, then you are free, free to take in the "new", the fresh energy of life! Now watch your breath, as it touches your nostrils, the temperature change in your nose, how it fills your throat, how it fills your lungs, how your chest expands, (even sideways) how your diaphragm lifts and relaxes. Now breathe out with a long conscious out-breath; let it go! Do not hold onto it. It has done its job, let it go! Pause briefly and inhale again, fill your lungs, feel your chest, feel your belly expand with the diaphragm, and at the highest point briefly pause and turn to breathe out, long, long and consciously.

"The moment you breathe deeply, more energy becomes available in your body. Where there is energy flow, there is motion. You can experience this motion in many different ways: as a sensation like tingling and numbness or vibration, or as emotion such as sadness, joy or anger. So therefore, if you are afraid to feel, one of the most effective ways to keep yourself from feeling is to control your breath"[2].

There are many activities that focus on breathing from Hatha Yoga to Tai Chi, Qigong or even a mundane activity like swimming. It is not the place here to go into various techniques, suffice to say that people with a distinct Metal imbalance, even more so than just every person, need to look at their breathing. For it is not just an exercise taking in more life-energy, but an important part in learning how to let go of what we don't need! This might be stale air or it might be commodities, past experiences, past grief and other emotions, past relationships, past attitudes. The biggest issue of all that needs to be faced, is to let go of the image we have of ourselves, of our grandiosity, cleverness and superiority - or on the other hand our smallness, unworthiness, timidity and loneliness; our individuality, our sense of isolation and separateness. Let go of who we think we are, and look into our deepest Self and find who we really are. Metal/Air energy then can help to cut away all pretence and in the clear light of cool crisp air show us our real Self. Learning to let go of our out-breath then heals our self-perception.

Believe me, this is one of the most difficult things to do. As mentioned before our self-perception is conditioned throughout life. A story illustrates this very aptly. A child and a middle-aged man are called up in front of an audience and asked to introduce themselves. The little boy gets up and says, "I am Jo Blokes. I am 5 years old!" (That is all he has to say.) The middle-aged man gets up. He thinks, sighs and starts an hours lecture, "I am Mr. Phil Jones. I am 5o years old. I have studied... lived in... I have been married... divorced... I have a car... I have been... I think... I feel... I want... "! The man has accumulated a lifetime of ballast. He has played many roles and identified with all of them. To let go of all this ballast and to see through it who we really are, is like being stripped naked of all social, psychological and philosophical conditioning. Who are we then, when we stripped of all this stuff we associate ourselves with – do we disappear? When we let go of all our props and conditioning, do we also loose all our fears our isolation? As for the essence that we will eventually discover - is my essence different from yours? The process seems endless, always more to let go off.

Conscious breathing is yet teaching us some other aspect. There is a distinct turning point in breathing, once at that point where there is fullest inhalation, once where there is complete exhalation. Each time the furthest perimeter is reached, a pause suggests, be aware of the turning point. You can not stay at the point of greatest expansion - either you decide to turn deliberately, consciously and out of your choice, or life turns it for you. The teaching here is two fold. From time to time we need to stop and think where we are going in life and we need to decide what to leave behind, what we need no more. If we neglect this shifting process, life will do it for us, it never stays still, it will turn us. We have the choice of consciously keeping what we need or let go. Indeed it seems that whether we do it by choice - or whether we are moved as a pawn in other peoples games, seems an essential difference. Letting go then has a very positive aspect, it empowers us to make our own decisions and choices, to take charge of our lives. Discovering and leaving the unwanted and unneeded also means, we can create anew, who we want to be. We can create our own destiny; we become pure creative force, life-energy. Choosing not to breathe properly is avoiding all these fundamental issues.

Breathing, as well as the activity of the Large Intestines has repetition and routine as one of their characters; to heal a Metal imbalance, therefore it might be worthwhile focusing attention on the routines in the persons life. We all have routines and habits. Imagine a smokers life: "every time I have a drink I crave for a cigarette", "when I have a break the first thing I do is light a cigarette" etc. But look at this wider: has the Sunday lunch become just a routine? Is the 7 o'clock walk with the dog just a habit, no longer enjoyable? How about the Gin and Tonic when you come back from work? Indeed the job - is it routine and not much else? How about the need for success and the craving for approval; is it just something we have got so used to, that it is an addiction? Do we still do, eat, talk, tell stories, the same way, when we are fifty years old as we did when we were twenty years old; or indeed are we still reacting in ways we learned when we were five years old to somebody who shouts at us? Is it not time to let go of all these?

These are some of the changes in our lifestyle we have to consider, some of the questions that have to be answered if we want to heal our imbalances in the Metal Energy. Let go, let go of the old and useless and turn to the now, towards what we need now. This can have very practical applications, like cleaning out a cupboard, or desk, or the loft. Sorting out the clothes we no longer need; give away those old books we used to read, change the food we have become so used to, e.g. move on; move into the now, as each breath is happening in the now.

This moving on, indeed movement or flow is also characteristic of Water Energy; thus one way to heal too condensed Metal Energy (Metal Energy that has got stuck) is to encourage Water Energy. Swimming can be a healing exercise, as is just about all movement and physical exercise.

On the other hand if there is too little Metal Energy, more focus, routine and self- discipline might be asked for.

Another important aspect in the healing of Metal Element is Earth (Earth is the mother of Metal energy). If there is a weak

Metal Energy, then maybe we need to encourage Earth, to find the centre and more than ever focus on such questions as: what is important, what is the centre in that person's life? To focus on that, to turn and change direction for it, to reaffirm our Centre, to strengthen it, can refresh our resolve to leave the superficial, the perimeter of existence and focus inward - on whatever level that may be for the individual.

In the Chen-Ko Cycle, Fire too has an important relationship with Metal. The Nei Ching says, "when people are hurt through extreme heat of summer they will get intermittent fever in fall"[3.] We know that Fire melts Metal; contemplating this, we can easily see the connections in the world around us, but also in our physiology. The lungs need humidity, the villi (little hair-like fingers) that moisten the air, will otherwise dry up. Then it will be easy for bacteria to invade, the body cannot process air if it is too dry; thus dry heat will parch the lungs; wither and shrivel the skin, or dehydrate the body internally. Fire, dryness and heat thus can damage Metal energy -literally and metaphorically. Emotions such as passion, a passionate love affair, a passion for sport or dangerous games, even a passionate attachment to a job can challenge Metal to self-destruction. On the other end of the scale, it might be healing for someone with too strong Metal tendencies to be exposed to such strong emotions; a passionate love might entice somebody out of their rut. Love and dedication for a certain sport might heal it, by forcing movement and exercise onto the person; a passion for travel might constantly provide the stimulus that makes the leaving of the old necessary etc. But Fire is dangerous for Metal to play with, something that is healing and softening to the edges might, - yet if Metal dwells too intensively with the fire of passion, or dwells too long on the outer periphery, it risk destroying itself. Fire melts Metal, destroys its life-giving energy.

The theme of letting go is beautifully illustrated by an Indian tale. In India monkeys are common, they are renowned for being attracted to whatever catches their attention, especially colourful items, toys or food. These monkeys become a pest, especially to farmers, for they steal items on the farm, fruit, nuts and other objects. To catch a monkey one puts food or nuts in a narrow necked jar. The monkey is attracted, puts its hand inside, grabs the food but cannot get the hand out. It is caught! His only salvation is to let go!

This tale is linked to the activities of our mind. Our mind gets attracted to this and that. The more attracted our senses get to the many objects in life like money, food, beauty, time or even energy, the more our mind holds on; the more caught we are. The Buddhists would say we are caught in *maya*, the world of illusion. Only if we let go, if we learn to do without, can we be free. However, of course this does not mean we should give these things up. We cannot give up food, we need money in our society etc., but it is more an issue of watching that these things do not become so important to us that they control us, like the monkey with his fist in the bottle. We have to learn to discriminate, to be aware of when it is time to let go, to turn away from it, what ever "it" may be. Thus discrimination is an important wisdom that we have to learn, which is associated with the sword of knowledge, of *Manjushri*.

How can we learn that? First we become aware of our senses, and train the awareness to be just that. To see without desire to possess; - to see without wanting; to dream even without wanting to have. To hear without wanting to hear the same song again, or need to buy the record. To taste the food and enjoy it, or the wine, or the air without wanting to eat or drink it for the rest of your life. That sounds easy; but how about the women who's touch we crave; the man who's smile we want to see "for the rest of our life"? How about the house we want to own, the garden we want to plant, to sit in and own for the remainder of our days? How about the comfort we are used to, the social level we have climbed to...? Our mind becomes attached to all sense impressions, like the monkey and its food! We all have such patterns and difficulties and need to let these go. Such Metal tendencies need to be faced and slowly through awareness and constant alertness, constant being in the here and now, they need to be re-examined.

Our thoughts, our mind itself, must be changed, even our lifestyle if we want to rebalance our Metal Energy. And this is so especially if we are dominated by the Metal Element. We have mentioned exercises that help, questions we have to ask ourselves, but even simple everyday things like food can help to rebalance Energy.

To strengthen and/or harmonise Metal Energy, we look for food that will strengthen and/or clear the Lungs and the Large Intestines, thus free the flow of *Qi*. Food that will moisturise air passages and intestines, or conversely depress humidity if there is excess in either of these. In accordance with the general recommendation of eating food suitable for where one lives, Metal energy is helped by food that ripens in the autumn and that grows in temperate climates. A range of vegetables such as beans, artichoke, beets, potatoes, spinach, watercress, seaweed and tomatoes are said to moisturise; onions, peppers, fennel, cabbage, kale and cauliflower, carrots and mushrooms decongest. Nuts and seafood are said to moisturise; red meat, dairy products and fried food are said to clog the system. Almonds, sesame seed, brown rice and all fibrous foods help with decongestion. Grapefruit, pears, oranges and especially orange peel, fresh ginger and glehnia-root are recommended to aid digestion. Astralagus, ginseng, radishes of all sorts are stimulating to the Lung organ network, as are tangerines (promote expectoration) water chestnut, grapes, apples, pears (lemons, mangoes, melons) blueberries, and strawberries are all thought to be beneficial for the tendencies of imbalance in the Metal Element.

To heal Metal Energy is then to foster the exchange between the world around us and the inner world; to be aware of the need to turn inward and to realise what is important to turn to. Then with gained insight and clarity, we have to "Let go of the rest!"

In fact a person that has Metal as their main characteristic might find that <u>the purpose of his or her life</u> is to learn to discriminate between "what I am" and "what I am not"; and to let go of "what I am not". Such a person has to learn not to hide behind rules of "I am all right", or " I am right", but surrender! By implication the greatest fear or danger for such a person is to be corrupted, to be misled, to stay at the outer periphery of existence, to calcify there.

"Such is the world, and one who feels there is
a fly trapped by that spider's subtleties;
If all the world is yours, it will pass by
as swiftly as the blinking of an eye.

You are a child, an actor on a stage,
don't seek for wealth unless you are a fool.

A whiff of danger; when your life's made plain,
which will be better, death or chastening pain?

Either give up your wealth or lay aside
The rash pretension of your crazy pride.
Your palace and your gardens! They're your goal.

Give up your restless pacing of the earth
To see the Way, look with the eyes of thought;
Set out on it and glimpse the heavenly court-
And when you reach that soul's asylum, then
its glory will blot out the world of men"[4]

Chapter 9

CHAPTER TEN

BALANCING THE WATER ELEMENT

Balancing Water Energy evokes the image of old fashioned pictures of young nymphs or goddesses pouring water from one container into another, from one jug into another, from one chalice into the other. Skilful, measured, smooth movement that takes care that nothing gets spilt, that the same amount is given and received - one into the other, the other into the one- a steady timeless flow. But it is not just the measure of water that is guarded, but the flow itself; to move too quickly, to let too much water, with too much pressure out of the container, will spill it, waste it and cause damage, but too little will equally injure. Thus balancing Water has the quality of fluid continuity. Yet this still is not enough. Water is equally accommodating towards poison or medicine. In water both dissolve un-judged - but the effects are different: one is detrimental the other healing and purifying. Water -like its opposite, Fire- purifies, cleanses; yet while Fire does it instantly (in its extreme as instant combustion - a powerful cleansing by transformation, in the vein of alchemy), Water does it gently; washes, dilutes and dilutes and transports the unwanted away. Patiently through continuous work it achieves that purifying transformation, but it has to work at it. While Fire, with one inspired action, can change a situation, Water might have to go over the same ground again and again - and again. In this way, a person with the main characteristic of the Water Element might be confronted with a similar situation again and again until it has achieved transformation. There is one exception- in the presence of the right fire, water instantly changes into steam!

In order to balance Water Energy, we can thus focus on three aspects: 1) to maintain an even, steady flow of energy in the related meridians and organisms. 2) a measured use of the available energy (especially kidney Qi); and 3) to ensure purity of energy suited to its cleaning task (again especially in the kidney organ network). For example, when "the kidney becomes blocked from fats, salt, cholesterol and stress, the amount of *Qi* that reaches the organs and lower back is diminished"[1]; or when the ancestral energy in the kidney organ network is weak and of poor quality, the slightest misuse (stress, diet or illness) will have a more severe effect than on people with stronger constitutions; or when emotions such as fear, melancholy or insecurity are experienced by the body over prolonged time, the back tenses up along its length and BL/KI contract and it will cause the backache, so common today.

The posture of a person can reveal whether a person has excessive, contracted Water energy, or its opposite too little, or even poisoned Water Energy. The Water meridians both run along the entire centre of the back (either side of the spine and down to the heels). We can again imagine our puppeteer. If he pulls the strings too tight, we can see a puppet with its head pulled back; the chest pushed forward and out, showing a strong front to the world, with the pelvis and coccyx pulled back; the legs apparently stiff from behind. The feet seem to lean possibly to the outside all the weight resting on the outside edge of the heel, in fact it might appear as though the person "digs their heels in", is inflexible and uncompromising.

By contrast, if the strings on the puppet are collapsed and too loose (for lack of Water Energy) the front of the puppet will seem collapsed, sunken inwards, not held upright and seemingly "without a backbone"; indeed as though without conviction and inner strength. From the back a person with pronounced Water characteristics will seem to have a low centre of gravity. People with a tendency to Water imbalances might, when they feel unobserved, stand with their hands on their sacrum, or indeed rub their sacrum. These people will appear as though, physically and mentally, they lack support in the back, which often is the result of failing support while growing up. They feel frequently tired in the back from constantly striving to hold himself/herself up.

Such people might play with their feet, specially rubbing the centre of the cross-arch where we find the start of the kidney meridian, which the Chinese befittingly call "the gushing spring". They might also be seen running their fingers over the centre of the scalp, seemingly massaging the Bladder-meridian; or indeed they might rub the inner corner of the eye, where BL starts. Children sometimes sleep with the thumb in mouth, yet index finger resting or rubbing on the inside corner of the eye. Other Water people might always choose to sit in a corner with their backs to the wall, or on the edge of a seat, and find it hard to explain their feelings. Their eyes might be shifting around the room and avoiding close eye contact or their eyes might gaze, or seemingly focused inwards. They might have big startled eyes full of fear, or reaching out plaintively for support. On the other hand the Water-person might appear outwardly strong, pushy, achievement orientated with high ambition and occupying much space.

Recognising Water characteristics in postures, gestures or in illnesses one aspect, but what can we do to balance the Water Element. How can we encourage healing in the Element that itself contains healing capacity? The latter has been recognised by man in every culture. Water's healing capacity has been used since ancient times; Goddesses and figurines connected to Water cults have been found in south-east Europe dating back to 6000 BC[2]. Celtic pagan traditions share ancestors with Hindu India, and it is not surprising that similar worship is found in Celtic Europe and India. In Both cultures we find sacred sites built around stepped wells, healing baths and hot tanks. Later temples or even Churches are associated with such wells.

Although one finds the like throughout all of India, my favourite spot is Ganeshpuri. It's a village north of Bombay in the Tansa River Valley where such water tanks have been and are used for both sacred ritual bathing ceremonies as well as for the village bath. These "tanks" are right next to a Shiva temple that is a step-down temple, where the symbol of Shiva (*lingam*) is bathed with the sacred waters regularly. The temple itself is very small and sunken, the walls constantly dripping with Water; the air loaded with moisture and even in the dry season, the steps down into the tiny area are slippery and wet. It feels as though this holy place is actually built into a hot spring. Water, spiritual energy and fertility seem inseparably woven together to generate the feeling of potent energy.

Sometimes such water tanks are incorporated in magnificent architecture. Some have the size of a football field and are surrounded by lavish architecture. In Polunnawaru, Sri Lanka's ancient capital, there is a temple complex that houses a bath shaped like a Lotus flower of ten meters in diameter. There the worshipper or priests took sacred baths, stepping down into the centre of the "lotus flower" probably accompanied by holy chants.

One of the most powerful experiences for me is linked to the tradition of Abishek. Abishek is a beautiful ceremony that can be observed in many Indian temples, where murtis (statues that are en-souled) are bathed with precious substances such as milk, honey, coconut water, oils and perfumed or pure water under the incantation of vedic *mantras*. The ceremony is performed with such love, such devotion and with such unrivalled care that the bathing itself is not only an act of worship, but the worshipper itself seems to be transcended by it. The bath-water itself is afterwards administered to the worshippers to impart healing for the whole person, body mind and soul.

Although we are familiar with the sprinkling of holy water in the churches, but to sprinkle blessed water on our head in order to dissolve and clean out the stagnant energy blocks and impurities might be less familiar. Even more strange appears to us the drinking of bath water of a holy statue or person.

Essentially all the practises are there to restore the quality of ones own Water Energy, be it from Indian temple tanks or holy rivers like the Ganges, or through the famous waters of Lourdes (France) and Polish and Spanish wells, that are attributed with miraculous healing powers. Within Britain too, many Scottish, Irish, and Cornish wells bear witness that water has been worshipped since more than 5000 years. The Celts and Norse tribes of old were not only remarkably clean (due to their worship of Water (e.g. saunas) but they used water for medical cures.

Water also was considered to be the door to "the Otherworld". "This 'Otherworld' seemed to have been thought of (not only) as 'another place', but also a state of consciousness"[3]. A place infinitely more alive and beautiful than this world and bathed in sweet light.

> "When all is done,
> will you sail with me in Pridwen, my ship?
> Will you come with me
> to the silver-circled castle
> at the back of the North Wind
> where there is peace between the stars
> and apple orchards grow?[4]

With this background it is surprising that "sea-water is the last to have come within the field of modern medicine"[5]. I remember as an asthmatic child being taken to the special healing places, where salt water was run down walls built of twigs, about five meter high. The air was saturated with fine spray to be inhaled; the patient walked slowly and with measured steps and expanded chest for deep breathing around such 'Salinen', or spend time even sitting wrapped in blankets within feet of the dripping water and read. This process is really not dissimilar to living near the sea - both nourish our kidneys and clean our lungs. Hot and cold bathes of salt water, swimming as a sport, gentle exercise or relaxation in pools or the sea, even bathing in hot sulphur springs are all part of common experience today.

We are familiar with spas, a Roman tradition, which has flourished in Europe until today. Baths are taken in hot or cold mineral springs and/or the water is drunk to cure various illnesses. Often the same water may be recommended for external or internal use, either because it is full of health-giving minerals, such as sodium, calcium, zinc and others, or because of it's purity. Hydrotherapy often accompanies such cures, and for centuries has included: alternative hot and cold foot-baths, pack-wrapping in wet cloths or sheets; compresses for inflammation and to lower fevers; steam to inhale; hip-baths or even jets to rinse the bowels in colonic therapy. Today water-births can be added to the list. Most of us will have experienced saunas, being sprayed or sluiced by water jets (many homes nowadays have Jacuzzis), or under-water-massage be it by bubbles or human hands. Hardly anybody takes a bath anymore without aromatherapy oils of one kind of another.

Prominent figures like Priessnitz of Bohemia or the Dominican Dr Kneipp in Austria, or Dr Gully in England, built on the belief that water is capable of curing every disease "by dissolving the diseased matter and enabling it to be expelled from the body"[6].

Water also plays a major sacred part in other traditions from the American Indians to the Incas, to Africa and to Australia.

Other less "watery" ways can be used to help the Water Energy of the body. As with the other elements, traditional ways of complementary medicine such as Acupuncture, Shiatsu, Massage etc. can be successfully used. To increase the flow and soften the character of Water Energy listening to music, dance and art therapy and all manner of slow exercises such as Tai Chi and Hatha Yoga can be recommended. Exercises that stretch the back of the trunk and legs are especially to be recommended. But equally and less straining is to just sit by a waterfall; listen and/or contemplate a still pond or a clear lake; listening to the sound of falling rain. Tuning into the lashing waves on a beach also helps to balance Water; it flushes out and dilutes the impurities of the emotional body.

To drink too much liquid though overworks the kidneys and then they tend to tire easily. A person with swollen areas below the eyes is showing such fatigue; the kidneys cannot cope with the amount of water. It is even worse if the person drinks a lot of toxins and stimulants, such as alcohol or tea and coffee, which tend to colour the "bags under the eyes" into dark rings; increasing dark areas signal severe illness. It would be good to eat a diet that does not put so much impurities in the body (that they need flushing out) so that the kidneys do not have to work so hard. What then would be good to eat for a person with the main characteristics of Water? Foods suggested for the Water Element are chosen for their ability to enhance the functioning of the kidneys, such as beans and salty foods (small amounts stimulate their work), barley and buckwheat in terms of grain, and all sea vegetables support the kidneys. Foods are also chosen for supplementing and regulating moisture. As illness in the Water Element is often connected to cold, warming food is essential to support the kidneys, such as ginger- root (as spice, tea or vegetable) garlic, chilli, mustard seeds, coriander and cardamom seeds. Since kidney energy is so important and of limited resources, to replenish the essence, dioscorea root is recommended, as are rehmannia root, black fungus and other mushrooms and the cornus fruit, all found in Chinese herbal shops. To conserve and act as a good householder towards our kidney energy is especially relevant if we recall, that kidneys have a special role as "vaults in which the inheritance of the ancestors is stored"[7].

The amount of life-energy available to us is connected to our kidneys and their condition. We have been dealt an unidentifiable but limited amount by fate, nature or God, we should look after it. If we mistreat it by eating the wrong diet (too many refined foods carrying chemical toxins; fat; cholesterol, too much salts etc.) or use too much of that energy by leading a harmful lifestyle(engaging excessively in sex or too much stress and/or continued fear and repeated shock) it will suffer. A dangerous lifestyles or abortions, misuse of drugs or abuse of our bodies in any way – will irreversibly deplete the Water Energy and an untimely death will follow.

Chapter 10

Thus to keep the amount of Water Energy in a steady and even flow, we have to assure that the lifestyle we choose is moderate and free of abuse. The body is the servant of our spiritual growth, through the body alone the soul can learn in this school of life; through the body alone our ability to evolve, to grow towards greater understanding, to higher wisdom, to greater illumination can be reached. Our hope for enlightenment is totally connected to the body, "understanding and protecting the body are acts of spiritual mastery"[8].

Ways of extreme austerity, as are performed by ascetics, are just as damaging to their life and spiritual paths - as are extreme pursuits of any sensual pleasure and misuse of the body's resources. Both extremes damage the ancestral life-energy housed in the kidneys, thus the Buddha advised the "middle path". Here again we are faced with the concept of balance, the character of the Water Element.

The balance of amount, flow and purity of Water are one, water is all these: it is constant movement, pure essence and continuous quantity. As we have seen previously, there is no division between matter and spirit, nothing exists, that is only material, or only spiritual. In fact in the Upanishads, the word for "different from" is the same as "interior to". "He who sees 'the waters' only as a colourless material liquid with certain physical properties will surely fail to know what that word really meant to mankind, nor will he know what water really is. He who, on the other hand, neglects or even despises the internal physical structure of water and does not bother to study its properties will equally miss the point"[9].

Water, containing "the movement of life of the airy element and the gravity and consistency of the solid"[10] holds with its all-permeating nature the role of a messenger, conveyor of divine, sustaining energy. We might experience this when we stand on the shores of the powerful, mysterious, fathom-less ocean and feel moved by its sight to a prayer, feel drawn into a sense of limitless space and time; feel literally at the edge of what we can perceive. This seems nowhere more obvious than standing on a sheer cliff of any coast, when mist draws in, touching the land, erasing its contours and smudging the limit between sky and sea. Air, Earth and Water seem just one.

Such dissolving of boundaries confronts the mind of the Water-person with its own greatest fear, which is to dissolve, to be extinct and meaningless. To balance such essential spiritual fear the Water-person seeks to protect itself, by seeking to give meaning to their lives, by seeking constantly new jobs, activities or partners and friends that protect them, or provide confirmation that life has meaning. They constantly seek confirmation that there is warmth, there is sun beyond the mist that erases all borders and boundaries. Such existential concern, as well as the fear of losing boundaries is ultimately connected to the fear of death. We have seen earlier that the season connected to the Water Element in the Chinese tradition is winter, a time of dying, where again under the layers of pure white snow, all boundaries are lost. The sense of dying and death associated with winter and water is the fear of being dissolved into nothingness, dissolved into the non-being, beyond the understanding of mind and ego.

To heal this fear, the Water person resolves to form strong attachment to people, friends, partners, teachers into which they put all trust; relying on the other's honesty and integrity in order to provide confirmation and stability. Since invariably situations and people are fallible, the search for such stabilising assurance "falls into the mist", and the search goes on ad infinitum. Until a new lesson is learned, in order to heal the thirst.

In the Vedas Agni the God of Fire is actually the "Son of the Waters", he originates in Water; Fire and Water belong together like Yin and Yang in the Chinese tradition. Even Celtic and Germanic traditions share that insight. Celebrations are held where the sun is reflected in a bowl of water, to symbolise just that. In the light of these traditions the search of the Water-person is actually linked to ancient recognition of the mutual belonging of Fire and Water. He/she then searches for the warmth of the Fire, the security, the confirmation of light; searches for the experience for its polarity, in order to become whole. To embrace one's opposite pole, heals an existential rift. Light and darkness both need to be experienced as one entity. Fire and its pole are essentially one. There are no opposites in the final union; in fact the search for union, for the ultimate belonging, needs to embrace both ends of any polarisation: good and bad, right and wrong, fear and security, need and desire, even male and female – all loose their boundaries. The Water-person by embracing Fire heals its ultimate separation in duality and realises that all is of the same essence. The observer on the cliff-top, the mist around, the ground we stand on, the air we breath, the ocean we look at, and the sky above are all of the same essence. One can not get lost, because there is nothing to get lost in. The love and warmth, even the fire, he/she craves is of the same essence; indeed; it is in oneself.

No more fear!
There is no getting lost,
for I am the way that gives direction;
There is no craving for security,
I am the house that gives security.
There is no impersonal cold
I am the love that warmth;
There is no loss of purpose,
for living my life is my purpose;
There is no hunger and thirst,
for I trust life will feed me,
There is no need,
For there always will be enough.
There is no sense of failure,
for I achieve what is needed;
There are no missed opportunities,
In God's perfect time I am there.
What is the use of being afraid, if fear has no object?
There is no sense in fearing even death,
since death has died already.
No more fears.
No more fears.

Svetaketu in one of the teaching stories in the Upanishads can help us to understand. In his search to understand the nature of reality, he is told by his father to place a lump of salt in some water; and to go back to check on it the next day. Coming back his father asks him to retrieve the lump of salt. He can of course, not since the salt has dissolved. His father then asked him to taste the water:

How is it?
I taste Salt
Take a sip from the middle - said he - how is it?
Salt
Take a sip from the end - said he - how is it?
Salt
Set it aside, then come to me ...

verily indeed, my dear, you do not perceive being here,
verily, indeed it is here.
That which is the finest essence, this whole world has
that as its soul.

That is reality. That is Atman; That art thou, Svetaketu.[11]

To dissolve in the ocean of divine love is not getting lost at all. The salt in the ocean is all pervasive. To surrender to the ocean, we give up nothing, - we gain all of it. No need to fear; no need to search, you are it, I am it.

O Waters, source of happiness
pray give us vigour, so that we
may contemplate the great delight

You Waters who rule over precious things
and have supreme control of men
we beg you, give us healing balm.

Within the Waters, Soma has told me,
remedies exists of every sort
and Agni who brings blessing to all.

Now I have come to seek the Waters.
Now we merge, mingling with the sap.
Come to me, Agni, rich in milk.
Come and endow me with your splendour.[12]

Chapter Eleven
Balancing the Wood Element

Picture a slice of freshly cut tree trunk; its colour rich golden green, still dripping wet with the moisture of each cut cell; revealing an inner pattern that seems to radiate from the centre outwards. Each ring is clearly distinguishable; on close inspection each cell can be made out, with its simple structured walls whose strength builds the whole tree.

To me this symbolises a balanced Wood energy. Let us contemplate it. Bold rings show the new growth that has been added each spring. They talk of a steady natural rhythm. Dormant withdrawn periods alternate with a time of rapid growth, stretching from the centre in ever widening circles. Each cell is structured in a controlled shape, governed by its own inherent biological laws that dictate the growth pattern and is in harmony with the adjacent cells. Each cell is filled with sap, rich nutritious moisture that rose up from the root, on its way to the branches and leaves expanding to all sides and up through the leaves seemingly reaching to the sky. Each cell is unique. Despite its blueprint each has its own unique character, like each leaf has its unique identity. Through eternal multiplication each constantly creates more cells, creates growth, is active, is building.

Balanced Wood Energy is aware of its interconnectedness. It is about creativity and growth with foresight, clarity and is confident with the strength of conviction. It is in tune with the repetitive pattern of cycles as a living organism. It is about acting according to that knowledge, going forward not withholding.

There is a beautiful story about the Indian God Indra, the greatest of the Hindu pantheon. It tells about Indra and his battle with Vritra, the one that resists and withholds. Vritra takes on the form of a cloud and holds back the life giving rains. It resulted in gloom and doom on the earth, there was only depression, sadness and darkness; there was no growth neither of plants nor human life. Indra decided to help the world. He drank three lakes of nectar, and thus armed, tackled Vritra, striking him with a thunderbolt in his back and in his face with a pointed dagger. When he had killed the demon, water burst from the clouds and from springs on earth and immediately growth started, the plains and fields started to bloom everywhere, trees started to sprout, light and joy was there again accompanying life and growth.

Withholding is - as can be seen, the greatest enemy of growth.

Analogous to the sap or life-force in Wood, is the Liver energy in the body. Its function is to mobilise and stimulate energy, to accelerate and expand. As we can see from the above story, one way to ensure its proper working is to make available plenty of Water Energy. Wood Energy represent that part of the Movement-of-Life that is representing expansion, outward and upward e.g. taking energy from the centre to the periphery.

During the course of human life even expanding growth as in the tree rings is rare, almost unthinkable. Influences and disturbances from life's movement usually distort our patterns and imbalances appear. Things happen and we react, but mostly not very appropriately, for example: we need to have control over various aspects, yet easily control becomes over-control, expansion can become over-expansion. We aim at a certain direction, but get influenced and torn this way and that; the path of the rising sap can be blocked and frustration and anger result and so on.

We can observe the resulting distortion in the posture. We remember that the energy pathways for Wood, are those of the liver meridian and the gall bladder meridian. The former rises, as we recall, from the big toe along the inside of the inside of the chin-bone, through the middle of the inner thigh. The latter descends from the side of the forehead, the side of the neck, trunk and legs literally along the side of the whole body. If we exaggerate and think of these lines as planks, then a picture arises of a man being held between two wooden planks. If these planks are contracted and squeezed together too hard, the body itself will be squeezed between those two planks. He or she will look inflexible, stiff and even squeezed out in the top, an appearance of being pushed upwards elongated in a tight vice, legs especially stiff and "wooden". This posture can be accompanied by a "wooden gait", which is due to surplus energy in the liver meridian on the inside leg, thus the legs becomes squeezed from inside and outside, as though in a vice.

On the other hand if there is no support from the wooden planks on either side of the body, in other words both GB and LV meridians are loose and slack without energy, then there is nothing to hold the body up. It will sag inwards, appear floppy, oscillating from side to side, without the strength to hold it up. Some people seem not to be able to walk in a straight line. They always seem to bump into the person walking next to them, their bodies and even their orientation physically and mentally sways from side to side, without direction, without purpose, like a tree in the wind. Some people with imbalances in Wood energy might hold their heads to one side, then the other, or craning their necks, straining out of the tight vice. Some might stand with their hands habitually pressed onto or resting on the hips. Some might habitually rub their flank, or rub the "seams of unseen trousers" in an attempt to ease the strain in GB.

Since the eyes are connected to Wood energy, some people's eyes reveal an imbalance. Crossed eyes or eyes where the right eye looks to the right, the left eye to the left, show a serious imbalance in the *Yin* meridian (LV).

Our feet usually also give clues about a state of our energy. If a person has a big toe overlapping the second toe, it is not only to be put down to "small shoes", but one could enquire whether the liver energy (meridian endpoint) is overpowering the Earth energy (second toe - stomach meridian).

Chapter 11

The gall bladder meridian runs across the top of the foot to the fourth toe. Not only have people often bunions on this toe (why?) but a look at their shoes might reveal that the outside of the shoe is especially worn just along the outside rim of the foot. Could it be that the person rests with most of their weight on the outer side of the foot, along the gall bladder and bladder meridians, again pointing at a typical wood imbalance? If the shoes reveal that the toe area is more worn than other parts it usually means that the liver energy is excessive[1].

So, once we have observed and found in the posture, habits or gestures, in illnesses of psyche, emotions or body tendencies to an imbalance in the Wood energy, what can we do to redress it?

Well, as with the other Elements, there are various ways of getting help from outside, such as Acupuncture, Shiatsu, Kinesiology etc. But then we are dealing here with an energy that is active. A person with strong Wood characteristic would probably want to do something themselves. Wood energy does not only "see the problem", has the vision of what to aim at, but also a plan of how to put it into action. Which reveals the quality of leadership, of giving purpose to self and others and putting that into practical action. So the Wood person wants to <u>do it!</u>

Since Wood energy is connected to tendons and ligaments which make movement possible, the obvious advice is to do exercises, martial arts, Qigong, Tai-chi, even walking. The Wood -person might be specially attracted to concepts of Self-Healing. It will give them the feeling of "doing" and of "control". There are various concepts offered: Do-it-yourself books fill the shelves of books-hops; Do-it-yourself Shiatsu, Yoga, Homeopathy etc., an ever- increasing popular industry, although this path is not without dangers. Most dangers come from our mind leading us astray, pride, anger and desires colouring our analysis - we see what we want to see, we cure what we want to cure! There is nothing wrong with this "placebo-effect", but the danger lies doing the wrong things, for the wrong reasons, for the sake of our ego.

One method I have come across pretty much excludes this: *Ngal-So*. The Tibetan way of Self-Healing introduced by Lama Gangchen Rinpoche. *Ngal-So* has several meanings. It means to relax the body and mind completely; *Ngal* refers to relative truth, while *So* refers to absolute truth; *Ngal* also means darkness, *So* means light (much like the Sanskrit: *Gu-ru*). Here like in all Buddhists thought, good health is a matter of creating good circumstances in the mind. Absolute truth persists beyond our mortal life. Part of healing then is to create good thoughts and shift our thinking from ordinary perception of relative truth, to absolute truth.

If we experience for example Physical pain, that is relative truth, which is experienced by the ordinary mind. On the absolute level we can appreciate that the pain is put there by 'ourselves', if we put it there, we can remove it.

Ngal-So creates thoughts and energy patterns by doing two things,

1) by focusing on other people's needs before our own, and

2) by developing positive mind energy through a combined praxis that integrates colour therapy, sound therapy, therapy to open blockages using gestures, syllables and symbols, as well as visualisations and breathing, in a sequence of prescribed steps, that set a daily practice of about half an hour, which befits anybody, and the energy created will go where needed.

Other, more quiet forms of healing might be suggested like sitting under a tree and feeling, or understanding the tree. "Listen to its healing talk" the American Indians would say. This would appeal to spiritual aspirants striving to the heavens, despite their roots being well grounded.

Chapter 11

And there is of course, as we have mentioned in the other sections, the area of food. Food specifically beneficial for balancing the Wood energy should be chosen for its ability to help distribute nutrients and blood, to activate and circulate *Qi* and for its ability to replenish blood and moisture.

So food with a stimulating as well as enriching character, such as sweet, sour, juicy and astringent food, is looked for. Nuts such as pine nuts, almonds, sesame and chestnuts are recommended. Honey is advised as a sweetener; vegetables are suggested such as leeks, carrots, spinach, beets, Chinese cabbage and watercress; fruits such as dates, cherries, blackberries and strawberries are recommended, as well as apples, pears, bananas, olives etc.; and of course all manor of beans, rice sea-foods etc. It is as well to keep in mind that foods should be chosen carefully, in accordance with the season and within the latitude in which one lives, yet much more detailed advice is needed than can be given here[3].

Wood energy is creative, as we have seen. The tree uses the other Elements -Earth, Water, Air and even Fire (Sun)- to assimilate to create something new. In a similar manner we take paint, water and paper and create a picture; we take an instrument, sound, a voice and create music; we take words, ideas, a pen and paper and create a poem or write a book. In another way we take food, water, thoughts, feelings, impressions and constantly create ourselves. One could say that this need to create is intrinsic in all that is alive, all that is created needs constantly to pro-create, or co-create. When this urge to create is frustrated, energy gets blocked and imbalances and illnesses result. Just think of the mental pain over infertility of a couple that desires a child; or the flare of anger over a burned meal; of the mental agony and dissatisfaction over spoilt plans for a certain lifestyle. Think of the resulting irritability because 'I can not go to a certain concert because I lack the money', or the irritation of not finding the right words to express oneself, or the impatience that ones arthritic joints will not allow one to go "just anywhere".

As the concept of homeopathy teaches us - like can be cured with like. The imbalances of Wood energy rising out of frustrated creativity might be healed by freeing creative energy, letting it flow into another branch, another direction. To find new and different ways of being creative might thus help to balance Wood energy. Many projects of art therapy can show the success of this. Even severely handicapped people found great fulfilment and improvement by getting involved in various creative arts, from dance therapy to painting, making pottery, writing poems on a computer etc. To channel creative energy into a new direction, - if a habitual one is blocked off, is thus an intrinsic way to heal Wood energy, even on a very physical level. We all have heard stories where a couple has tried in vain to have a child in all possible ways, then they adopted a child and soon after the mother is pregnant, the life energy freed. To become creative is a truly profound way to free Wood energy, but let us go even deeper.

From where does the tree get its strength? Why can it stand much weathering? What makes it able to sometimes survive thousands of years of extreme heat, cold, storm or even fire? (Redwood trees). They are rooted firmly in the ground (Earth Element), have a strong cell structure in their core and are full of moisture (Water Element) that allows each cell to be soft and pliable. Thus healthy trees have both, strength and flexibility. They adhere, with every ring of growth to their intrinsic growth pattern, to their own nature, to their integrity, their purpose, or as the old sages would say, their *dharma*. Yet, in all this strength, they are soft enough to bend to the wind, pliable enough to adapt to interplay with the outside world. If not, their branches will snap, the trunk will break.

From this observation I postulate, that Wood energy can be healed by living the right *dharma*. As the tree has its own *dharma*, its own suchness, its own purpose so has each person. To search for such purpose of one's life is the healing question that will affect the Wood energy. It is not so much the question of "Who am I" (Earth) or "What do I need to leave behind? (Metal), or "Where am I coming from, where am I going"

(Water) but more the question of "What am I here for?". Once I found the right *dharma*, I have to find out "How do I do it?" - for knowledge alone serves nothing, knowledge has to be put into practise otherwise it is useless.

It sounds completely mad to think that by doing some exercises, changing ones diet and thinking about the purpose of life - gallstones or arthritis or a choleric temper can be influenced. Yet practising the above will change energy, that is a fact and who knows what beneficial effects that may have on illness due to imbalances in the Wood energy.

Dharma means righteousness, right acting, right, noble duty. It is the highest goal of every living thing, the highest purpose, the inner most breath of the soul, "what am I here for, what do I need to do with this existence, what am I meant to do"? That is the question of the Wood energy. And that does not address the pleasurable, but the greater good in the long run. It refers to that which gives you true happiness, not momentary gratification of the senses (that would just be satisfying a desire). This is so for each action, each step you take, each thought you think; what helps you in the long run towards your own greater good? Is it possible, in our materialistic society, where many people believe only in more or less materialistic goals, to find their true purpose of life? Are the masses of disillusioned and depressed people in that state because there is no purpose to their lives?

How does one go about finding ones *dharma*? Ones own personal duty to the soul? It is said that the right purpose springs from the very core of ones being. To find it then, we must get in touch with our core. In Part II we mentioned "being spiritual" as the Wood quality of having or striving for a higher good, a greater sense of purpose, of reaching beyond the pleasurable gratification of the senses in daily life. For this the Wood-person needs periodic time of reflection. A tree grows in seasons, it bursts forth in spring, and withdraws in winter, its energy is cyclic. Similarly the Wood-person needs to withdraw and rethink its *dharma*; it needs to re-connect with the inner wisdom of what ones *dharma* is. Once conviction is re-established, one has found the right purpose then and only then, are we able to burst forth with the right action. The way to get in touch with this inner wisdom is, as we have been told time and time again - through meditation and contemplation. Only in the stillness of our depth will we find the answers to heal Wood energy. Fundamentally it can only be balanced by revealing to ourselves the purpose, which will lay down the fear of having wasted our life and save us from the ultimate frustration of being helpless to act on our true purpose.

There are steps on the way to answer this ultimate question, for instance every time we feel discomfort in our body, or life in general, we should ask ourselves, "what is this saying to me?" and once we understood, then we ask: "what can I do about it?" It is important to keep this sequence, otherwise mere wild action will only produce "wild, useless shoots"; detours, that will cost us; we may even loose our way. Eventually asking these questions in everyday life will enable us to take charge of our life and end those circumstances that bother us. We can then proceed to ask wider questions, such as, "how am I structuring my life? Are there any patterns I can see in my life; patterns of repeated behaviour? What are these trying to tell me? Why has this event followed another event in my life? What have I used and learned from the first, what not, so that I went through the second experience?". Nothing is an accident; we experience what we need to experience. What is it I need to experience? What have I always wanted to do and Why? What do I desire most and Why? If something really appeals to me I should do it, but why? Is this the divine will carrying me into a certain direction, guiding me? What is my purpose? Does the pattern of my life's experience reveal a certain truth of direction, my truth? my path?

Once the quest has revealed what we need to know, then it is in the nature of Wood, as we have seen, to act upon it. It acts not only for us, within us but, - as it is in the nature of Wood, (giving shelter, becoming furniture, tools etc.) it acts in respect of and for others. It seems to me that in order to heal Wood energy at the deepest level, in a high frequency energy field - it has to get involved with others, yes to create for, work with, even serve others! It can not stay in contemplation of its own truth forever and withhold its energy, it has to share it, come out and apply it to others.

For example: it is not in the "truth", in the "nature" of Wood energy to just create pictures in the mind, and dream on, (or even paint them in the back room secretly) but the pictures have to be put out. They have to be shown to others, exhibited, vented under the public eye, and eventually let go, sold. Music has not just to be written down, or heard in ones own ears, but played with instruments, performed in concerts etc.

We have considered earlier, that Wood energy is pulled into two or more directions. The tree stretches its branches this way and that; the wind blows the tree in all directions, the tree itself grows upwards and downwards with its roots. In a similar manner Wood energy on a soul level, can be said to have two directions. It has to focus inside to find its true purpose, its true *dharma* and it has to put it outside, practise it in the world. Only by satisfying both impulses can Wood energy be whole, can it fulfil its destiny of expansion.

The American Indians have a metaphor for it; with Wood energy one has to "Walk ones talk". The painted faces we are shown in films of the indigenous people of America were not there primarily to frighten the enemy, or hide behind, quite the opposite; it had a much more profound reason. The painted faces used in ceremonies as well as wars were showing the beauty and the achievement, the identity of the individual soul. The design and colour was chosen to express the individual's inner truth, or medicine. The painted face is a way of self-expression. It's an expression of who and what the wearer truly is - not what we on the outside perceive him to be. It allows others to see, and in a way open up their reactions to the truth of the wearer; the wearer offers his real Self to be relied on, to be used by others.

Wood energy rises from within and spreads outward. On the level of the physical body, the liver and gall bladder spread energy throughout the body. On the emotional level the anger and frustrations that rise, can be felt right into our toes. On a soul level, it is the purpose that has to be carried into interaction with the world - that is why we are here, that is why the Soul has a body in which it is incarnate.

Many people misunderstand meditation; it is not selfish, it is not cutting off from the world, but it is gathering the energy from the source, from the centre of our being to be able to act in the world in right action, according to the right *dharma*. If we do not know the right action, nor have the energy to act upon it, what is there we can give to the world: if I have nothing, I can give nothing. To give oneself, one has to have something oneself; for doing something right we have to understand what is right action; otherwise we give what does not belong to us, or we do what is not needed, we act inadequately. We shout at our children when they really need help. We give expensive presents when a kind, caring word is needed. We hide behind jokes and laughter when we want to ask for solace. We even kill, when we really are shouting for help.

To give of oneself, one has to have something

To do something right, we have to know what is right.

Nature is not a fool - a plum tree does not give us grapes, nor does a fire tree give acorns; but humans give what does not belong to them. Even if you raise money for some charity to help others, you are only using money, food, clothes or books that do not belong to you. Even if you give generously, providing well for your family, you are only using money, bits of paper to buy your family's love. Even if you are very concerned and spend your waking hours looking after the ill, or teach the feeble minded, you are only doing societies bidding. What are you giving of yourself? Oh yes, I hear the indignation in your voice, when you say, "But, but I give my abilities, I

Chapter 11

give my time?" Yes! But is your time yours? - Or is it just borrowed too? If you were true to yourself should your abilities, your time be spent differently. Are your reasons and your time borrowed, like your thoughts, your ideas, or your body?

> What is it then,
> that you can truly give of yourself?
> Listen to the silence within,
> open your heart
> to receive the gift
> the only gift, you can give.
> The love,
> the love, that is your Self.

Chapter Twelve

Balancing the Fire Element

Having looked at the Movement-of-Life and its energies we found, the Earth is the central focus, a point of balance. The Metal Energy contracts back into itself, descending. The Water Energy flows supportive, penetrating deeply here and there and from the depth rises to nurture growth. The Wood Energy then takes this impetus outside, to vigorous growth; it draws the life- energy up and outwards. In similar terms we can describe Fire Energy; it sparkles and dances around the furthest extension, it is on the surface, it is energy on the outside rim "easy to fly off". The picture of a circus act springs to mind, where a burning ring is held, with sparks flying off, through which the lions, clowns or acrobats jump.

A more reverent image is given by the image of Shiva Nataraj, where the God dances, creating the world out of his movement and sounds; this action is surrounded by a ring of flames. Fire Energy plays on the surface, decorating, celebrating life; it is like a frame to the picture, this very act of framing holds the picture together, enhances it and marks its boundaries.

Under the surface of our outer skin we find the tiniest blood-vessels, they give us a rosy glow, a healthy enhancing complexion, and they signal our outer boundaries; they are supplied from deep within. From deep within the body energy is supervised and held together by the heart. The heart's main task is to circulate blood through out the body to the outer periphery – and back.

In Chinese medicine the heart is also the seat of Shen, which regulates our awareness, our self-perception, presence of mind and our higher moral and spiritual faculties. It is an agent of communication, providing consciousness, sensation and feelings and through these faculties we shape our human identity, our personality; we shape how we see ourselves.

Chapter 12

The flow of energy around the outside yet being held in the deepest inner core, can also be observed in the flow of the meridians. The heart meridian flows from the upper frontal torso deep into the belly and resurfaces at the back on the soft inside of the legs. The small intestines meridian flows over the surface of the back (shoulder blades, sides) and descends deep into the pelvis and resurfaces in the front of the insides of the legs. These two run almost diagonally through the body, crossing deep inside the belly.

Imbalances can easily be observed in people's postures and gestures. Remember the puppeteer playing with his puppets? The main relevant meridian strings here cross through the centre of the body. The supplementary Fire meridian HC runs through the centres of the inner arm, the torso and inner legs; TH runs along the outside of the arms, body and leg to the second toe. To pull these "meridian-strings" too tight would result in a body folded in the middle, appearing as though the legs are drawn up towards the chest, opening up the knees like an 0. Arms might be tucked under, as in hugging oneself, or holding oneself together. Conversely when these meridians are too slack the body appears as too loose, without substance, not holding together.

Another way imbalances of the Fire Element show themselves from the outside is when we can observe broken vessels on the skin, especially in the face, around the nose and/or cheeks; furthermore the extremities, lips, nose and fingers start to acquire a bluish, purplish colour.

As for gestures such a person might acquire are those many variations of hugging (crossing arms over the chest, and rubbing the side of the arms to stimulate warmth and circulation). It can be observed that while (seemingly innocently) people usually have their thumbs on the heart meridian, or actually cup all four meridians around the elbow. People with Fire tendencies might rub the side of their neck, constantly try to straighten out their shoulder; rub the inside of the hand with the opposite thumb, such as pipe-smokers do, when rubbing tobacco in their palm. Gestures that draw our attention on the Fire Energy, or Heart Energy, include the many gestures of devotion, such as folding the hands so that two palms (centre HC) are facing each other; greetings where the palms are touching, or even bowing the head to the heart (*chakra*). In the opposite direction it includes beating the chest, crossing the arms in front of the chest to hide the heart (or indeed the opposite, such as opening he arms wide to embrace somebody, taking him/her to the heart).

Sometimes one sees people, resting their elbow on the table having the nail of the little finger dug into their front teeth (lower) while the upper teeth rest, or press exactly on the nail-bed. Here are the endpoints of the heart-meridian etc. (HT and SI), this thus is seen as a way to stimulate pressure-points. Sometimes one sees people sucking their little fingers, like a baby would suck a thumb for the same reason. Needy meridians in the legs might result in O shaped legs, for there is lack of vitality to hold the inside of the legs up; we might also observe a strained gait, that puts all the weight on the heals, (endpoints of HT, SI).

In the West we commonly sit with one leg crossing over the other. This is deemed mistakenly as especially elegant. It should be mentioned here, because it not only restricts circulation and blood-flow as commonly known, but it also interrupts the energy flow of all the Fire meridians (HC, HT, SI and TH).

Emotional imbalances of the Fire Element shows in people who have a volatile, restless disposition, or on the other hand might suffer from effects of trauma and shock, great sorrow or overwhelming fatigue due to stress and exhaustion of the whole body system. Constant need for attention, seeking distractions and disturbed sleep as well as devotion, that turns into religious fanaticism- or any fanaticism are disturbances of the Fire Element. Total withdrawal from a world that is experienced as hostile and un-supportive points also to imbalances and will eventually extinguish the flames of fire.

Chapter 12

So the question to be faced is, what can we do in order to help balance the distortions we can observe in the postures and gestures or in behaviour or illness as we have seen earlier in this work? How can we balance Fire Energy to exude warmth without burning; to give light without blinding; to be steady and tranquil without feeling bored; to be responsive to what life and circumstances give without hunting after each opportunity. How can we entice Fire Energy to be its best: joyful, celebratory, happy and content? William Wordsworth described the state beautifully:

With an eye made quiet by the power of harmony and the deep power of joy, we see into the life of things.[1]

There are as always the outside agents that can help, such as Acupuncturists, Shiatsu practitioners, therapists of zero-balancing, healers or other energy orientated practitioners who might help us to re-educate our body energy. They might help us to look at our tendencies and characteristic behaviour; because most of our lives (and possibly longer) - we have reacted to situations in a certain way, according to our predominant Element tendencies. But we do have a choice, we can choose to keep reacting that same way, walking that same way, attracting that same illness or we <u>can change it</u>. We can re-educate our body energy, and change ourselves.

- We can change ourselves.

Let us look at the physical level first: The main focus here lies in ensuring an even and steady activity of the heart, the right consistency of the blood and thirdly, the circulation of blood and warmth.

Tai Chi has been recommended by cardiologists for patients who have or are threatened with heart disease and patients having such things as palpitations, angina or hypertension. Tai Chi is a gentle exercise that puts no strain on the heart, yet strengthens the circulation and enriches life energy; the same can be said for some forms of Yoga exercise, as well as the

Makkaho exercises[2] advocated by Masunaga and Ohashi. Another home remedy worth mentioning might be that of rubbing your skin vigorously in the morning when you have your bath or shower, with a brush or hard sponge (*loofa*). Hot and cold alternative showers, cold water splashes and some other water treatments like jet-streaming, sauna etc. that are mentioned in the section about the Water Element are activating the circulation.

In the case of a too active Fire Energy more cooling water therapies, should be considered. Water is not only the polarity of Fire, but the Chinese believe that such opposites always carry each other inside, like *Yin* and *Yang* in its famous symbol. Water treatments then can especially be helpful in order to cool a raging fire and keep it within its boundaries. A person with a fiery temperament is thus well advised to take up swimming, have cooling drinks, eat cooling food and live in an appropriate climate and learn such calming techniques as meditation.

Water is not the only Element though that keeps the Fire in its place. To a lesser degree of course the Metal Element has to play its part. Blood needs to be properly oxygenated to carry out its task thus breathing correctly is of vital importance. Fire needs also the Wood Energy to provide energy to rise, and be available in appropriate amount for burning e.g. nutrients in their proper quantities and proportions. The Earth Element as the child of Fire has a special distinct influence. To have a good stable relationship, a home, care about ones origins and earth as the centre is another way of limiting or rather 'grounding' the Fire Energy. Such grounding can be influenced by what we eat. The activity of the heart, as we are all well aware, is greatly influenced by diet. Heart disease and the consumption of cholesterol, fatty foods, meats etc. are high risk factors and are opposite to a soothing intake of low dietary fibre. Diets are never out of the news, since in the 60's heart disease had become the most common cause of "untimely death".

Emotional stress too has long been recognised for its effect on the heart and circulation and many cures for such stress are now common knowledge. Businesses have stress councillors and stress release programs built into their systems. The answer to caring for the heart often lies not in such outside helpers, but simply in a change of lifestyle. A way should be found to remove the source of the tension and stress put on the heart. As we well know it is not just the heart, but the other organ-systems of the Fire Element that are involved. The problems in the affected person's life need to be found and solved, be it emotional trauma, respective lifestyle or physical heart conditions; they need to be found and solved.

Solved by switching to a better diet, a different job, a different place to live, a different relationship to others or even to oneself. Self-hypnosis, Auto-genics, Autosuggestion, Yoga, walking, painting, music, sports or swimming, anything that relaxing would help and then there is ultimately meditation.

As for supplementing the diet, depending on whether the Fire energy needs stimulating or cooling, such herbs as ginseng, lycii, rehmania, lily bulbs, poria root and carthamus flower, corn silk, honeysuckle etc. are recommended. These and others could help to balance and supplement the Fire Element - Nutritionist or herbalist should be consulted [3.]

As with all the elements, balancing food has two sides. A Fire energy that needs cooling should contain much cold food like salads and fresh fruit, whereas Fire energy that needs stimulating needs spicy and cooked, warming food, such as porridge, soups and stews. Any diet will of course not only effect the organs but the organ network, its emotional body and its spirituality.

My body metabolises everything I see, hear, smell and touch and turns it into me, just as surely as it ingests the orange juice.

As we have seen, Fire represents the furthest extension, the periphery, the surface, the completion of a process. What started with an idea and became a seed, was protected in the ground and nourished; it absorbed Water to grow and become a seedling. Under the warmth of the sun and further nourishment, it grew into a plant. It blossomed fruited and having fulfilled its task it was transformed back into pure consciousness, ready to start again.

Every day we also go through such smaller and bigger cycles, forever completing some, starting others. We say "goodbye" to a friend after completing a chat; we say "Amen" after completing the prayer; we do the washing up and complete the meal; we tuck a child into bed and complete the day; we sign a contract or a letter and complete the deal. It is finished. We move out of childhood to be an adult, we move from womanhood to that of wise crone, each stage needs to be completed, whether small or big. All day long, all life long we perform little acts of completion. Something has come to its furthest extension, to its highest goal so it can be completed and a new process starts. At some of these stages we are aware of the significance of such completion, and we accompany them with joy and celebrations, sometimes even appropriately with fireworks, candles and light. As outside, so inside. As it is in daily life so in our spiritual life, we complete a process of learning, an experience of purifying, an act of worship and at the pinnacle there is joy, celebration and even bliss.

> Let the heavens be glad before the Lord
> and let the earth rejoice,
> Let seas and all that is therein,
> cry out and make a noise
> let fields rejoice and everything that
> springs from the earth,
> then every tree shall sing
> with great joy before the Lord. (Psalm 96)

But then again we go through another winter of cold, of suffering, of deep contemplation, to reach another level of growth and insight, to a Summer of great blossoming and sharing the fruits of our insight, to yet another experience of celebration, joy and completion.

Wave after wave of such celebration, such joy, makes up our lives, even if we are not aware of it. Otherwise we can/could not exist, incomplete cycles, incomplete dealings with others and ourselves would leave unsolved problems, open wounds that will stay until we resolve them, stay until we complete them and be a burden and a problem that influences our body, mind and spirit. When life looks bleak and dark we need to call into our awareness where completion is needed. We need to focus on the problem, which has to be solved and bring it to completion, so that it can be let go of, released from the body and mind, so that the light can rise again.

Many techniques today are available to do just that, help ourselves to become aware of those issues that need completion. The ending will have to come is just as certain as one pulsation of the heart follows another, even though we are not aware of it. Everything that has started - needs an end; it is a cosmic law. Any action has consequences; any cause has an effect. What ever we have started however long ago, or unintended, it will seek its completion. When that is done, there will be joy. We need to trust this will happen. That trust as well as that joy after having completed an experience, that joy of being alive, the celebration of our lives comes from the heart. There is a time of joy when all is done. Joy and completion are intrinsically linked; it comes from hearts singing with the energy of love. This song of our heart carries that love to others, so that we can stand anywhere and suddenly we become aware that some struggle has been completed. Joy and love follow swiftly. We might stand in the bus, or ride in a full train, stand in a filled schoolroom or a secluded garden and suddenly that love pours out and we realise much to our own astonishment, " that just now, I love all these strangers, I love the whole world".

Why does this happen? They say out of grace, because a veil is suddenly removed from our hearts to let us see our true Self. The more frequently that veil is removed, and those waves of love flood us, the closer we are to that stage, the sages call Bliss or Ananda. That does not mean you go around all day grinning like a clown, it is not even necessarily accompanied by great emotions either, <u>but it is an inner awareness of being happy and secure in the universe, because there is nothing else.</u> In other words it is living in harmony with all there is.

Where and how can we contact such love, such bliss? Let's look at the *chakras*. We will find that although there are different traditions, in the main elements and *chakras* can be linked. The 1st and 2nd link to Earth and Water. The 3rd and 4th are linked to Fire. The 4th and 5th are linked to Air/Space. The 5th is also connected to Wood and the two final ones are linked to Ether/Space/or Fire(this time seen as light or spirit). The lower *chakras* 1 - 4 are associated with the physical realm, and in that sense, the Heart *chakra* is their highest. The upper *chakras* are associated with the spiritual more advanced realms, which puts the Heart *chakra* at the bottom of the loftier realm. The heart *chakra* thus has two aspects, or rather is seen as the cross point, as the "cave of divine splendour" and as such, is of the greatest importance. It is interesting to note here that the heart *chakra* is, according to the Oriental body map, situated in the diagnostic area (front and back) for the heart-protector and the heart. It houses a point of concentrated emotional Energy and physical *Ki*, the so called Bo-point for the heart-protector; and has similar contact points for the heart Energy at the back, between the 5th and 6th vertebrae, actually called "the path of God" (*Shin Do*). This concentrated area in the body of heart Energy or "Fire" then explains why it is said to be the stepping stone for the higher realms.

The Fire energy in the heart has been described from two different angles, the Fire of Purification and the Fire of Love, yet both can be said to be the same. In the Fire of Love all impurity, all *karma* will be burned, it is said all actions will find completion here. How can we open ourselves to this Fire of Love? It is also said that here resides the white light, that is the light of the individual soul, the jivatman; the individual divine energy. How can we get in touch with this light to help us with our task?

In a way we, through our own power we can do nothing, we can't "do" anything to it, but listen to the quietness of our heart; there we might sense the love in ourselves. For anybody seeking love- and who is not, it must be the most stunning revelation that love is not given to us from anybody; not from you, not from a husband or child, not from any agent outside ourselves. This love is in us! It is the nature of pure life energy, it is us, and it flows out from us, for us, to nourish us, to warm us and to give to others. We then are the source of love we give. We are, the instrument giving the love we need.

Earlier we ask how can we get in touch with the joy in ourselves. Now the answer is there, to look into ourselves, and discover that we are the source of that love and joy. In Indian philosophy our own being is characterised by three qualities: Sat (existence) chid (consciousness) ananda (bliss, joy). We exist, we are aware, and we are joy. Not bad! And Meditation is the one and only key.

To prepare for such deep meditations there are two useful ways I have come across. One is doing the right kind of exercise, like Yoga, Tai Chi or Makkaho exercises, to balance and quieten our body energy. The other is that of chanting. During my whole life I have never been considered as musical, but chanting is different. There is nothing more moving, more opening to the heart to me than chanting - chanting the name of God. What do you do? You repeat a simple, usually ancient, melody, filled with a few words over and over again. Usually these chants, *mantras* are in Latin, Hebrew or Sanskrit and one could well ask why? These languages are based on sound and have more open vowels in them than other languages. Re: Ave Maria or Hare-Rama for example; open vowels that open your breathing and thus your chest; and with it... the *chakra* ! You fill these words with your love, you breathe deeply, you concentrate on the object of your devotion. Heart energy then flows like a river, it is elating and touches you deeply. If there is no object of devotion for you - if you do not recognise a God to pray to - fine I say, chant anyway, worship yourself, pray to yourself - there is no difference.

> "Let the words of my mouth
> and the meditation of my heart
> be acceptable in thy sight
> O Lord"
>
> (Psalm 19.14)

The way of meditation and contemplation touches certain landmarks we have to pass. To be still entirely we have to grow comfortable with who we are. In other words we have to have answered the questions of the other elements. The Earth has asked us, what roles we play in Life and how we can detach ourselves from being needed in this role and that and instead focus on our centre? The Metal Element has asked us to strip away those parts or roles of ourselves that we do not need and find the "bare essentials". The Water Element then has asked us where does the real me come from or go to, with trust and without fear? The Wood energy asked: what purpose I have to fulfil here and acts according to it. Then the Fire Element has asked to accept and trust, in the last instance, who I am! I am sat-chid-ananda, not attached any more to the roles in society but delighting in the Universal play; rejoice in it, celebrate it. Of course these questions, this course of self- enquiry is a process of growth and does not have to follow the above linear sequence, nor does it come quickly, maybe not even in one lifetime. For the lessons to learn in each step are vast.

So we have become comfortable with ourselves, stripped of all that is not necessary and are left with the knowledge of our own divinity in which we rest. When we accept that, we and the rest of the world are one. When we feel secure in that connected-ness without fear of losing our ego, our possessions or our relationships, but aware that all this is borrowed, just there in one form or the other to serve. When we truly know that, we become aware that there is nothing left, but to fully surrender and trust the universe. In this trust we can look at ourselves in a different light and see that the way we are is perfect, we need not strive; there is nothing we are not, or cannot become. We do not need jealousy or desire because the other person, deep down, is also me. So what she/he has, I have, what I desire, I have got, even though in some other form. All we need is the awareness of being love, because everybody's heart is connected in the infinite energy that is God; all hearts, all beings are interwoven.

If I look at another person and see love in their eyes, it is nothing but a reflection of the love in me. Even more apparent; if I look at a picture of a person and see love in their eyes, surely it cannot come from the photograph, that is 'just paper', it must be a reflection of my own love; then love is inside me, all the time. So all that needs doing is ripping away the veil of my eyes, break out of my blindness open my heart to see the love in me. Yet since I am no different from you, there is only love in you. It is not 'my love', it is the power of love that has taken on my form; it is Love, that loves through me. I then have become aware of being thousands of forms of the Tao; a manifestation amongst many of the divine energies we call God.

> God is within me, I am within God
> "The Father and I are one"
> This is completion,
> Now let us celebrate.
> Celebrate by offering our service to God,
> a new seed to plant
> a new circle of life to start
> but each day, each deed performed
> as a joyous offer to the divine.

It remains to conclude:

As people, we have certain characters
and tendencies that make up our body and mind.
They create distress and illness.
To balance these tendencies we are asked to tune
into natures own energies, the five elements.

As people we are Soul-ful beings.
The Soul, Spirit or Self asks to look at
questions related to the above tendencies to lead
us back to a state of joyous health. Our Soul
asks us to choose to return to our origin,
a balanced state of mind, body and soul;
in harmony and joy with all creation.

As people we are blind to see the source
that frees us to do just that, thus we need
guidance. This guidance we find in the wisdom
of post and present masters, sages and saints that
have gone that way before us. Without such a guide
we cannot find our way.

With gratitude I bow to the one who guides me.

Chapter 12

Postscript

The Movement of Life as Seen by Sages, Saints and Scientists

Having come so far, the reader might well ask on what or whose authority I speak, and I can only point beyond myself. The reader has followed that there are FIVE ELEMENTS as the basic expression of the One Ultimate Energy. We live in interesting times, because the one energy, that has been clad in different garments by many religions has now increasingly been acknowledged by scientists. Somehow during the years of the countdown to the millennium our attitudes and experiences with science changed. What the world has seen so far as "matter", has in recent times with quantum physics been reviewed, its perspective opened. Not that science ever was closed, but we made ourselves a cage in which we only saw "what was scientifically proven; materially verifiable" This has changed. Scientists tell us that the universe - derives from something that exceeds these matrices. Science and ancient wisdom come together in battling for a language to describe what it is, that is BEYOND.

6000 years ago in India, the Vedic tradition began describing the ultimate indescribable beyond ordinary perception. And the process goes on; we still struggle with the same. Then, sages called *rishis* investigated the subtler realms and clad their findings in stories, here is such a story:

When Svetaketu, at his father's bidding, had brought a ripe fruit home from a banyan tree, his father said to him:

> "Split the fruit in two, dear son"
> "Here you are father, I have split it in two"
> "What do you find there?"
> "Innumerable tiny seeds"
> "Then take one of the seeds and split it"
> "I have split the seed"
> "And what do you find there?"
> "Why, nothing, nothing at all Sir."

Postscript

> "Ah, dear son, the subtlest essence of this fruit appears as nothing to you. Even if you cannot see it with your eyes, it is present nonetheless; the Being, that is the essence, which pervades everywhere and is all things, the supreme reality! - That is the SELF which lies at the root of all existence. That art thou, - Svetaketu."
>
> Chandogya Upanishad[1]

To me this story is a mirror of my own ignorance, arrogance and scepticism. Like Svetaketu most of my life I spend looking for this essence, the deeper meaning of life, and its purpose. What I saw was "innumerable tiny seeds", nothing else. And in my ignorance I believed I was clever for I was able to study and analyse, able to dissect the "fruit", and show that inside was nothing but "tiny seeds". Some were big, some seeds were small, some long, some short, some attractive, and tempting, some answers lasted many years some answers only satisfied me for month.

The father's appears a strange and unreasonable answer. I can see/feel my body; I experience my emotions, from joy to desperation, but the "Self"? My thinking mechanism, my inner computer had no concept of that.

The being, the subtlest essence that pervades everything can not be me, because I am limited to my body and my mind; "I belong to me". This is what my intellectual brain tells me, and more over, I am taught to be proud of it, by my culture that thrives on individualism. I belong to me. I am different from others, plants, the tree, my cat and my neighbour. In my eyes, to my perception, to my thoughts, this is obvious. The seeds are the seeds of the fruit and I am me, two different things, two separate existence; from the Latin word : *exist ere*- meaning: "to stand out"; I stand out from you and the rest, I am separate.

Splitting that seed, that smallest particle of matter, Svetaketu finds "no-thing" and most of us would agree. Yet his father has an entirely different view. Instead of looking at the object that one can taste, touch, see and put in a box and stick a label on saying: "Banyan tree seed"; - he, like many saints and sages throughout cultures, countries and times, looked at the split seed with different "eyes". They did not perceive things with the five senses; they thought them limiting.

How can our five senses be limiting us? Science has discovered so much; we have telescopes with which we can see galaxies undreamed of. Oh yes, our senses are excellent, but we can only see - where we look! We can only see what we want to see. The "other things we miss". There might be some things to perceive, but if we have no concept for what we see – we have nothing to register it with, nor language to describe it. It is a bit like a computer, using one language and being unable to read a "floppy disc" that is programmed in a different one. Let me illustrate this with another story:

> One day a frog from the sea paid a visit to another frog.
> "Where do you come from?" asked the frog of the well.
> "From the ocean", he replied.
> "How big is the ocean?"
> "It is gigantic".
> "You mean about a quarter of the size of my well here?"
> "Bigger".
> "Bigger, you mean half as big?"
> "No, even bigger!"
> "Is it...as big as this well?"
> "There is no comparison."
> "That is impossible! I have got to see this for myself."
> They set off together. When the frog from the well saw the ocean, it was such a shock that his head just exploded into pieces.[2]

It is near to impossible for us to imagine such a complete other dimension as described in Svetaketu's story as "nothing". In trying to understand this, lies the cradle of all religion, philosophy and science. Yet there have been always men who "knew" and they tried to communicate their understanding to us. But what did they understand? Passages of the Rig Veda,

Postscript

written thousands of years ago, read like a science manual, it makes me wonder. So let me tell you another story:

There was an owner of a big orchard, and he wanted to asses his belongings, so he advertised for people to come and research his peach -orchard. Many came. The next day work began. Some came to measure the circumference of the tree-trunks, some counted the peaches to asses the yield, some checked on the health of the trees, their age and growth rate. Some examined the soil and minerals, water and fertiliser used and so on. One man came and climbed up one of the trees and harvested as many peaches as he could. Then he sat underneath one of the trees, in the shade and ate the fruit. He just sat there until he was hungry again, then again, he went up a tree and collected peaches again and ate them. After a few days the owner came back and everybody told him what they found. When it was time to be paid, they complained about the one that had done "nothing" just eaten the peaches. The Owner said: "Well, you all have done good work, but only one of you knows what a peach really is, how it tastes, how it feels, what it does to your body; he is the only one who can now with his knowledge, asses "peach", understand "peach".

The sages of old, someone called them "inner scientists", observed the world in a very different way; they focused inside and observed their own mind and as there was no language for them to describe their findings they compared it to "things" that we could understand. In this way they compared the whole of creation to a cosmic Being, they called it *Purusha*.

> He pervades the universe
> even exceeding it in breadth,
> he is all that exists-all time is he
> what ever has been and is to come.
> Yet only a fraction of his glory is manifest.
> The rest remains unseen. (Rig Veda, X)

Another example of how the early "inner –scientists" tried to describe their finding can be found in another Indian scripture, the "Guru Gita". Here the Essence is compared to a "Guru", a "wise Being, or God":

> by whose reality the world is real,
> by whose light it is illuminated,
> by whose joy people are joyous.
> by whose existence the world exists,
> who shines through the form of the sun...
> who illuminates this world but whom the mind can not illuminate...
> by whose knowledge this world will
> no longer be perceived to be divided by differences
> whose thinking has no other thoughts
> who appears as the effect of which he is the cause
> He is the cause as well as the effect.
> All this universe appears in various forms
> but there is no difference from anything.
> It is merely an illusion of cause and effect.[3]

How could the wise man in those ancient times talk like this? They talked from an expanded awareness. They shut out the five outer senses, excluding these limiting agents; they directed their focus inside themselves. In that inner isolation they developed inner awareness, inner sensing. This we call meditation. They found that we do not understand the true nature of the world by looking at the outside. We can not perceive the truth about the world by looking at phenomena, because we are part of them. It is like trying to see your own eyes - it's useless, the eyes cannot see themselves! We are part of some great web of moving energy, as the Rig Veda states: "Though men call it by many names it is really One", to see things as separate is an illusion of our five senses. Only from the inside of the web, seeing ourselves as part of that web, can we begin to understand the essence of life! This is incredible similar to what W.K. Heisenberg declared at the beginning of this century, "the researcher can not stay objective, but participates in this happening". An investigating scientists always influences the result of the experiment, thus all science is subjective and the law of "interference" was established.[4] This was the door that led to quantum physics.

Once we have shifted our perspective from onlookers - to participants; from "outer-scientists" to "inner-scientists", we have a vantage point from where one can potentially "know" the essence of life, or Brahma, or God; energies beyond the normal human perception. "Beyond human perception" is according to the Oxford dictionary the definition of the word "divine". So once we have cast of the inherent human limitations of experiencing only through our senses, we can possibly perceive "the divine", that which is beyond human. And that is, I think, what Svetaketu's father referred to: "That are Thou" or better *Tat Twam Asi* ; a state, from where one experiences all of the same essence, only the form is different, there are seeds -or no seed, men , trees, flowers or cats.

A modern day philosopher, Henry Skolimowski, talks of the participatory mind, a mind which goes beyond superficial perceptions of phenomena outside, but participates in creating them. Such a shift of perception, he claims, is available to all; because we have it all, we just don't use it?[5] And we don't because we can't use it. We act within limited, conditioned mind-space, he calls it a mind-cone. The conditions are all the patterns and things we have learned during our life -time. This fits surprisingly well, to what we have been told over and over - that we use only part of our mind. But some individuals have always been able to look inside themselves, and gone beyond the limiting space. They found a different reality, one were all energies are interconnected, a unified-field.

If we look at the religious history of mankind, we see this basic insight shared by mystics of all religions, but their discoveries are obscured and mixed with beliefs, cultural traditions and expressions that distort it. Why? Because ordinarily we perceived with the "outer", normal senses, and we are attached to them! In India, the above awareness of life within one cosmic organism remained alive throughout thousands of years because individuals never lost touch with the know-how of experiencing this truth. Similarly Christian Mystics throughout centuries speak of the cosmic body of Christ, which is the same concept as *"Purusha"*. (To that more later) But in India as everywhere else these original ideas were clad in images and language easier to perceive with our senses. Many pictures of gods arose; nonetheless the gods remained images, "forms of the essence". Nirguna and saguna; form and formless are one. Shiva is the Lord of all (synonym for divine consciousness and the ultimate beyond) but he is represented in many forms, the most familiar is that of the Lord of Dance or Nataraja. A bronze statue from the 12th century where Shiva is depicted as personified universal energy. He is endowed with four arms; one hand holding a drum for the sound of creation, in the other a flame for sustaining light and transformation. Shiva dances on a demon, destroying what is not needed. The dance itself symbolises life as a great rhythmic process of creation and destruction, of death and rebirth. Creation, maintenance and destruction are the cycle of the universe. The three aspects are at times depicted as three different gods: Brahma, Vishnu and Shiva (their characters again are split in many lesser gods- even though it is maintained, always that form and formless are one.)

Basically this threefold cycle is in accordance with modern physicists who claim the world came into existence with sound and light; as the Big Bang, it expands than it exists until it shrinks in the Big Shrink, a pulsing dance? Listen to the following, it is a brilliant description of this cycle of existence.

> In the night of Brahman, nature is inert, and cannot dance
> till Shiva wills it; he rises from his rapture, and dancing,
> sends through inert matter pulsing waves of awakening sound,
> and lo!
> matter dances, appearing as a glory round about him.
> Dancing, he sustains its manifold phenomena.
> In the fullness of time, still dancing, he destroys all forms
> and names by fire and gives new rest.
> This is poetry, but none the less science.[6]

This paragraph is a rich source of Hindu thought. Shiva rests in Brahman (some source call 'it' Para-Shiva), some "Full Ground" that is beyond and holds all potential. Then out of his own will he sends out pulses. These pulses or vibrations are linked to light and sound. These pulses generate energy called Shakti and this energy takes form in matter. In this understanding objects are manifested, physical energy vibrations.

It is worth to skip to the beginning of this century where scientific research showed that atoms were not solid particles but consisted mainly of space in which extremely small particles moved around. If you tried to observe these small particles, they changed. The subatomic particles observed have dual aspects. Depending on how you looked at them, they are particles (matter) or waves (light). Einstein called these particles first *quanta*. Now scientists had to accept that quanta continually changed their nature; now particle, now wave; and even those were/are only probabilities. Matter does not even exist in a certain place- there are only tendencies for material existence-probabilities that occur. There is neither 'real' matter nor 'real' three dimensional waves, like water waves or sound waves. "They are 'probability waves'…abstract mathematical qualities" so Niels Bohr[7] declared in the "uncertainty principal". - It exists- it doesn't; it's real- its not, all dependent on perception.

Just as in the ancient Indian concept where Shiva is twofold, potential and potentiality; something before (light) and something that manifests into existence or matter. Anything that is matter is created and has to fall back into the ground from where it came. Anything that has a beginning thus also has to have an end, is impermanent; only the underlying energy, the potential is permanent. Shiva holds in himself both poles, birth and death; he creates and dissolves physical substances so that they can fall back so to speak to be re-absorbed. He is potential and potentiality. The two aspects are some times split into two "forms", Shiva and Shakti, but as in a married couple, they are really one.

How could the ancients know? It is so simple! We can re-experience the above concepts by simply turning inwards and watching our breath. We start being aware of "nothingness"- of absence of action, rest or pause before we breath. Then we are aware simply of the intention to breath, - then air floods into the lungs. There is expansion to its furthest limits. Then on the same wave of energy it sinks back again with the out-breath, - and again there is a fraction of stillness and the awareness of "nothingness".

That "nothingness" harbours the sense of potential, is a minute grain of potent stillness the sages call it, the portal of emptiness: *Brahma, Synyata,* Void (or the TAO). This void has an infinite creative potential...it gives birth to a new breath, but is symbolic for giving birth to an infinite variety of forms which sustain, and eventually are reabsorbs [8]. The collection of Vedic texts called Upanishads say:

> Tranquil, let one worship it
> As that form, which he came forth
> As that into which he will be dissolved,
> As that into which he breathes

This abstract view of life was observed, understood and honoured in five characters, five forms (albeit sometimes with different names), Agni the Lord of Fire, the goddess who is the beneficent mother Earth, Ether or the power of Faith, the supreme Spirit of Breath and Air, Varuna the shining God of Water. Thus the abstract was made manifest, took form in this world as FIVE ELEMENTS: Fire, Earth, Ether, Air and Water.

The insights of the few again and again drowned in the perception of the many that saw form only and worshipped it (pure materialism to day - or multitudes of gods in India – there is little difference). The masses of people trusted only their outer senses and developed a science and world view accordingly. Yet both share an aspiration to strive, to better, to evolve.

Postscript

Today some scientists look anew, trying to change perception:

In general, religions share the theory, that a superior Being or God created us physically out of some obscure substance and gave, or breathed human consciousness into it; this consciousness was given through grace or goodwill of himself. Man evolved by the grace of God – he fell, because he sinned by turning from that grace.

In past scientific theory we evolved from prehistoric "mud" crawling "out of the original soup into an un-populated universe and through a wondrous accident and neo-darwinian natural selection an organism developed with a complex nerve system"[9].

In one theory we are the shrunken version of a higher being, in the other a blown up version of lower beings. A humorous statement by Swami Anubhavananda might illustrate the point, "Those who believe in Darwin- are monkeys; those who believe in the Vedas are gods".

Now with new scientific thoughts, understanding dawns that we are part of energy processes, our individual being <u>and consciousness</u> is imbedded in energy fields, R. Sheldrake calls them morphogenetic fields; these fields are organised and connected within other fields, always smaller ones in the greater. In this way we are embedded with our body, family, society, culture, ecosystem, Gaia, the galaxy, the cosmos - and one might presume, we are also connected in higher cosmic consciousness. If that is so, than evolution or our aspiration is neither- "descended from"- "nor created by"- but are "aspiring to reunite", we strive for completion, - we evolve to one higher "Attractor"[10]. Surely in terms of the cosmic laws and the cycle of the elements,- to evolve towards completion is in tune- remember the Element of Fire.

The "Attractor" must be intelligent, have consciousness; this implies that matter too becomes consciousness, and consciousness becomes matter. Are both ways of looking at existence right and just referring to different points of the circle? Ascending or descending, is part of the same cycle, each cycle of existence might take aeons - again a thought that has been prevalent in many religions. We live, so they say in various "ages". It remains to ask are we ascending to consciousness, - to spirit? Or descending into darkest matter?

Teilhard de Chardin, a prominent modern mystic – sees everything drawn to the endpoint of OMEGA.[11] Now science ventures to agree. David Bohm talked of energy-fields in many depths and subtle dimensions, a super- implicate order; "merging into an infinite n^{th} dimensional ground"[12] This suggests both the above – ascending and descending could happen at the same time, different fields, different dimensions?

This evolving towards, this goal - orientation, is part of all major religions. Buddhism is no exception. Time and again people got stuck in the forms, the gods, the dogmas and forget that life is a dynamic moving process with the ultimate purpose of reuniting with the divine consciousness, (dare I say it) "the attractor".

Siddharta Gautama was a prince born (563 BC) into just calcified situation; he started a kind of reform movement to clear pompousness and attachment to the form, from the existing ways of worship. "It is not the knotted hair and the sprinkling of ashes, that make a Brahmin, but the practice of truth and love... neither abstinence, nor going naked, nor shaving the head, nor rough garments, neither offerings to priests, nor sacrifices to Gods will cleanse a man who is not free from delusion". This phrase is attributed to Buddha, but could equally stem from Martin Luther, or other Protestant leaders. The Buddha, taught against a backdrop of mindless, empty worship a doctrine of "mindfulness", as the way to enlightenment, to that state, where we are united with the divine consciousness and can thus see "life from inside". "I teach only two things, oh disciples, the fact of suffering and the possibility of escape from suffering". To stop suffering "one must conquer the egos craving for satisfaction"[13] This means one has to learn to control the mind, separate the illusions created by the ego from the reality, from truth.

Our mind limits us by putting labels and names; attributes and judgement on the energy (as we have seen above) and sees this one as good and wanted, that one as bad. The result is desire, we want the thing that appears beautiful to our eyes - we then attach our mind to the illusions and when we can't get it - we suffer. But, whichever object or quality we "think" they are and desire, - they all are temporary; they disappear again, because energy moves constantly, changes into a different form. This second part of Buddha's teaching therefore is called the law of impermanence.

We must learn to use the mind to transcend the mind (lojong), its attachments and illusions and return to the pure state from where we can be inner scientists and understand life as it really is, as changing; then we are en - lightened, we know! We know that we are all moving energy, it is said in the Visuddhi-Maggai VIII:

> "The being of a past moment of thought has lived, but does not live; nor will it live.
>
> The being of a future moment of thought will live, but has not lived, nor does live.
>
> The being of the present moment of thought does live, but has not lived, nor will it live".[14]

How is this fluctuation governed, what laws, what order is followed, or is it chaotic? Buddhism as a whole, and especially Tibetan Buddhism in the *Kargypta* order (the spiritual home of his Highness the Dalai Lama) pays great tribute to the lesser known, yet very crucial principle of "Dependent Arising"[15]. The Buddha taught that changeability, which results from impermanence, is not identical with chaos or arbitrariness, but is subject to a order that is generally known as cosmic laws, or causality.

Life-energy, in essence is constant, but it changes its expression. We can compare it to a river. The Water remains the same, but his micro-climate, his ground, the speed in which it flows, what lives and grows in it, etc. continually alter with every pebble that falls into it, with every rock that is in its way. - Yet the river still keeps its direction of movement and preserves its identity. Our problem is that, when observing that river, we fix our gaze on a particular section, we even judge that section, that experience, the people and events involved. It is like seeing one still-frame of a whole movie; we are blind to the rest and can't see the whole, what causes, what depends on what; or results in what. Yet we act and suffer as though that fragment is the whole river.

When a disciple asked the Buddha about this, he, of course could see the "whole river", could see exactly what events, subtle currents and energies led to the picture that was represented. It is said, he would know why a peacock had such extraordinary feathers, even though the reason for it might be millions of years ago. Looking at the whole web it is obvious why its parts are the way they are, all is one, albeit a complex one. Does that not remind you of D. Bohm implicate order of nth dimensions? But then who of us can look at the whole? On the other hand looking at one thread of a spiders web, - the thread seems a pretty silly waste of time, a sad useless piece of work. So we aspire to see the whole.

Although Buddhist doctrines vary, the teaching that life is all "One" is emphasised by all branches. The truth of Oneness of all life can only be fully realised, when false notions of a separate self are forever annihilated. In this truth Hinduism or Buddhism show no difference. Buddhist monks went to South East Asia and to the north into Nepal and Tibet and from there to China and Japan, everywhere creating their own version of the essential teachings. Ruth Fuller Sasaki, head of a famous teaching centre in Kyoto, wrote: "Only THIS -capital THIS is. Anything and everything that appears to us as an individual entity, or phenomenon, whether it be a planet or an atom, a mouse or a man, is but a temporally manifestation of THIS in form; every activity that takes place whether it be birth or death, loving or eating breakfast, is but a temporally manifestation of THIS, in activity. Each one of us is but a cell, as it were, in the body of the Great Self, a cell that comes into being, performs its functions and passes away, transformed into another manifestation. Though we have temporary individuality, that temporary limited individuality is neither a true self, nor our true self. Our true self is the Great SELF; our true body is the Body of Reality"[16]

In China, Indian metaphysic abstraction mixed with Taoist love of paradox and Confucian pragmatism (focus on life in the here and now). The essence of Taoism is collected in short aphorisms in the Tao Te Ching, attributed to Lao Tzu who reputedly states in the opening lines: "The Tao that can be expressed is not the eternal Tao". In the beginning we hinted at the same when we have said that really it is impossible to communicate the nature of the essence, the Absolute, or in the words of Chuang Tzu:

> If it could be talked,
> everybody would have told their brother[17]

As with the Indian sages, the Taoist philosophers withdrew from outer life, mainly into isolated spots of nature to meditate upon the order of things and gained their insights from observation of nature and focused inwards.

> The softest thing in the Universe
> Overcomes the hardest thing in the Universe
> That without substance can enter where there is no room
> Hence I know the value of non-action.
> Teaching without words and work without doing
> Are understood by very few[18].

The most widely known symbol of Taoism is that of *Yin* and *Yang*. In Taoist perception the One is expressing itself in a paradox, or as opposites. Ultimate truth is only revealed when both opposing poles are seen as ONE. Thus to describe Yin and Yang as two opposites does not capture the true essence of the symbol. Like two poles they cannot exist without each other, they are always together; talking about one, always implies the opposite. They define each other, they produce and destroy each other; they are a rhythmic cycle between two polarities in constant flux. With this fluid understanding of Yin and Yang we see that duality is only a play - or a dance as the image of the dancing Shiva who's movement manifests and destroys itself continuously, or a law of impermanence as Buddhism will have it. The Indian Poet-saint Janeshwar Maharaj, Lord of knowledge, King and poet (1271) describes the mystery:

> That One who exists, when nothing else is,
> That One who is seen, when nothing else is
> That One who is enjoyed, when nothing else is
> That One Alone is [19]

Although this might sound simplistic to the Western intellectual, the implications of this "simple truth" are far reaching. To give just a few examples:

If you are basically of the same essence as your enemy, you can not hate him, for hating him means hating yourself!

If 'You' are of the same essence as the trees, how can you cut them down , for you are cutting into our own essence!

If 'You' are of the same essence of the Earth, how can you poison it with pesticides, and cover it with tarmac, you poison your own skin!

If 'You' are of the same essence as Water and Air, how can you pollute them, it is polluting your own life!

If 'You' are of the same essence as other creatures, by killing them, you kill yourself.

Postscript

The list could be endless. The basic truth might sound reasonable to us, yes - we must not cut trees, poison earth, air, water etc. but then we have to go just one step further. We have to realise that the One that is talked about, is not just "out there" in the environment, but means us, is inclusive of you and me, - that is difficult. Even if we attempt to treat the environment with respect and love, can we treat ourselves with respect and love? What does it mean? If we are divine essence, if you are divine essence, do you look after yourself as you would look after God? Honour and love your neighbour as they self, as one divine essence? It is so hard to imagine, because of the image we have of God- and worse, we forget it is "just an image". How can we worship the Absolute if it is beyond what we imagine?

Tukaram, another Poet-saint of Maharashtra (1608-1649) sings about it:

> Who is the one that conceives?
> Who is the one that is born?
> I cannot fathom your love of form
>
> Who is the one that asks?
> Who is the one that gives?
> O Benevolent One
> I cannot fathom your form of love
> Who is the one that experiences?
> Who creates the experience?
> O Benevolent One
> I can not fathom your form of love.
>
> Who is the one that manifests?
> Who is the un-manifested one?
> O Benevolent One
> I cannot fathom your love of form
>
> Says Tuka
> It is you everywhere
> and you are everything other than you.[20]

Postscript

The concept of seeing the world "out-there" as "objective" and simultaneously as subjective is hard for us because basically it is defying the programming of our mind. As we said, our mind depends on the senses - by and large they react to matter only. We have to literally go "out of our mind" to fully understand the universe subjective. That is why – again most sages insist - we have to leave our mind and sink into our heart. We have to learn to perceive from a different angle. This is not unlike modern science and philosophy. Henry Skolimowski talks of bursting the walls of the mind-cone[21]. David Bohm talks of the "holomovement", the universe is a dynamic, moving hologram, where everything within has access to understanding everything else[22]. The trouble is, we have to resign ourselves to a language of metaphors, examples and analogies to communicate it – even if we experience it.

Ken Wilbert states that as a small child we have naturally a similar, holistic perception. A child feels totally at one with the environment, for it there is no distinction between the outer world and the inner world. It is easy to observe. The child smiles at friend or foe- it cannot distinguish. It touches the flame of the candle with the same eagerness as the ice-cream, unaware that one will hurt. The child still sees the world undifferentiated, without judgement, without discrimination. I am not for a minute advocating that we should behave in the same way, but the state of mind that is behind such behaviour is what we need to explore. We can describe it as a state of innocence that is reached not because we cannot discriminate, but precisely because we use right discrimination. We must learn to distinguish between the outer appearance of things and the inner truth. To use discrimination to reach such a holistic view of the true nature of things, is a major aspect of two lesser- known concepts of Asian wisdom.

In the Himalayas, cut off for thousands of years from much disturbance, original Hinduism and Buddhism created two brands of philosophy, which gained increasing influence in this century. They have many similarities: Tibetan Buddhism and non-dual Kashmir - Shaivism. Srong-bcasgampo, the Tibetan

Postscript

King in 616 AD sent for Buddhist scripts from Kashmir and ever since Kashmir played an important role in transmitting Buddhism from India to Tibet. Tibetan Buddhism has become very attractive to the west through the teachings of many honourable Lamas and H.H. the Dalai Lama. Sogyal Rinpoche writes in his book on Tibetan Buddhism how discrimination can be used to strip away our false perception and all that obscures our true nature of Ground Luminosity, or "Clear Light where consciousness itself dissolves into the all encompassing space of truth."[23]. Sogyal Rinpoche describes three levels, or states of this light, of potential energy: the ground (base), the rising (activity) and the created object (manifestation). *Dharmakaya, Sambhogakaya, Nimanakaya.* This threefold rhythm we found in the stages of Shiva and know from the Christian principle of the Trinity.

Kashmir was from the first century BC a centre for spiritual studies, where great councils took place regularly attended by more than 5oo monks and scholars who exchanged wisdom and learning. Although Kashmir-Shaivism is said to date back into furthest antiquity its main proponent lived in the 11th century, Abhinavagupta. According to an ascetic called Vasugupta, after a revelation he found a stone "on which were inscribed the Aphorisms of Shiva (the Shiva *sutras*) consisting of some eighty brief statements that describe the very abstract notions of a 'doctrine of vibration'"[24.] Its tenet being, "that the entire universe is nothing but conscious energy and that everything in the universe is nothing but consciousness expressed in different forms..."[25] In fact everything that exists is a "ray of the light of consciousness. Consciousness has two aspects: Light and awareness"[26]. The light is the same as the "Clear Light" of Buddhism which is the source of space and movement. "In fact the ancient Sanskrit word *akasa* describes space as 'Space of consciousness' through which things 'step into visible appearance' become corporeal or manifest"[27]. Consciousness as universal essence is called Shiva, or "the heart of the Lord"[28] and is seen as omnipresent, omnipotent and omniscient and endowed with self-awareness. Of its own free will it obscures its self-awareness, and thus limits its consciousness. This limitation gives rise to "frustration, unrest, action"; this action sets waves of energy free. Creative energy, "Shakti" manifests form. Just as it is the nature of fire to burn, similarly it is the nature of divine energy to manifest itself in a playful game that is without judgement.

The separation of the One into two (similar to the Taoist concept of Yin and Yang) and further into manifestation of "real form" takes place in Kashmir Shaivism in no less than thirty six steps or *tattvas* that bring extremely subtle energies down to less subtle energies. Only in the second half they become linked to the senses and only in the last four stages (32 to 36) energy is in such a gross state that it can be perceived; in the final step energy manifests in the FIVE ELEMENTS, components of the physical world. Consciousness has taken form.

Now we can see the importance of discrimination. The higher and finer we tune our awareness the more we can see subtler energies, behind what our senses perceive. Suffering only appears because our mind perceives only the gross, separate reality. It is under the illusion that things happen to US, instead of realising that we are It; suffering can be transformed by the awareness of unity of all beings. Things just happen, we just exist there is nothing but beneficial, creative, intelligent energy, we could call it love, life- energy or in its purest form , it is called bliss (*ananda*). Active Bliss surely is Love! Hildegard von Bingen calls it greening power: VIRIDITAS.

> We are that creative energy with our own part to play
> structuring the world; we are co-creators in the process of
> life; or as a Buddhist would say: we all have our *dharma*
> to live, or as a Hindu would say:
>
> Love is the firstborn, loftier than the Gods
> The father and men,
> Altogether mighty
> To you we pay homage

> Greater than the breath of Earth and Ether
> or of Waters and Fire .
>
> Beyond the reach of Wind and Fire
> the Sun or the Moon
> You, O Love are the eldest of all
> altogether mighty
> To you we pay homage.
>
> Atharva Veda; Av 1,2,15, 20,24-[29]

In the West we have been stuck in a split perception of sacred and secular. As a result we are left with a fragmented society that gets further and further involved in creating more diverse parts, dissecting, analysing, looking at bits and forgetting the whole. This is termed the Cartesian world – view and allows people "to treat matter as dead and completely separated from themselves and to see the material world as a multitude of different objects assembled into a huge machine. Such a mechanistic world view was held by Isaac Newton who constructed his mechanics on its basis and made it the foundation of classical physics"[30]

It started in the 6th century BC - until then science, philosophy and religion were not separate. The sages of the Milesian school of Iona had the same aim as their eastern brothers, to discover the essential nature of things they called *physi*s. The Milesians saw no difference between spirit and matter, animate and inanimate; all forms of existence were manifestations of life and spirit. In fact all things were supported by cosmic breath, *pneuma*. Heraclitus saw the world as a dynamic and cyclic interplay of opposites and any pair of opposites rested in unity he called *Logos*... the word.

But soon the divine principle was lifted to that which <u>stands above</u> the world. With that, the first step was taken in the shism of spirit and matter that lead to the dualism, which characterises Western science and philosophy. Democritus was the first to mentioned atoms as the base building blocks that were not divisible, pure matter. Yet Plato became quickly his opponent, strangely predicting something like quantum physics. If we think of an atom as a thing, Plato argued, then it must take up some space, therefore it can be cut in half to occupy a smaller space. Anything that can be cut in half is not the smallest constituent of the material world. By this impeccable reasoning, Plato demolishes the argument. "Whatever it is that builds the world, it must be something, so tiny, that it occupies no space, or be of a different nature, such as indivisible matter... or energy[31].

In those days people like Pythagoras (born 582 BC, a contemporary of Buddha Gautama) and his followers still felt that the "highest level of spiritual experience came from contemplating the essence of all reality." He believed that music, astronomy and mathematics were all interconnected and that cosmic wonder and intellectual delight were part of the same experience. The Pythagorean brotherhood became a religious order with ascetic rules of life. Their basic tenet was that human beings reflected the whole universe within themselves.

Even in the great traditions of Judaism and Christianity mystics have seen beyond the separation. From early prophets Isaiah and Ezekiel to the Hasidic tradition and mystics like Baal-Shem-Tov to such honoured sages as Rabbi Nachman of Bratslav, every Rabbi, every mystic of Judaism was filled with yearning and devotion for reunion with the divine - deve kut, or *Ein Sof* for nothing exists outside the divine energy, as it says in the Psalm: "God is the sun and the shield", the cause and the effect.

Christian mysticism begins with Jesus who experienced the Ultimate expressing itself in the word *Abba*, which is translated as "Father", a term relating to a unique intimate relationship, a union between father and son, creator and created. This certainly is the "mystical tradition which is the very life of the Church. Without that it has no meaning at all"[32]. The metaphor of "relationship" means there are inherently two entities involved, one who relates and one who is related to, which is

Postscript

quite different from the statement "I am the father" which is without duality yet "the two become One"[33] Thus Jesus can say of himself:

> I am the way; I am the truth and I am life
> ...if you knew me, you would know my father too
> ...I am not myself the source of the words I speak to you
> it is the father who dwells in me, doing his work
> Believe me , when I say that I am in the Father
> and the Father is in me,...
> ...the Spirit of truth...you know him, because
> he dwells in you and is you..
>
> John 14. 4...21

On a deep level there is "One; you converge on the original source"[34]. But there is a fundamental difference in the interpretation, of how the relationship between the One and the many forms is seen. In the East, they <u>are it;</u> in the Christian Tradition, they <u>have a</u> 'relationship', a communion. "We are one and yet distinct, there is never total loss of self in consciousness, there is pure identity, because love involves two, and yet the two become one"[35]. And herein lies the mystery. The word "love" itself has taken on a different meaning from what we have learned from the Vedic texts. It is no more ground of all existence, but an expression of relationships so there remains some measure of duality at least for mainstream Christianity; there is God and the Self, the human being.

Increasingly through history the description of the Ultimate got clouded and separated out, into a hierarchical God figure and the rest of creation as represented by the churches. This attitude calcifies into a doctrine that mystics right up to our time have rejected.

And there have been many Christian mystics throughout our history, we just have lost track of them. There are such outstanding people as Francis von Assisi, Mechthild of Magdeburg, Julian of Norwich, Niolas of Cusa to name just a

Postscript

few and not to forget the anonymous author of "the cloud of unknowing". These can stand side by side with the mystics of the East.

One outstanding figure is the 11 th century mystic, Hildegard von Bingen, a scholar, musician, painter, medic and writer. Her mystical experiences started at the age of three, but like so many, at first she dared not to speak of them. At eight she took the vows of a nun and later, on the following command, she began to write an account of her visions. " Oh weak person... speak and write what you see and hear... speak and write those things not according to human speech or human inventiveness, but according to the extent that you see and hear those things in the heavens above in the marvellous-ness of God. Bring to light those things by way of explanation..."[36] Her main book is called "Know the Ways", it contains her visions, paintings and music. She also wrote a medical book called *Causae et Curae;* her art work is collected in a further book as "Illuminations" She approached any subject in a scientific, analytical manner much beyond her time. Her scientific thought never let go of the connection that "all science comes from God". For her the link between science and spirituality is art and she states that

> "God has arranged all things in the world in
> consideration of everything else"[37].

Her visual interpretations are detailed and indeed illuminating. In one, she gives the image of the cosmos as an egg, a living organism, - which is itself the cosmic Christ containing the torch or Sun as the Christ-light. For her the cosmic Christ, or Christ consciousness finds its incarnation in us and our life's work. "God resides in all of us", we are the instruments of divine peace which is non-other, than returning to our origin the bliss of Christ -consciousness. There is a drawing of the "cosmic wheel"; a loving God figure has as his chest the wheel that is the cosmos. Another picture shows a beautiful *mandala* where inexhaustible, prolific growth and the regenerative process of life is depicted as a cosmic tree... and many more. All of these *mandalas* have five inner circles. Hildegard wove her *mandalas* out of the FIVE ELEMENTS. They were recognised as constituting the essential elements of cosmos and human body. To create peace one needed to create equilibrium and harmony between the FIVE ELEMENTS within the human body and nature. "Inner Peace is the cause, outer peace is the result" might be a Tibetan slogan but if so, Hildegard must have know it.

FR.M.D. Chenu, a great scholar and contemporary of Hildegard says: "the whole penetrates each of its parts, we are one with the universe. It is a single whole and thus it has sacramental character. Even without people contemplating it, the sacramental universe is filled with God."[38] A sentiment surely in tune with any mystic and moreover with D. Bohm idea of "holomovement".

Both Hildegard von Bingen and her earlier compatriot Meister Eckhardt stem from the Celts who settled in the Rhineland and who were reputedly closely linked to nature which shows in Hildegard's rich connections and were linked in their spirituality, to the Hindu Tradition[39]. For the Celts, the earth was a living organism, with every rock, animal, tree and flower imbued with the same spirit that flowed through women and man. The power of the Elements was revered and part of everyday life, and they took form in a rich culture of myths of gods and goddesses. Their mystic traditions were, and are still, cultivated by the druids.

Meister Eckhardt. (1260-1327) became a Dominican friar and left much literature. He wrote: "When you pour a drop into the stormy sea, the drop changes into the sea and not the sea into the drop." And furthermore: "If I am to know God, in such an unmediated way, then I must simply become God and God must become me. I would express it more exactly by saying that God must simply become me and I must become God, so completely one, that this 'he' and this 'I' share one 'is' and in this 'is-ness' do our work eternally. For this 'he' and this 'I', that is God and the soul, are fruitful as we eternally do one work"[40].

Postscript

Thomas Aquinas, set out his *Summa Theologicae* to remind the influential Roman Catholic theology that "the light of reason burns in every human being... and the difference between divine revelation and scientific inquiry result from false reasoning;" yet when he had a mystical experience of great intensity on the day of St. Nicholas in 1273, he realised that "everything that I have written seems to me like straw, in comparison with the things that I have seen and that have been revealed to me." In total awe he downed 'his tools'; and thereafter never wrote another word. "This episode illustrates the staggering nature of mystical rapture... (and) presumably direct knowledge of that mysterious background of pure consciousness... ultimate reality"[41].

Teresa of Avila writes for her nuns in the 16th century: "All the harm comes in not fully understanding that He is very near, but in imagining that he is far away... Even in the midst of our jobs we must withdraw into ourselves, even if it is only for a moment, and remember that I have that company within myself...strive to remember that the one with whom you are speaking, is present within you. When you listen, remember that you are hearing the One who is very close to you...All one need to do, is go into solitude and look at Him within oneself...the Lord is within us, and there we must be with him." (The Way of Perfection).

A hundred years later Angelius Selisius, hailed as the European Zen poet sums up both mystics from East and West writing, "the wise have one wish left; to know the whole, the Absolute. The foolish lose themselves in fragments and ignore the root."[42]

Turning to Islam we come across the same world wide problem, on one hand the established calcified structure of the religion, and on the other the wise-man and mystics. Mainstream Islam is adamant there is no God apart from Allah. Another exclusive religion that fosters separateness... "if there is one unforgivable sin in Islam, it is that of associating anything or anyone with God apart from the Prophet

Postscript

Mohammed"[43]. On the other hand Islam has produced a fine mystic tradition, Sufism.

> The universe is like a mirror of God
> the mirror that shows His majesty and glory,
> the mirror in which He Himself is reflected
> as is the heart of man,
> It is the mirror of the universe,
> if the traveller aims to know God;
> he must look into his own heart.
>
> Aziz a -Nasafi (7-8 th century C.E.)

Kabir and Rumie are probably the two most well known mystical poets of the later part of the Sufi tradition. Rumie was a scholar of astronomy, mathematics, theology and thus a scholar of his culture; Kabir by contrast was an uneducated weaver, working in a crowded back street of Benares.

> Every form derives its nature from the void;
> if a form dies, its eternal nature will survive.

> Regard the Soul as a fountain, all creatures
> as rivers;
> While the fountain flows rivers swell-

> Dismiss grief from your mind and drink your fill
> This spring will not cease, its waters are eternal.
>
> Rumie[44]

> Are you looking for me?
> I am in the next seat.
> My shoulder is against yours.
> You will not find me in stupas,
> Not in Indian shrine rooms,
> nor in synagogues, not in cathedrals;
> not in masses, nor in kirtans,
> not in legs winding around your own neck,
> nor in eating nothing but vegetables.
> When you really look for me,
> You will see me instantly-
> You will find me in the tiniest house of time.
> Kabir says: student, tell me, what is God?
> He is the breath
> inside the breath.
>
> Kabir [45]

Islam, as we have seen, starts with the concept that God is separate from his creation, but those who wait until he calls them with a loving heart, will find union in him. But even so, the soul still retains some trace of individuality. Junayd of Baghdad shows that identification of the self with God is only 'the first isolation' of the soul, it is kind of a trap that God sets for those that are spiritually proud. God shatters that experience and changes it into an I-Thou relationship in which then God appropriates it and the soul submits in total love, accepting all. Thus each Soul has a unique relationship with God, including suffering that turns to joy. This tradition seems thus to have elements of both the Hindu concept of unity and the Christian concept of the relationship of I-thou, the latter being responsible for the well known poetry of love, that stems from this tradition.

In the American Indian Tradition man is entirely embedded in nature and both are in God. The Ultimate is "the great Mystery". It is the source of everything, including other universes and galaxies; it lives in everything and it is everything. Embracing all of creation, it is thus distinctly different from other Western religion which are so centred on

Postscript

human existence that they seemingly divorce themselves from the rest of creation.

The Great Mystery of the American Indians is seen as self-regenerative and eternal, like a filled void in which there is a vibrating core, or primal energy source; it is limitless and it is thought, form, spirit, consciousness. It is the origin out of which all form arises and into which they fall back, it is itself the creative flow of the energy that is all the universes. This is incredibly similar to the ideas of Kashmir Shaivist teaching.

Mystics in this tradition, called Shamans or Medicine Man and Women, let their insight traditionally infuse the whole culture, and thus <u>their concepts</u> are the wisdom-culture or "religion". The structure of their world, the teaching of the children, the poetry, the passages of life, their ceremonies, are all touched and understood as divine forms of the great spirit. One of the Tools is the Medicine Wheel. It shows how many life forms relate to each other and what process they run through in physical life - an essentially cyclic movement that is seen in four groups; planting/gestation, birth, growth and change, and death and rebirth. In the phases of the Medicine Wheel we find the characters of the FIVE ELEMENTS as the four Clan Chiefs; four directions, or four shields which are moved by the Spirit-Wind; the fifth Element.

Not only is creation linked and expressed in these five tendencies, but the Four Winds bring change, the four directions teach us the secrets of Life; the animals guide us with their wisdom, the plants give us knowledge and healing etc.

Much can be learned from this tradition which holds the Earth as its central, sacred domain and that is filled with the awareness that all is divine consciousness, all is divine wisdom. We just need to learn and listen in the inner heart, to their teachings.

Chief Seattle delivered a speech in 1885 in answer to President Franklin Peace, whose government had proposed reservations for the Indian Tribes of the North West of the U.S.A., which meant uprooting the tribes from their natural habitat, or limiting their movements in their natural habitat. "Every part of this earth is sacred to my people. Every shining pine needle, every sandy shore, every mist in the dark woods, every clearing and humming insect is holy in the memory and experience of my people... what is there to life if a man cannot hear the lovely cry of the Whippoorwill, or the arguments of the frogs around the pond at night... the smell of the wind itself cleansed by a midday rain, or scented with pinion pine. The air is precious to the red man. For all things share the same breath, the beasts, the trees, the man... if all the beasts were gone, men would die from great loneliness of spirit, for what ever happens to the beasts also happens to man. For all things are connected. Whatever befalls earth befalls the sons of the earth... one thing we know... our God is the same God... he is God of man... and his compassion is equal for the red man and the white"[46].

In the "global village" of today the boundaries between East and West seem to blur. His Holiness The Dalai Lama, the fourteenth, exiled from Tibet settled in Dharamsala, northern India but teaches most frequently in the West. Bede Griffiths, a Roman Catholic monk, lived in India wearing the saffron *kavi* (habit) of the Hindu holy man. Ramakrishna, Vivekananda, Rabindranath Tagore, Sri Aurobinda, Ramana Maharishi Shree Ma, Swami Chidvilasananda, Swami Anubhavananda, Shri Amma and many more have come to share their teaching. In addition to which the West is gradually waking up to its own rich tradition. Hopefully we can remember the sacredness of the universe. When the West can acknowledges that, healing of the individual and the environment can begin in earnest.

Precondition for this in society, as much as in the individual is the "letting go" of self and self-importance. It is in the law of the Elements that one has to let go of the useless, before progress can be made. Letting go includes national arrogance as much as the individual pride and pain of separatism. Mystics

Postscript

of East and West agree that ultimately everything is interconnected, everything is One regardless of whether it is born or unborn, man-made or growing; whether the smallest cell or the biggest universe - all is One.

> In God all things are one
> He does not separate
> with me as with a gnat
> does he communicate
> A raindrop becomes the ocean
> when it falls in the sea
> Thus does the soul become divine
> on seeing its divinity
> It is as if God played a game
> immersed in contemplation;
> and from this game
> all worlds arose
> in endless variations.
>
> Angelius Silesius [47]

Can we experience any of this and make it real for ourselves? Close your eyes and breathe out, then open again. Imagine the book in front of you is actually not a book at all, but vibrating energy in a certain form. Can you can hear the sound of its vibration, is it pleasant? Does the desk vibrate at another pleasant frequency, deeper? Can you influence that sound, change the sound by introducing other frequencies like bells, music, chanting. Can you create good vibes?

Soft focus your eyes and draw your attention that the book is energy in the form of light. Imagine you can see the book as light? If both desk and book are made of energy or light waves, should they not radiate, like a lamp? Your arm rests on the desk as well, is that too radiating light? Are the different lights of arm and desk compatible, does it feel comfortable? How does the zone where arm touches desk feel? Does the desktop when imagined as light, feel less hard to the arm that rests on it? How about the fluid zone, where does "desk-ness" end, where "arm-ness"?

Postscript

An interesting game, that might give you a feel for the implication of such altered view. What was seen at first as a solid desk or a book became something different. Our mind is conditioned to see it like solid. But can you expand your awareness to see any of these objects as different forms as changing energy? With that thought does your arm feel less heavy on the desk, the desk less hard... are you creating your own reality? If you are then letting go of the conditioning of the mind it will make way to see everything in constant flux. Nothing is solid or constant, or isolated or permanent. Life has started to become Movement-of-Life.

Think of a row of dominoes, when I flick one, the whole row falls over, one by one, carrying the initial movement. So if I move my arm, or even tap a rhythm with my finger, will the vibrations carry on to effect the desk... change the vibration of the desk... effecting the ground the desk stands on... effecting the rhythm of to the earth underneath... how far? Or is it going on and on and on?

Fair enough these are all inanimate objects. What if I touch the cat, hug my daughter, etc. are the effects of these actions changing in their inherent vibration and will they go on, changing, changing ... to New York, San Francisco, Tokyo etc.? What if I give a *Shiatsu* to a person, touching them with my hands, my vibration, changing their vibration, changing their energy field. What if I shout in anger at my daughter is my anger disturbing the peace in the still mountains of Tibet? Is my action carried around the world by the movement-of-life?

Taking sages, saints and scientists serious would change our life, it would give us back the power to change ourselves too. Is it not time to take that wonderful opportunity. For two thousand years and more the development of thought and science in the West was based on the notion of the hierarchical separateness of the creator from the creation. At the end of this century this development can come to an end. Although the implications have not filtered down into everyday life and attitudes, nor even into all strongholds of science, yet impermanence has shown its face again. Isn't it time, that we woke up to it?

"Every subatomic interaction consists of the annihilation of the original particle and the creation of new subatomic particles. The subatomic world is a continual dance of creation and annihilation, of mass changing into energy and energy changing into mass. Transient forms sparkle in and out of existence, creating a never-ending, forever newly created reality"[48].

What an enormous chance for us to recreate ourselves!

NOTES

Prologue
1. Deepak Chopra, Quantum Healing. Bantam Books. New York 1989. p178-180
2. Henry Skolimowski, The participatory mind, Arkana, London, 1994

Chapter One
1. S. Masunaga, Zen Imagery Exercises. Japan Publications, Tokyo - New York 1987 p16
2. R. Gerber, Vibrational Medicine, Bear & Co, Santa Fe, 1988 p67
3. S. Masunaga, i.b.i.d. p 44-60
4. i.b.i.d. p 51
5. D. M. Connelly, Traditionelle Akupunktur, (original title) Traditional Acupuncture. The Law of the Five Elements. Fuldaer Verlagsanstalt; Dritte Auflage. p20
6. Deepak Chopra, Quantum Healing. i.b.i.d. p45-46
7. S. Manunga, i.b.i.d. p14
8. R. Gerber, i.b.i.d. p209
9. See Gandharva Music Therapy for example in: Perfect Health, Deepak Chopra, M.D. Bantam Books 1992
10. For further information about illnesses and their meanings, see Louise Hay, You Can Heal Your Life, Eden Grove Editions 1088. and: Heal Your Body, Eden Grove Editions 1989
11. G. Parrinder, The Bhagavad Gita, Sheldon Press, London, 1974
12. A.K. Ramanujan, Speaking of Shiva, Penguin Books 1987, p.19.
13. R. Gerber, i.b.i.d. p 22
14. Deepak Chopra, Quantum Healing, i.b.i.d. p 49
15. i.b.i.d. p 49
16. R. Gerber, i.b.i.d. p 32
17. i.b.i.d.
18. Thich Nhat Hahn, Peace is Every Step. Bantam Books 1992, p123
19. Barbara Ann Brennan, Hands of Light. Bantam Books 1988, p41
20. i.b.i.d. p49
21. i.b.i.d. p53
22. Manvela Dunn-Mascetti, Saints, Boxtree, London 1994 P245/5
23. Linda Johnson, Daughters of the Goddess, Ycs International Publishers, St Paul, Minnesota. p.10
24. B. A. Brennan, Hands of Light i.b.i.d p61 ff
25. The Lord of Caves is a reference to Shiva, for the dome of a cave is a metaphor for the sky, which is a symbol for the vast receptive curved vessel that becomes the ground of new creation.
26. Darshan, monthly magazine of Syddha Foundation: 1985, Vol.23. p102 - Lama Prabhu, other verses in: Speaking of Shiva, translated by A.K. Ramanujan Penguin 1987, p143 ff
27. R. Gerber i.b.i.d. p128

28. i.b.i.d. p369
29. i.b.i.d. p131
30. Lama Anagarika Govinda, Tibetan Mysticism, Samuel Weiser, Maine 1969 p.134
31. i.b.i.d. p.178
32. Dr F Ross, The Lost Secret of Ayurvedic Acupuncture, Lotus Press, Wisconsin, U.S.A. 1994,p.32
33. Physics for Science and Students of Engineering. Halliday, Resnick. John Wiley and Sons, Inc 1965, p 901-902
34. Lama Anagarika Govinda, Tibetan Mysticism, i.b.i.d. p.73
35. i.b.i.d. p.179
36. i.b.i.d. p.183
37. The above list is compiled after: B. A. Brennan, Hands of Light. p 48 & 73; R. Gerber, Vibrational Medicine i.b.i.d. p 130; and Klaus Volmar, Journey Through Chakras. Gateway Books 1989
38. Further information on Ayurvedic Medicine: Deepak Chopra, M.D. Perfect Health. i.b.i.d.; Scott Gerson, M.D. Ayurveda. Element Books1993 and: The Lost Secret of Ayurvedic Acupuncture, Lotus Press, Wisconsin, 1994, Dr Frank Ros.

Chapter Two
1. Similar exercises: Stephen Levine, Healing into Life and Death and Meditations. Gateways. 1993
2. R. Gerber, Vibrational Medicine i.b.i.d. compiled after p 172-178
3. i.b.i.d. p 27
4. Ohashi, Reading the Body, Ohashi's Book of Oriental Diagnosis. Aquarian/Thorsons. 1992
5. S, Masunaga, Zen Imagery Exercises. i.b.i.d. p 55
6. Deepak Chopra, Quantum Healing, i.b.i.d. p 200
7. R. Gerber, i.b.i.d. p 29
8. M.U. Hatengdi, Nityananda, The Divine Presence, Rudra Press, Mass. 1984, p 35
9. Sakala Sant Gatha, ed. by T.H. Avate, Poona, 1923
10. Beinfield/Krongold, Between Heaven and Earth, Ballentine Books, New York 1992, p 35
11. Sonia Moriceau. Excerpts from guidelines compiled for Shiatsu practitioners.
12. Karlfried Graf Duerckheim. Hara, The Vital Centre of Man. Mandala Books. 1989
13. B. A. Brennan, Emerging Light, Bantam Books 1993, p 289
14. i.b.i.d. p 306
15. Benjamin Hoff, The Tao of Pooh. Mandarin Paperback. 1991, p 39

PART I

All references of anatomy or physiology are based on: Ross & Wilson; Anatomy and Physiology in Health and Illness, Kathleen J. W. Wilson OBE. Churchill Livingstone, Edinburgh et al. 1990; Seventh Edition.

Chapter Three
1. Beinfield Korngold; Between Heaven and Earth, a guide to Chinese Medicine, Ballantine Books, New York,
2. 1991, p87
3. Chief Seattle's Vision; How can one sell the air? The Book Publishing Company, Summertown, 1992, p20/21
4. Ilza Veith, (Neiching), The yellow Emperor's Classic of Internal Medicine, University of California Press,
5. Berkley, 1884, p.112
6. Hildegard von Bingen, Heilkunde, Otto Mueller Verlag, Saltzburg. P.84/106
7. Dr. Franz Ros, Ayurvedic Acupuncture P.20 ff
8. T.Y.S. Lama Gangchen Tulku Rinpoche Ngal-So, How to Relax
9. Body Speed and Mind, Institute of Propsychic Tibetan Medicine, Milan p.15
10. Ilza Veith, Nei Ching...p.177-179
11. i.b.i.d. p.28
12. Barbara Brennan, Light Emerging, Bantam 1993
13. Graf v. Duerckheim, Hara, the Vital Centre of Man, Mandala Books, London 1989, p.49
14. Debbie Shapiro, The Bodymind Workbook. Element Books. 1990, p.73
15. Ilza Veith, Nei Ching, p.141
16. Lama Anagarika Govinda, i.b.i.d. p.65ff
17. Ilza Veith, Nei Ching,...p.119
18. Ilza Veith, Nei Ching,...p.109
19. H Wilheims; Chinese Horoscopes; Pan Books London; 1980, p.31ff
20. Jamie Sams; Sacred Path Cards; Harper, San Francisco, 1990, p.279
21. Ohashi/Monte, Reading the Body, Aquarian, London, 1991, p.90
22. Dr. F. Ros Ayurvedic Acupuncture i.b.i.d. p.51
23. Lama Anagarika Govinda, Foundation of Tibetan Mysticism. p.144ff i.b.i.d.

Chapter Four.
1. Magda Palmer, The Healing Power of Crystals. Arrow Books London 1990; p.15
2. i.b.i.d.
3. Anne McCaffrey; The Crystal Singers; The Ship who Sang. Corgi Books, 1968,69
4. Lama Anagarika Govinda, Foundation of Tibetan Mysticism. p.147
5. i.b.i.d. p.153
6. W. Ohashi: Reading the body, i.b.i.d. p.96

7. Plotinus, in : Stephen McKenna, First Ennead, Faber & Faber, London 1962
8. Shakespeare, As You Like It. Act II, Scene VII. The Complete Works of.., Oxford University Press London...1962, p 1226
9. W. Johnston, The cloud of Unknowing, Fount, 1997
10. Ilza Veith, Nei Ching p.103
11. Jamie Sams, Sacred Path Card I.b.i.d, p.101
12. Ilza Veith, Nei Ching, p.147
13. Shaykh Fadhlalla Haerri, Sufism, Element, Shaftesbury 1990, p. 49.
14. Giovanni Maciocia, The Psyche in Chinese Medicine. European Journal of Oriental Medicine, 1/1 Spring 1993, p. 16/17
15. Ohashi/Monte Reading the Body; i.b.i.d p.164/165
16. Alan Isaacs et al. The Physical World. Penguin Books, 1976, p.82
17. Hutchinsons Encyclopaedia. i.b.i.d. p.1239
18. Ilza Veith, Nei Ching. 207/141
19. E. Kuebler-Ross, On Life after Death, Celestial Arts, Berkeley, 1991 p.78
20. Ilza Veith, Nei Ching. p.120
21. M. Sky; Breathing. Bear and Company, Santa Fe; New Mexico 1990; p.35/36
22. Thich Nath Hahn; The Sutra on the Full Awareness of Breath. Berkeley, Parallax Press. 1988, p.53
23. Swami Chetanananda; The Breath of God, Rudra Press, Cambridge, Massachusetts, 1977 p.23/24
24. M. Hatengdi/Swami Chetanananda, Nitya Sutras; Rudra Press, Cambridge, Massachusetts, 1973 p.165
25. Lama, Anagarika Govinda, The Way of The White Clouds. Ride Books, London, 1992 p.244.
26. Swami Chetanananda, i.b.i.d. p.23
27. Beinfield/Korngold, Between Heaven and Earth. i.b.i.d. p.119

Chapter Five.
1. Hildegard von Bingen, Heilkunde, Saltzburg. p.77
2. i.b.i.d. p.96
3. Dr. Frank Ros, Ayurvedic Acupuncture, p/24
4. Lama Anagarika Govinda, Foundation of Tibetan Mysticism, p.178
5. T.Y.S. Lama Gangchen, Ngal-So, How to Relax, p.17
6. M. Fox, Meister Eckhardt, Meditations with i.b.i.d. p 51/52
7. J & C Matthews, Celtic Wisdom, Element Books, Shaftesbury, 1993,p.26
8. after Ilza Veith, Nei Ching p.133
9. Jamie Sams, Sacred Path Cards. Harper Collins, 1990, p.107
10. Gopi Krishna, Living with Kundalini; Shambala, Boston 1993; Swami Chetanananda, The Breath of God. i.b.i.d. p.23/24
11. A. Tomatis, For further information contact: Tomatis Centre, Eccleston Square 26, London SW1 1 NS
12. W. Johnston, Cloud of Unknowing, Faunt, 1997, p 30 ff

13. Lama Anagarika Govinda, Foundation of Tibetan Mysticism i.b.i.d. p.180 + 187
14. Hildegard von Bingen. i.b.i.d. p.75
15. Nor Hall, The Moon and the Virgin, Harper/Row, New York 1980, p.44; T Suttrim Allione, Women of Wisdom, Arkana, London 1986, p.31/32
16. Ilza Veith Nei Ching; after page 120
17. Lama Anagarika Govinda, Foundation of Tibetan Mysticism, p.272
18. Beinfield, Krongold, Between Heaven and Earth; i.b.i.d. p.42
19. Hildegard von Bingen i.b.i.d. p.78

Chapter Six.
1. Dr F. Ros, Ayurvedic Acupuncture i.b.i.d. p.24
2. Swami Chinmayananda, The Holy Geeta, p.652; 922ff Chinmaya Mission Trust, Mumbai , 1996
3. Lama Anagarika Govinda, Foundation of Tibetan Mysticism. i.b.i.d. p.137
4. T.Y.S. Lama Gangchen, Ngal-so, i.b.i.d. p.78
5. i.b.i.d. p.106
6. Lama Anagarika Govinda, Foundation of Tibetan Mysticism, i.b.i.d. p.115ff
7. T.Y.S. Lama Gangchen, Ngal-so, i.b.i.d. p.175
8. J & C Matthews, Celtic Wisdom, Element Books, Shaftesbury, 1993, p.40
9. Ilza Veith, Nei Ching p.180 i.b.i.d.
10. after Ilza Veith, Nei Ching. p.133
11. Hildegard von Bingen; Mathew Fox; Illuminations; Bear and Company, Santa Fe, 1985, p.32
12. Jamie Sams, Sacred Path Cards, Harper Collins p.89/90
13. Lama Gangchen. Ngal-So, p.59
14. R Panikkar, The Vedic Experience, Dayton, Longman, Todd; London 1977; p.206
15. Lama Gangchen; Ngal-So, p.+ 73/74
16. A. W. Reed, Aboriginal Fables, Reed, Sydney 1965; p.137.
17. Swami Hariharananda Aranya, Yoga philosophy of Patanjali; State University of N.Y Press, 1981, p.76.
18. G. Parrinder, The Bhagavad Gita, Sheldon Press, London 1974, p.38 Bh. G. vi; 34/35.
19. Dr. F. Ros, Ayurvedic Acupuncture p.55

Chapter Seven.
1. R. Panikkar, The Vedic Experience. i.b.i.d. p.169.
2. Sadguru Sant Keshavadas, Gayatri; Kegan Paul, London, 1993; p.125
3. Hildegard von Bingen; Heilkunde; i.b.i.d. p.244
4. S. Masunaga, Japan, Publication, Tokyo/N.Y. 1989 p.71
5. J . Sams, Sacred Path Cards i.b.i.d. p.29

6. Hildegard von Bingen, Heilkunde, i.b.i.d. p.128
7. i.b.i.d. p.112
8. Hildegard von Bingen, Heilkunde i.b.i.d. p.57ff
9. W. Ohashi, Reading the Body, i.b.i.d. p.90ff

PART III

Prologue
1. B. Ingles and R. West; The alternative Health Guide; Michael Joseph Ltd. London, 1983, p.7
2. After: Dhammapada Eknath Easwaran, Penguin Arkana, London 1986, p.78
3. Lama Anajarika Govinda, Foundations... p. 247
4. Milaripa, Autobiography of Tibetan Yogi, i.b.i.d. p.246
5. Lama Gangchen, Ngal-So - Healing 111, i.b.i.d. p. 87/88
6. A. Young, Miracle or Mirage, Spiritual Healing, Devoers Company, California 1981 p.72 / 128 f.
7. Farid-Ud-din-Ahar, the Conference of Birds, Penguin Classics 1984 p.166

Chapter Eight.
1. M.H. Woodcott, A. Schumway Cook Development of Posture and Gait across the Life Span. University of South Carolina Press, 1989.
2. Ilza Veith. i.b.i.d. p.149
3. Lama Gangchen, Ngal-So 111 i.b.i.d. p.153
4. C.A. Meier, Healing Dream and Ritual, Daimon, Switzerland, 1989 p.1
5. i.b.i.d. p.52/53
6. Jamie Sams, Sacred Path Cards i.b.i.d. p.141
7. V.W. Odajnyk, Gathering the Light a Psychology of Meditation, Shambala, London 1993
8. Ilza Veith i.b.i.d. p.148
9. i.b.i.d. p.55
10. Beinfield, Krongold, Between Heaven and Earth. i.b.i.d. p.332
11. Ohashi, Reading the Body, i.b.i.d p.171
12. These books might help for further information: An Introduction to Macro-biotics, Oliver Cromwell, Thorsons 1987; Food for Thought, A new look at Food and Behaviour, S. Miller, J. Miller, Prentice Hall, Inc, 1985; Food and Healing, A. Colbin, Ballentine Books 1986. For further information a nutritionist should be consulted.
13. Ilza Veith, Nei Ching, i.b.i.d. p.148
14. Rom: Open Secret, Versions of Rumie, Threshold Books, Putney, 1984.

Chapter Nine.
1. Ilza Veith, Nei Ching, i.b.i.d. p.139; 140; 146.

2. Bruno Hans Geba; Breath Away Your Tension. Random House, New York, 1973, p. 38
3. Ilza Veith, Nei Ching p.117
4. Farid-Ud-din-Ahar, The Conference of Birds, i.b.i.d. p.109

Chapter Ten.
1. Ohashi, Reading the Body. i.b.i.d. p.126
2. Janet and Colin Bord; Sacred Waters, Holy Wells and Water Lore in Britain and Ireland, Granada, 1985 p.2
3. Vivianne Crowley, Phoenix from the Flame, Aquarian/Thorsons, 1994, p 61
4. Susanne Cooper, The Dark is Rising Sequence. Penguin, Harmandsworth, 1984, p. 763
5. Ingles and West. Guide to Alternative Medicine, Michael Joseph, London 1983 p.25
6. Ingles/West, Guide to Alternative Medicine. i.b.i.d. p.24
7. Ohashi, Reading the Body. i.b.i.d. p. 54
8. i.b.i.d. p.58
9. R. Panikkar, The Vedic Experience, Darton, Longman and Todd, London, 1977, p114
10. i.b.i.d. p. 117
11. Upanishads i.b.i.d. Chapter 6; p. 248
12. R. Panikkar i.b.i.d. p.120/121

Chapter Eleven.
1. For further information, also on shoes and feet and the other elements see: Ohashi, Reading the Body, i.b.i.d p.143 ff
2. For further information please contact: Kunpen Lama Gangchen KLG, Institute for the Propagation of the Tibetan Medical Tradition, Via Marco Polo B, 20124 Milan, Italy.
3. For further reference to food and herbs refer also to Beinfield/Krongold, Between Heaven and Earth, i.b.i.d.

Chapter Twelve.
1. from: Tintern Abbey - William Wordsworth's The Prelude, ed. by Carlos Baker, Holt, Reihort and Winston, New York 1965.
2. to be found in Masunaga/Ohashi, Zen Shiatsu, Japan Publication, Inc. Tokyo,NY,1977
3. for further information see: Beinfield/Krongold, Between Heaven and Earth. i.b.i.d.

Postscript
1. Changagya Upanishad, sixth Prapathaka, twelfth Khanda; The thirteen Principal Upanishads, R. E. Hume, Oxford University Press. 1979
2. S. Rinpoche, The Tibetan Book of Living and Dying. Rider, London, 1992

3. Shri Guru Gita, Sri Skanda Purana, Ganeshpuri, The Nectar of Chanting, 1987, v.36-42
4. W. Heisenberg, Physics and Philosophy, Harper Torch Books, NY 1958
5. Henry Skolimowski, The participatory mind. Arkana, London 1994
6. A. K. Coomaraswamy, The Dance of Shiva. The Noonday Press. 1969, p 78
7. Fritjof Capra, The Turning Point. Flamingo, Fontana. 1982, p 69
8. Fritjof Capra, The Tao of Physics. Fontana. 1980, p 223
9. R. Sheldrake, Mc Kennan, R. Abraham Denken am Rande des Undenkbaren (Org. Trialogues at the edge of the West) Piper Muenchen, 1998,.p.167
10. i.b.i.d. p.28 et all
11. Teilhard de Chardin, Spirit of Fire, Orbis Books, New York 1996, p.176
12. David Bohm , in R. Weber, Dialogues with Scientists and Sages , Arkana London 1990, p.25
13. Nancy Wilson Ross, Three Ways of Asian Wisdom. Touchstone. 1966, p 81
14. Lama Anajarika Govinda; Foundations of Tibetan Mysticism. Weiser, Yorkbead 1969, p.72
15. T.Y.S. Lama Gangchen, NGALSO - Self-Healing 111. LGPP Milan 1994, P.45
16. N. Wilson Ross, i.b.i.d. p.145
17. F. Capra, Tao of Physics, i.b.i.d. p 30
18. Lao Tzu, Tao Te Ching. Wildwood house. 1973, p 43
19. Sakala Sant Gatha Kashinath Ananta Joshi, Sant Vanmaya Prakashan. Mandir Poona 1975, translated by Anand Mudra
20. Dilip Chitre; Says Tuka: Selected Poetry of Tukaram, New Delhi: Penguin Books India Pvt. Ltd.1991
21. H. Skolimowski, The participatory mind, p.265 ff
22. D. Bohm, in R. Weber, Dialogues with Scientists and Sages. Arkana, London 1990,p.46
23. S. Rinpoche, The Tibetan book of Living and Dying, i.b.i.d. p.259
24. Mark S .G. Dyczkowski; The Doctrine of Vibration, State University of New York Press 1987
25. Swami Muktananda, Introduction to Kashmir Shaivism. Ganeshpuri. 1975 p.1 & 3
26. Mark S.G. Dyczkowski; The Doctrine of Vibration, i.b.i.d. p.60
27. See Lama Gangchen, NGALSO, P.136 f; and Lama Anagarika Govinda, i.b.i.d. p.137
28. P. E. Muller - Ortega, The Triadic Heart of Siva. State University of New York Press 1989
29. Raimundo Panikkar, The Vedic Experience Darton, Longman, Todd; 1977, London p.242f
30. Fritjof Capra, The Tao of Physics. i.b.i.d. p 21
31. Deepak Chopra, Quantum Healing, Bantam Books, 1989, p. 128

32. Father Bede Griffith, in: Dialogues with Scientist and Sages .i.b.i.d. p 173
33. H. Zahrnt, Die Sache mit Gott. Piper Munchen. 1966 . p 170 - 171
34. Father Bede Griffith, i.b.i.d. p 170
35. i.b.i.d
36. Hildegard von Bingen/Matthew Fox, Illuminations of Hildegard of Bingen. Bear & Co. 1985, p 28
37. i.b.i.d. p 14 - 15
38. i.b.i.d. p.15, 18 - 20
39. i.b.i.d. p.16
40. Matthew Fox, Breakthrough; Meister Eckhardts Creation, Garden City,1980
41. Amaury Riencourt, The Eye of Shiva. Condor Books. 1980, p 38-39
42. F. Franck, the Book of Angelus Silesius, i.b.i.d. p 51
43. Manuela Dunn-Mascett, Saints, the chosen few. Boxtree, London 1994 p.102 ff
44. Jalo Luddin Rumi, Where Two Oceans Meet, interpretations by J. Cowan, Element; Longmead 1992
45. Swami Chetananda, The Breath of God. Rudra Press, Massachusetts. p XV
46. Chief Seattle, Summertown, Tennessee, 1992
47. F. Frank. The book of Angelius Silesius, Wildwood House, 1976, p54-55
48. Gary Zukav, The Dancing WU-Li Masters, Bantam, NY, 1980, p.197

ABOUT THE AUTHOR

Dr. Christa-Maria Herrmann, a German by birth, naturalised British, after many years of study and world wide travel, lives in the far west of Cornwall with her daughter.

Although she originally studied Theology (Lutheran), her studies soon expanded to Education, Psychology, Philosophy and Art. (M.A; M.ED; Dip. Theol; Dip. Ed; DAD). Different teaching jobs in various countries followed; the last in Monash University Australia, where her work on Self-awareness started. From the eighties she worked as a well recognized potter, exhibiting world-wide.

Extensive travel and life in Asia (Hong Kong, India, Japan) awakened her interest in Eastern philosophy and led via the Zen-art of Raku to deep involvement in Meditation and Healing Arts i.e. several years as a practitioner of complementary medical practices. She has practised Sattipathana (mindfulness) and Siddha Yoga for many years.

1997 she made her doctorate in Eco-philosophy. Since, she talked world-wide on conferences and workshops (incl. the House of Lords) about inter-religious spiritual awareness and a need for new ethics based on the "Five Elements" and was presented with an Award for contributions to World peace in 1997. (Lama Gangchen Peace Foundation; NGO/UN).

The many different strands of her education and varied experiences provide the background for her writing;

The Five Elements, Volume I
  - *The Movement of Life through Body, Mind and Spirit*

The Five Elements, Volume II
  - *A Contemplation of Relationships.*

The Way of Raku.

Guru and Disciple
  - *Contemplation of a Sansktit hymn.*

Web: http://www.5element.org.uk/cmherrmann/
Email: cmherrmann@5element.org.uk